EARLY MODERN LITERATURE IN HISTORY

General Editor: Cedric C. Brown
*Professor of English and Head of Department, University of Reading*

Within the period 1520–1740 this series discusses many kinds of writing, both within and outside the established canon. The volumes may employ different theoretical perspectives, but they share an historical awareness and an interest in seeing their texts in lively negotiation with their own and successive cultures.

*Titles include*:

Anna R. Beer
SIR WALTER RALEGH AND HIS READERS IN THE SEVENTEENTH CENTURY
Speaking to the People

Cedric C. Brown and Arthur F. Marotti (*editors*)
TEXTS AND CULTURAL CHANGE IN EARLY MODERN ENGLAND

Martin Butler (*editor*)
RE-PRESENTING BEN JONSON
Text, History, Performance

John Dolan
POETIC OCCASION FROM MILTON TO WORDSWORTH

Pauline Kiernan
STAGING SHAKESPEARE AT THE NEW GLOBE

Ronald Knowles (*editor*)
SHAKESPEARE AND CARNIVAL
After Bakhtin

James Loxley
ROYALISM AND POETRY IN THE ENGLISH CIVIL WARS
The Drawn Sword

Arthur F. Marotti (*editor*)
CATHOLICISM AND ANTI-CATHOLICISM IN EARLY MODERN ENGLISH TEXTS

The series Early Modern Literature in History is published in association with the Renaissance Texts Research Centre at the University of Reading.

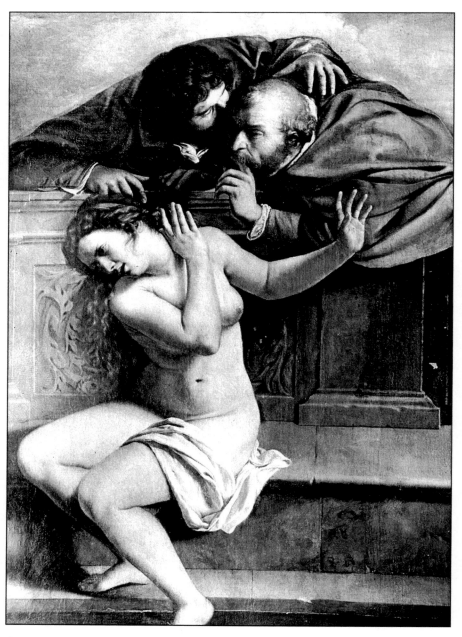

Susanna and the Elders by Artemisia Gentileschi (*courtesy of Schloss Weissenstein, Pommersfelden/Bilarchiv Foto Marburg*)

# Writing Rape, Writing Women in Early Modern England

## Unbridled Speech

Jocelyn Catty

LIBRARY ST. MARY'S COLLEGE

First published in Great Britain 1999 by
**MACMILLAN PRESS LTD**
Houndmills, Basingstoke, Hampshire RG21 6XS and London
Companies and representatives throughout the world

A catalogue record for this book is available from the British Library.

ISBN 0–333–74028–9

---

First published in the United States of America 1999 by
**ST. MARTIN'S PRESS, INC.,**
Scholarly and Reference Division,
175 Fifth Avenue, New York, N.Y. 10010

ISBN 0–312–22181–9

Library of Congress Cataloging-in-Publication Data
Catty, Jocelyn, 1971–
Writing rape, writing women in early modern England : unbridled
speech / Jocelyn Catty.
p.   cm. — (Early modern literature in history)
Revision of the author's thesis.
Includes bibliographical references (p.        ) and index.
ISBN 0–312–22181–9 (cloth)
1. English literature—Early modern, 1500–1700—History and
criticism.   2. Rape in literature.   3. English literature—Women
authors—History and criticism.   4. Women and literature—England–
–History—16th century.   5. Women and literature—England–
–History—17th century.   I. Title.   II. Series.
PR428.R37C38   1999
820.9'355—dc21
99–18161
CIP

10   9   8   7   6   5   4   3   2   1
08   07   06   05   04   03   02   01   00   99

Printed and bound in Great Britain by
Antony Rowe Ltd, Chippenham, Wiltshire

# Contents

# Acknowledgements

This book could not have been written without the encouragement and support of numerous friends and advisers. I am indebted to Hannah Betts, Hero Chalmers, Danielle Clarke and Helen Moore for many helpful suggestions. I am also grateful to audiences at the *Women, Text and History* seminar organised by Emma Smith and Margarita Stocker in Oxford, and at the Reading University English graduate seminar organised by Cedric C. Brown, for the opportunity to air material from the final chapter, and for their many helpful comments.

The research for the book was enabled by a British Academy scholarship and generous support from Jesus College, Oxford. I am also grateful to Julia Briggs for the loan of her microfilm of the manuscript of the *Urania* sequel.

I am indebted to Katy Willison for her dilligent translation of Greek and Latin texts for Chapter 6, and to Lord Justice Auld for providing me with information concerning current rape laws. I am grateful to Danielle Clarke for allowing me to make use of her unpublished doctoral thesis on women and translation, and to Corinne J. Saunders for allowing me to read and quote from her forthcoming book on rape in medieval literature. I have also greatly appreciated the support and interest of Nicholas Jacobs and David Womersley while at Jesus College. I have benefited greatly from the advice of Cedric C. Brown as general editor of the *Early Modern Literature in History* series, and Charmian Hearne at Macmillan. Thanks are also due, as always, to the support of Jon, Barbara and Benet Catty.

My greatest debts of thanks are to Dennis Kay and Helen Cooper, as supervisors of the doctoral thesis of which this book is a revised version. Professor Kay inspired me to undertake doctoral research in the first place and guided the project from its inception, while Professor Cooper contributed invaluable advice and support in its final stages. Ros Ballaster and Helen Hackett also gave valuable advice when examining this work as a thesis; since then, I have benefited hugely from Dr Hackett's painstaking reading, advice and encouragement. The revision of thesis into book has also been facilitated by the advice and friendship of Paulina Kewes, who has ensured that I remain in touch with the most recent developments in the field and whose close reading of the book has been invaluable.

# Abbreviations

| | |
|---|---|
| *ELH* | *English Literary History* |
| *ELR* | *English Literary Renaissance* |
| *MLN* | *Modern Language Notes* |
| *OED* | *The Oxford English Dictionary*, 2nd edition, ed. J.A. Simpson and E.S.C. Weiner, 20 vols (Oxford: Clarendon Press, 1989) |
| *PLL* | *Papers on Language and Literature* |
| *SEL* | *Studies in English Literature* |
| *STC* | *A Short-title Catalogue of Books Printed in England, Scotland, and Ireland and of English Books Printed Abroad 1475–1640*, compiled by A.W. Pollard and G.R. Redgrave (London: The Bibliographical Society, 1926) |

Contractions in primary texts have been expanded and italicised.

# Introduction

> One W.G. getting a copie...put it forth excedingly corrupted: euen as if by meanes of a broker for hire, he should haue entised into his house a faire maide and done her villanie, and after all to bescratched her face, torne her apparell, berayed and disfigured her, and then thrust her out of dores dishonested.
>
> *(Gorboduc*, The P[rinter] to the Reader)[1]

When, in 1570, John Daye sought to assert the superiority of his edition of *Gorboduc* over the previous one, rape provided a powerful metaphor for illegitimate publication. In imaging the text as a raped woman, he was hardly radical; in fact, writers of this period pervasively trope the text as a female body and publication as an exposure and invasion of that body akin to rape.[2] Yet, although he goes on to describe the woman as ready to 'play Lucreces part, and of her self die for shame', and although he presents himself as arguing that the 'fraude and force' used against her relieve her of any blame, he carries on:

> the authors...were very much displeased that she so ranne abroad without leaue, whereby she caught her shame, as many wantons do. (sig. Aii)

The ambivalence of his presentation of the woman – 'done... villanie' yet 'wanton' – is characteristic of representations of rape in the early modern period, as well as of attitudes to print. (If any publication is the 'rape' of a text, after all, how is one to mark out an illegitimate printing from the rest?) In restoring the text to what the authors had originally written, as he claims, Daye reclothes it and sends it 'abroad among you'. Where the image of rape figured the illegitimacy of the original printing, this legitimate publication too is a making available of the woman/text. Either act prostitutes its object.

Daye's concern here, of course, is with literary property, officially the authors' (but in reality his own) ownership of the text. The theft of the text by unlicensed printers is thus readily figured as an act of appropriation of a woman which could be either abduction, seduction or rape. Although, today, the word 'rape' denotes the violent sexual appropriation of a woman against her will, it derives from the Latin *raptus*, meaning theft, and was originally used for the abduction

1

of a man's wife or daughter, regardless of whether the sexual act took place, and regardless of her volition. In the early modern period, both senses of the word were available. Even when the word 'rape' is used to signify non-consensual intercourse, then, the act represented is surrounded by an intense ambivalence, both about the woman's role and her moral status.

Rapes and attempted rapes proliferate in the literature of this time. As an act perpetrated by men against women, with drastic implications for the victim's moral and social status, the act of rape is an extreme expression of the power-relation between men and women. Research into rape over the last two decades has concluded that, despite social sanctions against it, it is and has been an intrinsic part of Western society's subjection of women.[3] Literature, along with the visual arts, inscribes this violence in culture.[4] While the need to address this area of literary history has now been well established, attention to the portrayal of rape in the early modern period is long overdue.[5] There are accounts of rape in medieval French literature, for example, but no comprehensive study of rape in English literature of the early modern period has yet been written.[6]

The period 1560 to 1630 also witnessed the emergence of the woman writer.[7] Several aristocratic women publish literary texts in which they both contribute to the literary and political culture of the age and also, inevitably, reflect on the conditions facing any woman taking up the pen. The injunction to women to be 'chaste, silent and obedient', as is now well known, rendered literary activity for women potentially problematic, despite the commendations for learning which some of these writers received.[8] Yet classical myths depicting women telling stories associate this activity with resistance to rape, and these myths are of course an influential part of the cultural heritage of the early modern period.

By investigating the portrayal of rape, I hope to uncover the functions it fulfils and the attitudes to women it conveys. Further, I hope to reconstruct the cultural context for the representation of female mental and sexual autonomy, and of rape, by women writers.

By 1594 the story of Lucrece's rape had become, in Shakespeare's words, 'a theme for disputation'.[9] Debate, the guiding principle of Renaissance education and rhetoric, frequently takes rape stories as its subject,[10] and is also often presented as intrinsic to the rape situation. Debate may take the form of the rapist's mental struggle with the idea of rape; more commonly, however, it manifests itself in a competition between the 'male' art of persuasion and the 'female' art of *dis*suasion, in such a way as to exert tremendous pressure on women's eloquence as conceptualised at this time. Rape thus paradoxically functions as a means of identifying women as either possessing or lacking the cardinal female virtue: chastity. The rapist 'tests' the woman for this virtue by defining rape as a failure of her eloquence. Yet at the same time, rape alters the sexual status of its victim, who loses her honour, whether virginal or marital, and becomes an 'unchaste' woman. She is then no longer containable within the tripartite definition of the 'good' woman: as virgin, wife or widow. The rape situation, moreover, both necessitates and circumscribes female utterance: legitimises and silences it. We shall see that portrayals of rape both contain and reflect wider attitudes to female sexuality and discourse.

The early modern dichotomy between chastity and wantonness is crucially linked to women's writing. As critical work on gender and women's writing has established, authorship and sexual conduct are problematically interlinked for women by the cultural equation of chastity and obedience with silence, and eloquence or action with promiscuity.[11] Autonomy in writing thus figures sexual autonomy in a variety of ways. Although in some cases this may manifest itself on a biographical level, my concern here is not with biography, but with the ways in which texts written by women negotiate ideological circumscriptions and associations, whether in terms of genre or the concerns addressed within the text.[12]

By combining my study of rape with a study of women's writing, then, I do not seek to offer solely a comparison between men's and women's writings about rape in this period. The paucity of explicit portrayals of rape in texts by women, relative to the proliferation of rapes in male-authored literature, would itself create an imbalance in such a project. The writers considered in Part II are writers whose works register the connection between women's sexual autonomy and their autonomy in language: concerns which emerge both as the writers fashion female characters and as they negotiate their own discursive positions. They also engage with rape in various ways: whether as a narrative function or as a figure of the power-relations between the sexes. The work of Lady Mary Wroth, in particular, explicitly and frequently deals with rape, using it as a narrative and ideological tool which proves an integral part of her portrayal of female identity.

The issues of 'identity' and 'interiority' have been controversial in recent thinking about the early modern period.[13] Katharine Eisaman Maus has argued persuasively that while early modern ideas of 'interior truth' may be 'philosophically defective', this 'neither limits the extent of, nor determines the nature of, the power such ideas can exert';[14] we shall find this a useful basis for the concerns about identity and self-determination which emerge from what follows. Rape is significant in defining identity, both because it alters the victim's sexual status and because it raises a number of important questions intrinsically concerned with identity. We shall also find that women's texts return insistently to the question of women's identity or self-definition. Although the idea of 'autonomy' must necessarily differ from ours in a culture in which arranged marriage was common, at least among certain classes, this does not detract from the way in which these writers explore ideas about how to determine and define their 'selves' for the scrutiny of the world.

Rape is a violation and negation of female sexual autonomy: the most extreme, though by no means the only such negation in this period. As a private (sexual) crime with public (political) significance, it transgresses the same boundary between the two which works against female authorship and public(-)ation. Rape is both a sexual (and usually social) destruction of the woman and a figurative silencing, according to one strand of associations. It figures the denial of autonomy which disables and disempowers female authorship. At the same time, its destruction of chastity is a destruction of the very virtue which is implicitly antithetical to female authorship. It is perhaps fitting, then, that there should be an alternative, mythological tradition, typified by Philomela, which associates rape with the production of female utterance.

The significance of 'male' and 'female' rhetoric in rape situations highlights the role of voice. In representations of rape, moreover, whether a view is expressed by a character, or directly by the narrator, or seems to be implicit in the narrative, necessarily affects its impact. The connection between rape and women's utterance is particularly complex, finding different manifestations depending on genre and on the gender of the writer. Female discourse may register or figure resistance to rape, whether through cries for help or attempts to dissuade a potential rapist. In the texts discussed in the first part of this book, the female voice is a 'ventriloquised' one, that is, created by a male writer.[15] Women's writing, on the other hand, may represent resistance to male ideological prescriptions for or characterisations of women. Whether overtly polemical or not, it thus may function as an expression of critical reading. These two functions converge figuratively in the myths of Philomela and Arachne. Philomela saves herself from imprisonment and initiates revenge against Tereus for raping her, despite his removal of her tongue, by narrating her story in weaving: a resistance which also involves rewriting his fiction of her death. Arachne condemns the gods' rapes of mortal women, again by weaving, and thus contravenes the usual narration of these tales as love stories.

While the originary myths of women's narrative provide a model of resistance, revenge and rewriting deriving from rape, an alternative model of women's utterance is provided by the 'swansong'. I use the term 'swansong' to cover a variety of situations in which female eloquence is at once validated and circumscribed by the imminence of death.[16] In particular, in the 'female complaint' poems of the 1590s, the speaker is a ghost, her speech already authorised by her death. The two models of women's language thus converge in the preoccupation of this sub-genre with female sexual shame, and are exemplified in Shakespeare's *Lucrece*, which images its heroine as a 'pale swan in her wat'ry nest' (l. 1611). Lucrece's utterance – her reporting of her rape – is validated by her approaching death. This book will trace the parallel between these two models of women's discourse.

The 'Unbridled Speech' of my title both figures the relation between male discourse and rape (whether in threats by characters or in the inscription of rape in culture by authors) and, as the defining feature of Elizabeth Cary's heroine Mariam, represents the power of women's eloquence. The first part of the book will explore the portrayal of sexual violence against women in works by male writers, separated into genres, while the second will focus on women writers, treated individually. In the introductory chapter to Part I, I outline the concerns and methods of rape criticism, and consider the cultural and semantic complexities of the idea of 'rape' in this period. The introduction to Part II considers the implications of women reading and writing about rape, and focuses on specific examples of direct engagement with this subject, chiefly from polemical and conduct literature by women.[17]

It will be apparent that this study follows the work of at least two strands of recent criticism. In its treatment of the portrayal of rape it contributes to the project of unveiling the inscription and mystification of rape in literature. It also engages with the ongoing study of women's writing.[18] It is perhaps unusual in juxtaposing material on male with material on female writers: recent studies of gender issues in early modern literature have tended to exclude women's texts,[19] while studies of 'women's writing' have usually been exclusively so.[20] That the book considers male writers in Part I and female writers in Part II will inevitably impute to it an 'oppositional' structure; as I have indicated, however, this is not my exclusive aim.[21] Nevertheless, the book is perhaps oppositional in less direct ways: namely, in its implicit awareness of the function of writing as critical reading or rewriting. This is not to imply that women's writing is able only to respond to male writing or definitions of female sexuality; the idea of writing as critical reading is by no means limited to women's writing. It is, however, important in relation to the texts considered in Part II, which, as we shall see, also contribute to and sometimes transform cultural understandings of women's self-determination and discourse.

# Part I
# Writing Rape

# 1
# The Meanings of Rape

What can bee well or safe vnto a woman, when she hath loste her chastitie. Alas *Collatine*, the steppes of an other man, be now fixed in thy bedde. But it is my bodie onely that is violated, my minde God knoweth is giltles, whereof my death shalbe witnesse.

Painter, *The Palace of Pleasure*[1]

Tales of rape – attempted, achieved, resisted – pervade Elizabethan and Jacobean literature. The influence of classical literature accounts for a proliferation of allusions to Lucrece, Virginia and Philomela, whose stories are made available in English translations by Painter, Pettie and others, while Ovid's *Metamorphoses*, made popular by Golding's translations of 1565 and 1567, takes rape as its prototypical metamorphosis and provides a model of rape as foundation myth, as well as one in which it is readily glossed as 'love'.

Literature participates in the discourses that shape perceptions of rape. By writing rape, it not only reflects such perceptions, but inscribes rape in culture, imparting to it both ideological and narrative functions. Just as there is a 'deep interdependence between rape and society's institutionalization of women's subjection',[2] so literature deploys rape while participating in this subjection. Lynn Higgins and Brenda Silver argue that literature inscribes male power and female subordination by troping rape as '"natural" and inevitable'. In their pioneering study of rape in literature, they advocate the rereading of the representation of rape so as to uncover the ways in which it is normalized or mystified. This necessitates reading rape 'literally', that is, reading the violence back into texts which have made of it 'a metaphor or a symbol' or which represent it in ways which displace the trauma.[3]

My definition of 'rape' in this study is the modern one, sexual intercourse without the woman's consent.[4] Any study of its representation, however, needs to take into account the various early modern definitions of the word and their ideological implications. In his sociological study, Lee Ellis acknowledges that 'one can argue that [the term "rape"] should only be used to refer to whatever criminal behaviour happens to be legally defined as *rape* in a given society at a given point in time', but argues that this would hamper any efforts to understand rape as a 'cross-cultural phenomenon'.[5] Sylvana Tomaselli too suggests that 'each usage of the term seems to capture some relevant aspect of the problem even if none encompasses them all', but that it is necessary to avoid the potential amorphousness implied by this openness, whereby forced sex could not be considered in itself, as distinguished from abduction or arranged marriage.[6] I shall keep the issue of rape separate from these important, related questions. To make my discussion clear, I shall refer to 'rape' in inverted commas when I wish to indicate that the term is being used in a historically-specific or ambivalent way, and with no inverted commas when signifying the modern definition.

The goal of reading literally in order to demystify is more complex than it might seem. To read literally is not to read naively, or to be unaware of the various functions rape fulfils and the ideologies it upholds. On the contrary, it is only by *adding* a literal reading to the equation that we can appreciate the deployment and manipulation of rape in literary texts. In the early modern period, rape is often deployed as a political allegory, or defined in terms that privilege its political significance over other concerns. Rape may be an expression of political tyranny, or function as a crime against other men. 'Political' readings (or writings) of rape, however – that is, readings that privilege these functions of rape – can mask the power-relationship between the sexes upon which rape is always based and which it enforces. This is not to deny that the representation of rape may fulfil such roles. On the contrary, it is essential to recognise them: not only as part of the spectrum of narrative and ideological functions of rape, but to highlight the fact that it is the female body that is always the site of contestation at these moments.

My investigation of rape, then, is located firmly in relation to the sexual ideology of the period. It is not possible to approach these texts in order to infer the 'psychological effect' of rape except as it is represented. When social circumstances and sexual ideology affect so profoundly the depiction of the rape victim's predicament or distress, it is difficult to distinguish between such causes and any modern perception of 'trauma'. Rape narratives are, however, usually predicated on a notion of female distress, however circumscribed. In referring to 'trauma' in connection with these works, I shall be alluding to the pain, fear or feelings of violation attendant on rape. My interest is thus in the way such feelings are represented; in the alternative concerns which marginalise them; and in the ways in which inscriptions of female distress generally serve alternative purposes.

Self-destructive responses to rape or assault, such as self-mutilation or suicide, are well documented today.[7] Yet as they appear in Renaissance literature, they relate to ideological imperatives and constraints on women – the troping of female beauty as responsible for rape, and the idea that rape pollutes the victim. While the definition of rape as a 'property crime', which we shall see to be implicit in some representations, needs to be balanced by an awareness of its significance for the woman, the two are not mutually exclusive. A woman raped would necessarily have been concerned with the loss of her marriage potential or with the possibility of bearing an illegitimate child, probably more than with the traumatic nature of the rape. Moreover, stock motifs in the rhetoric of rape, such as the idea that a woman's 'no' means 'yes', play a significant role in the troping of rape as normative, but may also reflect a historical contingency, whereby women were obliged by the constraints of ideology to act 'coyly' and say 'no' despite, or as part of, their own erotic agendas. Such considerations do not detract from the exposure of the rhetoric of rape and its justification of violence against women. They do, however, point to the complexity of the situation to which contemporary economic and ideological factors give rise.

In choosing to look at literary representations of rape, I shall be exploring representation, rather than the 'truth' about rape in a particular historical period. I shall not be positing an unproblematic correspondence between 'literature' and 'life'; indeed, even legal records cannot be taken as wholly representative of contemporary attitudes, since rape appears to have been under-reported.[8] Rape is very much a *represented* crime, whether it is represented in the testimony of a complainant or defendant, or in a 'literary' text. In her study of pornography, *The Pornography of Representation*, Susanne Kappeler firmly defines the object of her enquiry as 'representational practices, rather than sexual practices', and argues that 'pornography is not a special case of sexuality; it is a form of representation'.[9] In that depictions of rape are a form of pornography (and Kappeler's argument that 'high' and 'low' culture should be seen as part of a continuum is helpful here), a comparable argument can be made for them. The implications of Kappeler's work have already been applied to the study of rape in literature, in Amy Richlin's study of rape in Ovid.[10] As we shall see, the representation of rape raises questions about the nature of representation in itself.

The *Gorboduc* printer's reference to the raped woman/book playing 'Lucrece's part' illustrates the popularity of Lucrece's story and
the ease with which that story can be appropriated. It is a story that
exemplifies the attitudes of early modern writers towards rape and
its victims. Painter introduces the tale with the words, '*Sextus Tarqui-
nius* rauisheth Lucrece', and later refers to the act as a 'rape' (ff. 5,
6v). Yet these terms are by no means straightforward in delineating
the crime. 'Rape' descends from the Latin '*rapere*', which signifies
theft or, if its object is a woman, abduction.[11] This definition of 'rape'
as 'abduction' is still available in the early modern period. Yet it also
carries the meaning 'violation' which it signifies today.[12] The coexistence of these two definitions of the word accounts for much of the
complexity surrounding the issue of rape.

Violation and abduction are related by historical and ideological
circumstances. When a woman is defined as the possession of a
man, rape is inevitably seen as a 'property crime', the theft of daughter from father or wife from husband.[13] That this sexual theft may
coincide with abduction heightens the conflation of the two. Yet
while the term 'rape' conflates rape and abduction in such a way as
to foreground the latter (a phenomenon mirrored by the term
'ravish'), the word 'deflower' is used interchangeably for rape or sexual
initation.[14] When signifying rape, 'deflower' may be used of married
women as well as virgins; conversely, it insidiously defines sexual
initation as an act of violence. In the cases of 'rape' and 'ravish',
then, the theft of the woman from her male owner is paramount
whether or not it has a sexual dimension; with 'deflower', it is the
sexual act which is foregrounded. Both words, in different ways,
may marginalise the woman's sexual volition.

The semantics of these terms are closely involved with the history
of legal attitudes to rape. As Elspeth Graham points out, legal dis-
putes played a key role in the definition of identity, by seeking 'to
establish boundaries to the self through the rightful protection of
property'.[15] Rape law is, by extension, an important way of defining
the identity of women and of families (when the woman's body as
property guarantees the honour of husband, father and wider family). The legal term during and beyond the medieval period is the
Latin one, 'raptus' (seizure), a term that gives prominence to abduction. Yet it would be a mistake to imagine that the treatment of rape
in law before the early modern period had no conception of the act
*as* a sexual act. Corinne Saunders has demonstrated that Anglo-
Saxon legal codes evidence a sense of the violation to the woman's

body effected by rape.[16] It is after the Conquest that this awareness is undermined with the arrival of Norman tradition and the terminology of 'raptus'. Saunders argues that 'legal writing after the Conquest is informed by recollections of the distinction made between rape and abduction in the Anglo-Saxon period'.[17] The reversal of this shift thus begins to be seen in the sixteenth century. Nazife Bashar points out that the statutes of 1555 and 1597 treated rape separately from abduction, and argues that this shows the emergence of the legal definition of rape as a 'crime against the person'.[18]

By 1616, John Bullokar defines 'rape' in his dictionary as 'a violent rauishing of a woman against her will', without mentioning abduction; he does not define 'ravish', perhaps thinking its meaning well known.[19] However, a compendium of laws relating to women, T.E.'s *The Lawes Resolvtions of Womens Rights* (1632), provides much evidence of the words' semantic complexity in its long section on 'rape'.[20] The conflation of rape with abduction and elopement pervades this text. The author's preoccupation with the original Latin meaning of the word (theft) leads him to define the 'two kindes of Rape', first, as 'when a woman is enforced violently to sustaine the furie of brutish concupiscence: but she is left where she is found . . . and not hurried away' (pp. 377–8) and, second, simply as her removal (regardless of any sexual consequences). The location of the woman is still paramount here. He cites Lucrece as the paradigm of the woman forcibly violated without being abducted, but for his second model cites Helen: certainly the paradigmatic stolen woman, but one whose volition in the removal and its sexual consequences is highly ambiguous.

The definition of 'ravishment' which emerges from this distinction disregards the woman's volition. A 'damsell within age' may not be 'rauish[ed]' 'with her consent or without' (p. 380); moreover, 'rape' and 'ravish' signify not only abduction, but elopement. The section treating the 'ravishment' of unmarried maids distinguishes between a woman consenting and not consenting, but only to establish the different penalties for the crime, with a view to its economic implications (pp. 385–90). The terms also cover adultery, often regardless of the woman's consent. Another section distinguishes between adultery with and adultery without consent, the woman's volition affecting her role in the litigation; but both cases are defined as 'rape' (p. 390). Despite the writer's abhorrence of 'hainous' rape (p. 378), the most detailed case-study concerns the consensual marriage of a widow against her family's wishes; she forfeits her lands because she 'assent[ed] to the rauisher' (pp. 399–400).

Bashar notes a conflict between the attitude to rape evidenced by legal statutes – that it is a heinous crime meriting severe punishment – and the low reporting of rape and proportionally low conviction rate.[21] Overt social condemnation of rape thus clashes with actual practice as reflected in the courts. She argues that this conflict may be the result of medieval law (based on the definition of women as male property) being applied in an age which has come to define rape to some degree as a crime against women.[22] Conviction thus seems to have become less likely once the volition of the woman became part of the equation. Yet Bashar finds that in early modern rape trials the defence was usually to claim that the sexual act did not take place, rather than to claim, as often today, that the woman consented. In the legal context, she concludes, the woman's volition was 'still fairly irrelevant'.

Not only do the words 'rape' and 'ravishment' signify theft as well as forcible coitus, but 'ravishment' also has a metaphorical significance which works against women. Figurative 'ravishment' indicates 'transport, rapture, ecstasy'; to 'ravish' is thus 'to transport with the strength of some feeling, to carry away with rapture; to fill with ecstasy or delight; to entrance'.[23] As Gravdal explains, the literal signification of 'ravish' presupposes a male subject, but in the figurative sense 'it is the female who is ravishing, who causes the male to be "carried away" and who is responsible for any ensuing sexual acts'.[24] This semantic phenomenon gives rise to a useful rhetorical tool, whereby rape is 'erased behind the romantic troping of ravishment'.[25] Although female beauty is a passive attribute, not disturbing the idea that a woman is the passive recipient of male desire, it is also credited with the power to 'ravish'. As Ellen Rooney argues, 'victimisation is read as the sign of seductive force', and so women are charged with complicity, at least, in sexual violence against them.[26] The language of courtship exemplifies this topos; its irony becomes apparent when the subservient male renders powerless and rapes the female.

Lucrece's story provides a *locus classicus* for the coexistence of the two definitions of rape, one as a 'property crime', the other as an act in which the woman's volition is crucial. In Painter's version, Lucrece's description of the rape as 'by violence [carrying] awaie from me . . . a pestiferous ioye' (f. 6) retains the semantic associations of the word. Yet the definition of 'rape' as theft *of*, rather than *from*, a woman is also a key part of this story, in which rape is seen as a crime against her husband as much as against Lucrece herself. Shakespeare is later to underline Lucrece's status as male property, when he depicts her husband and father competing for the right to mourn her.[27]

At the same time, female volition has a role to play in Lucrece's story. Its importance in defining her moral status is heightened because rape is instrumental in 'dramatiz[ing] a problematic about the relationship between the body and the mind': a relationship which is a major preoccupation of the age.[28] Lucrece's assertion, 'it is my bodie onely that is violated, my minde God knoweth is giltles' (f. 6), places her story at the centre of this debate and initiates centuries of controversy.

Whether the mind and body are discrete categories or are mutually implicating is a vexed question in the early modern period, and one which is at the centre of thinking about interiority at this time. For women, the question of whether the mind is affected by actions done to the body also finds a context in a pervading suspicion of both. Because they are defined by their sexual status (the tripartite system of maid/wife/widow, on the one hand; the opposition chaste/ unchaste, on the other), the relative invisibility of the female genitals and female sexual pleasure produces great anxiety in male thought. The female body seems unknowable, and the female mind equally so.

Rape makes significant the difference between two definitions of chastity. Chastity is frequently presented as an ideologically informed state of mind; a 'chaste' woman is one who chooses to live by its principles, preserving her virginity or remaining faithful to her husband. Yet the forcefulness of arguments for an opposition between mind or soul and body following rape, perhaps paradoxically, would seem to confirm that the basic definition of chastity is as a physical state. Rape, after all, tends to be seen as a *pollution* of the female body, regardless of the victim's volition, as is shown in the assertion by Lucrece's friends that 'her bodie was polluted, and not her mynde' (f. 6).

This definition of chastity as a physical state contributes to the blurring of the boundary between rape and seduction which sees all forms of female 'unchastity' as threatening moreover, perceives women as ever vulnerable to temp attack on 'chastity' becomes an 'assault', whether pe

force predominates. The resultant ambiguity facilitates the conflation of rape with all forms of illicit behaviour. The common function
of rape as a chastity test is predicated on a concern with resistance
(although problematically if that resistance fails, as we shall see).
Complicating the issue is the fact that female sexual denial is usually
figured as the active decision to be *chaste*, rather than to reject an
offer on any other grounds. Social or ideological factors thus often
coexist with the problematic idea of female sexual choice to the point
of rendering the latter invisible.

Popular and quasi-medical theories also shape the discourses of
rape. The belief that female orgasm was a prerequisite of conception
led to problems when a woman fell pregnant following rape.[29] This
belief adds to the problems surrounding the rape of a married
woman. A major concern in such cases is the possibility of illegitimate offspring being foisted on the 'wronged' husband. Yet if this
were to take place, the pregnancy would reflect, retrospectively, on
the 'rape' of the wife, whose resistance could be called into question.

The equation of 'consent' and orgasm further problematises the
perceived relationship between body and mind. *The Lawes Resolvtions*
records that if a woman conceives, 'there is no rape; for none can
conceiue without consent'.[30] Shakespeare's *Lucrece* is to suggest the
possibility that a genuinely resisting woman may be betrayed by her
body's responses, in referring to Lucrece's 'accessory yieldings'
(l. 1658).[31] If the body and mind are conceived of as separate, of course,
this should have no implications for the woman's mind or soul. In
practice, however, such an event (or the idea of it) strongly challenges
that opposition.

Even if the mind may be unviolated by any act perpetrated on the
body, it cannot be *read* except by the signs the body provides; physical evidence must, if it can, prove mental or moral innocence.
Lucrece's destruction of her polluted body attempts to provide such
evidence: paradoxically, by destroying the evidence. Her motivation – to ensure she is never cited in mitigation by an 'vnchast or ill
woman' (f. 6) – does not resolve the problems thrown up by this paradox. It also implies an apt awareness of herself as text: her suicide, as
much as the rape itself, is to prove endlessly re-readable and open
to interpretation. Not only does Lucrece's suicide seem to undercut
her claim to virtue, it is also inimical to the Christian religion, provoking Augustine's famous query: 'if she be an adulteresse, why is
shee commended? if shee bee chaste why did shee kill her selfe?'[32]
Augustine's anxiety is in part the product of a clash of cultural

values. The Roman culture in which Lucrece's story is located has been described as a 'shame' culture; in this context a raped woman's shame and loss of reputation were sufficient to justify suicide. Christian culture is, by contrast, one of 'guilt', in which the emphasis on conscience led Christian commentators such as Augustine to seek a 'guilty' reason for suicide, such as enjoyment of the rape: 'she her selfe gaue a lustfull consent' (p. 30).

The iconography of female martyrdom plays a significant role in the representation of rape. It provides a precedent for the complex relation of mind and body, whereby the true self is located in the mind or soul, but is marked by the endurance of pain. Where the torture involves rape, Augustine argues that 'the body is sanctified by the sanctification of the will', as, Vives notes, 'a comforting vnto our Christian women that endured these violences'.[33] Suicide still presents problems, however, and Lucrece's story is often cited alongside those of Christian martyrs and saints in this context. For Augustine it is no more justifiable to kill oneself to prevent rape than after it: if there is no reason for the latter, 'how much lesse ought this course to bee followed before there bee any cause?' (p. 29). However, an early Christian tradition represented by St Jerome unproblematically lauded such suicide.[34]

Female martyr stories, as Helen Hackett points out, were based on the 'belief that the virgin body was pure and holy, and that chastity ... could achieve spiritual purity', and she argues that 'just such an identification of different kinds of bodily purity seems to have become attached to Elizabeth [I]'.[35] The rhetoric of chastity thus has an added resonance in the Elizabethan period. Iconography surrounding the Queen, moreover, frequently defines chastity as *inviolability*. As Louis Montrose has argued, Elizabeth's virginity is figured as the inviolability of her country, and invasion as an attempted rape which this inviolability thwarts.[36] Such iconography may relate to an assertion of the power of chastity which we shall find prevalent in rape material. The troping of chastity – and frequently also beauty – as all-powerful contributes significantly to the belief that only suicide can prove a raped woman innocent of sexual desire and enjoyment.

Lucrece's story evidences an ambivalence about the feasibility of rape which intensifies the anxiety concerning the female role and heightens the necessity for suicide. While (as in most rape scenarios) the man's threats or violence serve as a measure of the woman's chastity, the alternatives he gives her verbally do not admit of rape as a physical possibility. When Lucrece will not 'yelde to his requeste' (f. 5v) Tarquin threatens her not with rape, but with infamy through sexual slander. Painter, translating Livy, portrays the rape as necessitating a female choice. Yet the language betrays its own ambivalence: 'She *vanquished* with his terrible and infamous threat. [*sic*] His fleshly and licentious enterprise, *ouercame the puritie* of her chast harte' (my emphasis). The syntax too is ambivalent: is it Lucrece herself or Tarquin's 'enterprise' that overcomes her purity? Ovid says that she 'yielded, overcome by fear of scandal'.[37] Despite the sympathy for Lucrece in both versions, she is seen as yielding. The terms of Tarquin's threat, after all, do not allow for anything other than yielding or refusing and being murdered. Although this does not interfere with the definition of the act as a rape, the words 'rauish' and 'defloure' (f. 5v) which the story uses, are sufficiently ambivalent to fail to elucidate the matter. It may give rise to such seemingly paradoxical arguments as William Vaughan's, that 'Lucrecia was an adulteresse, because she consented for that time, though it were against her will'.[38]

Conflicting ideas about female desire complicate the notion of resistance. Some medieval and Renaissance commentators contend that a virtuous woman should experience no desire outside marriage, so that her resistance of an assailant will be motivated by chastity. Others, however, argue that for sexual resistance to qualify as virtuous, it must be the resistance of a temptation rather than of an act for which the woman has no desire.[39] Resistance, then, relates problematically to virtue.

Moreover, Rooney has argued that the active/passive dichotomy which is attributed to rape as its defining feature – distinguishing it from the 'equivocal' situation of seduction – is problematic because by this formulation the woman's 'resistance (her activity) goes unread'.[40] The tension she suggests between the conflicting female roles of passivity and resistance is still more complex in the early modern period. While her claim that resistance is what 'makes rape rape' is true for the modern sense of 'rape', it is clearly not valid for its original sense as theft: a crime in which the woman is by definition an object, whose volition is irrelevant. Kappeler's analysis of the 'willingness of the victim' in pornographic representation is helpful here. She argues that 'the woman-object consists of body alone, without the dimension of a human will. When it is new, intact, it bears the seal of its "unwillingness" in its virginity'; hence, she suggests, 'male culture's historical obsession with female virginity and

the act of deflowering'. This may help to explain the use of the word
'deflower' interchangeably for rape or sexual initiation. However,
once initiated, women are conceived of as becoming insatiable. 'The
willingness of the female victim,' she concludes,

> is...the cultural state of woman, coded by the patriarchal eco-
> nomy of the exchange of women....The willingness of the woman-
> object is the natural state to which she has been returned through
> the offices of men. Willingness and unwillingness are thus expres-
> sions of her body, not determinations of her mind.[41]

Kappeler's argument provides a helpful gloss on the familiar
dichotomy in early modern sexual ideology between the belief that
women are pure and the belief that they are naturally evil.[42] It is pertinent not only to the conception of rape, but to that of seduction.
Where the difference between the two is commonly seen as hinging
on the woman's mind, Kappeler's argument gives rise to a different
model, whereby rape is the overpowering of the female body by
male force while seduction is its overpowering by desire. Both scenarios are located in the physical. This model is potentially very helpful in looking at early modern texts, in which the destruction of the
woman's (physical) chastity is often of greatest weight, rather than
the role of her (mental) volition in the sexual act. Yet this privileging
of the physical coexists with a deep concern over how to identify a
woman's mental state. A tendency to collapse rape and seduction
into each other thus clashes with a need to distinguish between the
two. The resultant tension is characteristic of early modern representations of women's sexual 'falls'.

The story of Susanna and the Elders exemplifies the proximity of
seduction, rape and slander. Thomas Garter's play *The Commody of
the moste vertuous and Godlye Susanna* (1578) reveals the Elders'
'temptation' of Susanna to be poised between attempted seduction
and threatened rape, as they intend to enjoy her 'through love or
might' (l. 664):

> Nay, nay Madame, we meane not so, we meane to haue our will,
> Doe you consent you shall vs fynde both sure and secrete still.
>
> (ll. 759–60)

An emphasis on the rhetoric of 'persuasion' employed by the sexual
aggressors, and the role of 'dissuasion' in fending off unwanted

advances, gives rise to an alternative model of the sexual fall, where-by rape is the failure of a woman's eloquence (often reflective of an inadequate virtue) and seduction is the triumph of the man's persuasion. Where male persuasion should presuppose a female counterpart of being either convinced or unconvinced (saying 'yes' or 'no'), female dissuasion should presuppose a male counterpart of either being dissuaded from his sexual goal or not being dissuaded. (Male) persuasion thus implies a scenario of (attempted) seduction, while (female) dissuasion implies one of (threatened) rape. That the two tend to be presented instead as counterparts contributes to the confusion of verbal with physical force.[43]

A powerful tension operates, then, in representations of rape, as of women more generally. Two interpretative forces tend to com-pete in such material, deriving from the opposed definitions of rape as a crime against the woman and as property crime. One defines female sexual conduct categorically as either innocent or guilty, leading respectively to approbation or condemnation, but acknow-ledging the woman's volition as a factor. The other defines as illicit all sexual activity that is not 'chaste' (marital), without regard for her volition, and therefore condemns the woman as well as the act. This phenomenon is clearly connected to the conflation of rape with abduction. Comparably, the presence of rape in a narrative has different generic consequences, causing it to develop into either tragedy or tragi-comedy. This hinges not only on whether the rape is achieved or not, but on whether a raped woman commits suicide (producing tragedy) or marries her rapist (a happy ending).[44] If she dies, there is a further possibility that good will be made out of the rape, most notably with the expulsion of the Tarquins fol-lowing Lucrece's death – and in this case the story is assimilated into history.

Lucrece's story illustrates the tradition in which rape is at once an expression of political tyranny and a moment of weakness which leads to the tyrant's overthrow. In the terms of Aristotle's political formula, 'one of the primary reasons that tyrants are ruined is that they offend the honor of their male subjects by raping and violating their wives'.[45] Machiavelli's discourse, 'How Women have brought about the Downfall of States', attributes power to the rape victims:

> First, we see how women have been the cause of many troubles, have done great harm to those who govern cities, and have caused in them many divisions .... We read in Livy's history that

cuntcave 333

the outrage done to Lucretia deprived the Tarquins of their rule, and that done to Virginia deprived the Decemviri of their power.[46]

In both stories, the women's bodies are displayed publicly in order to incite political action, literally held up as symbols of male tyranny and as incentives to political uprising. The rape or attempted rape is exploited in the interests of political action, and the idea of sexual violence as a woman's traumatic experience is written out of the narrative in favour of its 'greater' political significance. It is possible to see this narrative progression as empowering for the women, whose lives have such momentous effects. Yet such power achieved so passively might be seen, like the eloquence of the 'swansong', as not empowering at all. Like all uses of rape narratives for supposedly 'greater' ends, this exploitation of the woman might be seen as a kind of 'symbolic' rape.

If early modern thinking about rape exhibits significant tensions, a comparable clash has also arisen more recently. Where rape was traditionally perceived as motivated by desire, Susan Brownmiller's pioneering study, *Against Our Wills: Men, Women and Rape* (1975), argued radically that rape is primarily an act of power and aggression that deploys sexuality, rather than being 'about' desire *per se*. Despite plenty of clinical evidence to support it, the idea that rape is motivated by power (or the urge for power) rather than sex continues to be a contentious issue.[47] Moreover, as Teresa de Lauretis demonstrates, defining rape as 'violent' rather than 'sexual' presents its own problems, exemplified by Foucault's attempt to desexualise and thus decriminalize rape.[48] As Monique Plaza argues:

> rape is sexual essentially because it rests on the very social difference between the sexes. . . . It is *social sexing* which is latent in rape. If men rape women, it is precisely because they are women in a social sense.[49]

It is for this reason, she argues, that the victim of rape is always symbolically female, even in cases of male rape; the argument can be extended to allegory, in which a 'raped' country, for instance, is by definition female.

The representational strategies that implicitly give women the responsibility for rape exist in tension with the actual power-dynamic

between the sexes. This is not just available to a 'modern' perception, but is actually the basis for the strategies themselves. Giving
women the blame for rape counterbalances an overt condemnation
of it; and this condemnation itself exists in a profound tension with
the desire to reproduce rape of which all representations give evidence. As Jonathan Crewe has argued, '"writing rape" ... threatens
merely to reinstate rape'.[50] Writing (about) rape writes the rape into
literature, inscribes it in culture. It is, not least, a form of writing
(about) women: thus 'enforcing' certain perceptions of women's
roles, bodies and minds. Without needing to enquire into the inten-
tions of the individual writer, we can see that writing rape cannot be
a neutral activity. As such, it raises questions about the nature of
representation itself.

When the body of Lucrece or of Virginia is displayed to incite
revolution, it functions as an emblem of rape (whether achieved or
not), a visual narrative. Yet its display also incites or necessitates a
voyeurism which we shall find to be inevitably bound up with the
representation of rape. The act of rape itself proves congruent with
both voyeuristic intrusion and narration. A woman held up to view
is 'disclosed': the word 'dis-closure', opening up, figures its own
relationship to rape. Rape discloses/ascertains a victim's chastity,
sometimes because to be raped is defined as yielding, but more
commonly because rape defines a woman's sexual status by creating
it. It also casts her from the closed system of categorising chaste women. Rape is, however, a secret, hidden crime, usually taking place
without witnesses, perhaps (as with Lucrece) in bedchambers, its
effect on the victim hidden within the recesses of her body. How
rape is disclosed to others, then, becomes equally significant. It may
be disclosed by the victim, which may or may not be empowering.
Her disclosure, whether in literature or in a legal 'disclosure', may
constitute a narrative; but the rape is always already disclosed *by*
the narrative.

Rape is thus by its nature an act of intrusion comparable to narration, a resonance which many early modern texts exploit. Nashe's
depiction of the rape of Heraclide in *The Unfortunate Traveller* (1594) –
observed by the narrator, 'through a cranny of my chamber
unsealed' – is infamous for its deployment of voyeurism to reflect
on the nature of writerly authority and the reading experience.[51]
Heraclide's rape, which is described at length, also exemplifies an
important function of the rape narrative: to titillate. This function underlines the inherent voyeurism of rape as a narrative act.

Criticism of the 'gaze' has established that its hypostasisation of its female object is analogous to rape; Nancy Vickers' application of this theory to the early modern period focuses on the blason as the literary device which most invites the gaze, and on Shakespeare's *Lucrece* as self-consciously exemplifying the way in which the blason thus renders its object vulnerable to rape.[52] More generally, Gravdal has argued that male readers are intended to enjoy a voyeuristic pleasure in reading about rape, and that 'a male audience enjoys watching forbidden scenes of erotic pleasure ... if the text manages the taboo in an acceptable way'.[53] Caroline Lucas further suggests that lurid descriptions of rape indicate the (male) writer's enjoyment.[54] More recent work on desire and the gaze, however, has suggested that the gaze may not always be gendered male. Valerie Traub's insistence on the 'interplay of power and erotic desire' in the reader or viewer has opened up the way for readings of early modern texts to allow for titillation for the female reader of a scenario in which the female character is disempowered.[55] This perspective will be helpful in looking at the implications of a woman writer manipulating desire.

In the following chapters, I examine a large number of texts which contain rape or attempted rape. I define 'rape narratives' as any in which a sexual threat is articulated, since the portrayal of attempted rape reveals as many attitudes as does that of accomplished rape. The material which appears in these chapters shares several attitudes to rape. However, different genres frequently treat them in different ways, sufficiently to necessitate genre-based study. The rhetoric of rape as it appears in romance sometimes gains an ironic distance in the drama, where all ideas must be voiced by a particular character. Other attitudes which were largely unchallenged in the romances become the subjects of debate later on. This may, of course, owe as much to the passage of time as to the exigencies of genre.

As we move from Elizabethan translated and native fiction, through Elizabethan poetry, to late Elizabethan and Jacobean drama, rape becomes increasingly prominent. In chivalric romance rape attempts usually fail, with successful rapes set in the past. The poetic genres which involve rape tend to play on the confusion between rape and seduction, or feature failed attempts; this emphasis is predominantly shared by late Elizabethan drama. In Jacobean drama, sexual violence as spectacle becomes extreme; yet, paradoxically, the actual moment of rape necessarily takes place off-stage. The exception to this progression is found in Elizabethan native fiction. Not bound by the conventions of chivalric romance nor the contingencies of the theatre, the novellas are free to stage rape, and do so, sometimes in lurid detail. It is to fiction that I now turn.

# 2
# Damsels in Distress: Romance and Prose Fiction

Lucrece's story exemplifies most of the attitudes characterising Elizabethan rape fiction. The *Palace of Pleasure*, in which it appears, along with other novella translations, exerted huge influence on subsequent prose writing in the period.[1] The rape narrative is a standard feature of the equally popular chivalric romance, which became available in translation from the 1570s, opening up the market in terms of both class and gender. The number of romances increases dramatically to the last decade of the century.[2] Once the romances become available to a female readership, they are increasingly associated with it, and references to women's appetite for romances increase.[3] Whether women's apparently increasing consumption of romance itself gives rise to the central focus of native prose fiction on female characters is a vexed question. While Caroline Lucas believes that it does, Lorna Hutson has argued that this focus is rather due to a preoccupation of the genre with masculine agency, now displaced from military prowess to the art of persuasion.[4] The incidence and portrayal of rape in romance, then, exists in relation to, rather than in spite of, its posited female readership.

## RAPE AND RESCUE IN CHIVALRIC ROMANCE

Surely saide *Palmerin*, I must needes venture my selfe again those, that will take vpon them to vse cruelty to any faire Lady.

(*Palmerin of England*, i. f. 152)

Rape is a stock motif in romance. Gravdal argues that it is intrinsic to the genre, which 'by its definition must create the threat of rape ... so that knights can prove their mettle'.[5] The importance of rescue in this scheme (displaying the rescuer's prowess) means that the majority of the rape scenarios (roughly two-thirds of them) feature attempted rather than successful rape.[6] Even narratives

25

concerned with successful rape tend not to stage it. Many feature a giant or tyrant who is prone to raping women as a sign of his power, and whose rapes are reported rather than staged; the report is often followed by a staged instance of attempted rape, which is foiled by the hero.[7] Others are reported as part of a description of war, real or threatened.[8] I have found only two scenes which stage rape. One follows the report of multiple rapes by a giant, and the story is told by the victim, who is then avenged by the hero (*Amadis*, pp. 39–42). In the other, the narrator's husband rapes her four sisters in front of her – another exception to the usual narrative pattern (*Palmerin*, iii. ff. 112–112v).

The 'distress' of threatened damsels is represented visually by various physical motifs. The women have loose or dishevelled hair, or are tearing their hair or faces. Their language at this point is generally inarticulate: they are weeping or screaming. The setting too provides a visual marker, as most attempted rapes take place in a wood.[9] The rescuer is alerted to the scene by hearing the cries of the woman or women under attack, and/or by catching sight of them, or by being told the story by another woman – either a witness or another victim who has escaped. The knight rescues them from their attacker(s), after which they are overcome with gratitude. A woman who has narrowly escaped violation shows no further sign of distress, and sings the praises of her rescuer. One is 'verie ioyfull' that she had seene so warlike a knight' (*Mirror* iii(1). sig. Gg4v).

Two definitions of knightly ethos clash in these narratives, one based on male–female, the other on homosocial relations. Palmerin's speech (above) exemplifies the former, which establishes women as needing defence, and true knights as bound to protect them. He draws a significant equation between sexual threat and male heroic action when he tells a woman she 'shall finde [knights] as ready to defend you, as your enemy dare presume to molest you' (i. f. 81). A rape-and-rescue narrative demonstrates not only the power of the rescuer over the rapist, but the power of both males over the female. Female beauty has a dual effect: both an incentive to rape and an incentive to rescue, it stimulates both males into action.

In the homosocial system, the knight's duty is to support his fellow knights. An episode in *Palmerin* brings out the conflict between the two. Palmerin meets a knight who reports how a third, Felistor, is about to ambush and then marry by force a woman who has refused his marriage proposal. Palmerin assumes that the knight is urging him to help the woman; to his surprise, he turns out to be demanding help for Felistor. Palmerin stubbornly defines knightly ethos according to the heterosexual model: 'It better standeth with your credite, to defend the cause of a distressed Lady, then to be an instrument whereby her honour may receiue such disgrace' (ii. f. 10v).

Two knights in *Palmerin* attempt to rape a woman in revenge for their defeat by the men of her court, arguing, 'we should ease our anger on this Damosell' (ii. f. 109). Rape thus becomes a male weapon against men, as well as a gesture of male solidarity. In one case, male revenge provides the imperative for rescue as well as rape. In the *Mirror*, the Queen of Mauritania is abducted by a giant as revenge on her husband for the destruction of the giant's people. The hero remembers that this king has defeated him in the past and decides:

> that if fortune did fauour him to rescue & set at libertye this Ladye, not for to let hir passe, till such time, as the King did come in hir demaund ... [H]e would not deliuer hir but with mortall battaile. (ii. f. 289)

The irony of the phrase 'set at libertye' here becomes increasingly apparent.

The knightly ethos of rape is also predicated on the division of all knights into good and bad. The fight over the body of the woman thus becomes a symbol of the battle between good and evil. However, conflicting definitions of the knightly ethos, and the sense in which all battles in rape narratives simply demonstrate male competitiveness, frequently undermine this convenient opposition. Several moments also suggest explicitly that a 'good' knight may be as dangerous to a woman as a 'bad'.

The idea that a rescued woman is beholden to her rescuer sometimes gains a sexual significance. In the *Mirror*, Pastora asks her rescuer, 'what reward can I ... giue ... but to put my selfe into your handes, that with mee you may doe your pleasure, hauing a respect vnto my honour' (*Mirror*, ii. f. 306v). The last clause barely mitigates the sexual overtones of the speech, particularly as the phrase 'to do/ take one's pleasure' was a common sexual euphemism. This sexual indebtedness becomes explicit when rescue is followed by a demand for sex.[10] One rescued woman in *Palmerin* lies with her deliverer, who then abandons her.[11] Palmerin himself rescues a woman whom he then entreats to 'bestow that on me by gentlenesse, which the vncourteous Knights would haue taken from you perforce'. Her response is not given; instead, the narrator coyly comments that 'if it were incident to his purpose, hee is best able to answere it, if not, then there was no harme done' (ii. f. 109).

Two earlier scenes in the work gain significance in this context. In both cases, the rescued woman is frightened of her rescuer. One woman runs away when her attacker has been defeated (ii. f. 13). The other asks her rescuer to leave, as the attack has frightened her. His amusement at 'the little trust the Lady reposed [in] his company' (i. f. 168) is difficult to share. Female consent is written out of these narratives. The scenes are certainly not presented as rape narratives; rather, a formula is being established whereby the defeat of a rapist entitles the conqueror to exactly the goal of the 'bad' knight, that is, sexual pleasure. This formula helps normalise rape, by defining women as male possessions.

## SLAVES OF FOLLY

Tis hard to stop but harder to retire
When youthfull course ensueth pleasure vaine,
As Bears do breake the hives and weake defences
When smell of honie commeth to their sences.
                    (Ariosto, *Orlando Furioso*, XI.1)

Chivalric romance aestheticises rape as a normative male action. Although the standard pattern of rape and rescue normalises rape predominantly as the practice of evil characters, several tendencies emerge which justify it in behavioural terms, rather than as a generic requirement. The troping of rape as an expression of love or uncontrollable desire, as seen in Ariosto (above), implicitly excuses rape even while condemning it. The focus may foreground the battle between good and evil within the man; alternatively, he may be portrayed as weak, succumbing to the greater (though passive) power of his victim.

In the *Mirror of Knighthood*, a woman contests the definition of rape or abduction as the expression of love, telling her abductor, 'if like a good Knight ... thou haddest procured my good will, it had not bene much I had yeelded to thy request: but since thou hast imployed thy force vpon a poore weake Lady, I will rather bee my owne murtherer, then consent to any such thing' (iii(3). sig. M3).

The force of her position is undermined, however, when she eventually falls in love with and marries him.

The raped or threatened woman coming to pity or even marry her attacker is a common phenomenon. Such characters implicitly or explicitly define rape as an expression of love, rather than as a traumatic sexual crime. In *Palmerin*, a knight asks mercy of his victim:

> she (beholding the amiable countenance of him that would haue forced her) was supprised with exceeding greefe, so that she pittied more to see him so neare his death, then she required reuenge for his dishonest enterprise. (ii. f. 10)

In such cases, not only the women but the 'good' knights may concur with the rapist's opinion that rape expresses love. Palmerin, despite his condemnation of rape attempts, persuades three women he has freed to marry the men who had imprisoned them, citing 'the great estimation [they] made of them, [and] how also the cause of [their] sharpe dealing, was onely because they denied [their] loue' (i. f. 153v).

Where women marry men who have tried and failed to rape them, the marriage cannot function as a restitution of female 'honour'. In the novellas, by contrast, marriage often functions as recompense for an actual rape, reflecting real-life contingencies.[12] In Painter's story 'Alexander de Medices' the rapist is compelled to marry his victim and 'the marriage [was] made in presence of the Duke, with so great ioy and contentation of all partes, as there was rage and trouble for y$^e$ rape of the Bride'.[13] This neat equation seeks to cancel out the rape, writing the issue of female consent and desire out of the story, and conflating all male sexual behaviour as 'love', whether aggressive or not. Alexander commands the rapist to 'loue hir so dearely, as fondly heeretofore she was beloued of thee' (f. 168v).

In the novellas, both the translations of the 1560s and 1570s and native prose fiction, the absence of rescuing knights produces a greater balance between actual and attempted rapes than in chivalric romance.[14] They also show greater flexibility about the relative social status of attacker and victim. Where the sexual status of victims in chivalric romance is rarely mentioned (and if it is, the woman is likely to be a virgin), there are more married victims in the novellas. This variety naturally produces a greater range of social implications hinging on the rape or attempted rape. In both chivalric romance and the novellas, the victims are usually of a relatively high social class, which highlights the function of rape as a weapon in male power-games.

The concept of blind male desire as a categorical imperative ennobles the male characters in these works. They may also be troped more explicitly as heroic. In Bandello's 'A Modern Lucretia', translated by Fenton, this paradoxically coexists with a justification of the rapist as weak. Although he is first referred to as a 'detestable palliard and common enemy of the honour of women', he is then immediately represented as a noble character with a fatal flaw: 'one vice that is detestable darkeneth the credit of a number of virtues!' (p. 340). He becomes a 'slave of folly', a 'fond youngling and pupil of Cupid' (pp. 346, 342). Combined with this sympathy for male weakness in the face of female beauty, an extensive use of military metaphors tropes sexual advance, assault and rape as heroic. It allows the 'poor gentleman' (p. 342) to be imaged as a 'valiant soldier that will not leave the assault for one repulse' (p. 345). The woman's body is imaged as a castle or fortress, the man as a 'valiant soldier of love' (p. 348). His determination to rape signals his bravery: 'seeing he could not prevail by policy nor win the fort by summons or offer of composition, he determined ... to use the uttermost of his forces and perform his conquest whatsoever it cost him' (pp. 357–8). Token condemnation of the rapist's actions cannot counterbalance such a characterisation of his sexual aggression as heroic and erotic as well as natural and unavoidable.

Such explicit sympathy for the rapist is quite rare; the rhetoric justifying rape is more often employed by the rapists themselves, which allows for a certain amount of distance between the reader and the ideology. Yet it is only an extreme version of the idea that rape expresses love, which implicitly condones sexual violence. There are, however, two further strategies for justifying rape. Rape may be written as something else: especially as seduction. Still more insidiously, the responsibility for rape may be placed with its victim.

## VIRTUE AND INVIOLABILITY

> But I know this assuredly, that if she guiltlesse bee,
> God will defende the innocent, from cruell destinie.[15]

If God is prepared to save the virtuous from a 'cruell destinie' which is frequently rape, we must ask how it is that a supposedly virtuous woman can come to be raped. Elizabethan rape fiction manipulates the implication that a rape victim could not have been virtuous enough, and uses rape to enforce chaste conduct in the posited woman reader.

Lucrece's story shows how the belief that rape is physically impossible produces a new definition of rape as 'forcing a woman to yield'. This definition coexists with the mass of evidence in prose fiction that men are physically capable of raping women. Bandello's 'The Villainous Abbot' provides an early example of the 'forced to yield' definition of 'rape'. The victim of the monk's attempted rape throws herself into the sea, preferring to die rather than 'to *yield forcible* offering of the first-fruits of her virginity' (p. 283; emphasis mine). In *Palmerin*, some knights 'endeuoured by their faire speech to allure [the woman] to their lust, but when they sawe she would not consent, they would *vrge* her to it *perforce*' (i. f. 168; emphasis mine). Women are often threatened with death if they do not yield, which implies that only 'yielding rape' is a physical possibility; in *Palmerin*, for instance, the knight threatens to 'cut off her head, if she refused to obey his lust' (ii. f. 107v). Several attempted rapes actually culminate in murder, as though this were the only alternative to 'yielding'.

The strongest evidence of this attitude appears in the *Mirror*, in an episode which rewrites the story of Tereus and Philomela. This reworking alters the original in one important respect: when Herea (Philomela) resists, Noralindo (Tereus) murders her, rather than raping her. Again, the language of sexual threat is confusing. The possibility of force is the basis of Noralindo's 'determined purpose towardes hir' (ii. f. 68), but his speech is contradictory:

> Doe not thou thinke O cruell *Herea*, that thou canst delyuer thy selfe out of my hands, except first thou graunt vnto this my desired will, and if not, I doo promise . . . to put thee vnto the most cruell death that euer was deuised for any Damosell or maide. (ii. f. 68v)

He thus ends by threatening death as the only alternative to 'yielding'. His final threat, 'either liuing or dead I will performe my will & pretended purpose', suggests murder might follow (or precede) rape, but this never occurs. His murder by strangulation suggests that he makes a conscious decision to kill her – she does not simply die because of the physical violence he has been using in the rape attempt. In this version of Philomela's story, the women are denied empowerment and revenge as well as language. Yet if this alone had been the writer's agenda, Herea could have been murdered after rape. The alteration of the story, and the language which accomplishes it, suggest that the writer was exploiting a prevalent belief.

Such examples, however, exist in tension with plenty of evidence of male capability of force. Painter's Lucrece may be 'forced to yield', but in his 'Alexander de Medices', the miller's daughter is raped by force: 'in dispite of hir teeth' (f. 162v). The same clash occurs in *Palmerin*, where Polynarda fears 'that violence might wrong her beyond compasse of sufferance' (iii. f. 65v); when Tamerco decides to 'rauish her immediatly', he 'had euen then accomplished his wicked desire' if Palmerin had not appeared (iii. f. 66v). When a giant abducts Candida we are told that 'if he could not by faire meanes haue compassed his desire, in brutish manner he would haue rauished her' (iii. f. 259v).

Native fiction manifests the same tension. In Lodge's *A Margarite of America* (1596), Philenia and her husband Minecius die defending her 'honor'.[16] Although it is clear that Arsadachus intends rape, demanding 'my pleasure of thee' (p. 29), Philenia seems to think that she is choosing between death and yielding, despite her awareness of his physical power:

> since neither teares, nor tearmes will satisfie thee, vse thy tyranny (for better were it for me to be buried with honor, then bedded with infamie). (p. 30)

In *Euphues Shadow* (1592), however, Servatia is raped by force.[17] *Robert second Duke of Normandy* (1591) actually includes two directly contradictory episodes. Robert murders Lady Beaumont because she will not yield.[18] Yet earlier, his rape of a nun is described with lurid emphasis on the force used, and the victim 'resisted euen in conquest' (p. 18).

The ideological implications of this tension are tremendous. Although a woman is apparently not to blame for a 'yielding-rape', this definition subtly allocates a degree of responsibility to her. However resolutely she may have clung to the ideal of chastity, however she may have resisted, if verbal threats or physical violence induce her to *yield*, she is technically consenting. As we know from the dilemma over Lucrece, she is stained not only passively, by being the recipient of sin, but because she has engaged (for whatever reason) in illicit sexual behaviour.

The tension between rape as force and rape as forcing to yield thus concerns not only physiology but also the issue of female response or resistance. As we know, the idea of resistance is problematic. While in chivalric romances it is a measure of the assailant's power, in novellas it is essential for the woman's lack of desire to be absolute in order to establish her in her function as paragon of chastity. In both cases, female desire is written out by the conflation of the lack of desire with the principle of chastity. Only in the rare examples where a rape attempt follows the woman's rejection of a marriage proposal (that is, a licit sexual advance) is it possible to read the woman's resistance as a sexual choice rather than an ideological one.[19]

The idea that rape is physically impossible lies behind the strategies for blaming its victims. The prevalent motif of dishevelled hair exemplifies the duality of rape's portrayal. Loose hair is associated with sexual initiation – legitimately, in the case of brides.[20] Hair that is not only loose but dishevelled frequently signifies rape in romance, whether the woman has been raped, is under threat of rape or is reporting an attack on a friend. However, it may also signify general distress or distraction by love. The *Mirror* shows the intersection when Lidia is traced by the hair which she has pulled out and scattered in a trail (suggestive of violence), but turns out to be a victim of love and not rape (ii. f. 103). The association of rape and female sexual activity through this motif may relate to the belief that rape is forcing a woman to consent; both shift a degree of responsibility onto her.

While the rape narratives thus try to deny the existence of female desire, it is a belief in female desire which lies at the root of the strategies they use to shift the blame for rape onto the women themselves. These strategies are part of a rhetoric used by rapists as well as narrators, whereby female beauty is all-powerful, love irresistible and rape, therefore, an inevitable submission of the male to female allure. This rhetoric is both a weapon to use against women and a sign of fear of their potential power. As rhetoric, it renders women vulnerable by creating an idea of female power which turns out to be illusory and a means of blaming them for rape. But the fear of female sexual power seems to be real, and this anxiety informs the portrayal of rape.

Just as female beauty may be blamed for rape, assertions that beauty and virtue are their own protection also give women the responsibility for rape. The idea that a woman's beauty gives her power over men is a cover for its justification of male sexual violence. In *Amadis*, rape is described as an appropriate response to beautiful young women, when some would-be rapists describe their behaviour as 'such . . . as beseemeth women of their age' (p. 84). Yet beauty may be given as a reason for rescue, 'seeing hir to bee a verye fayre woman, and without anye desert to bee thus so euill intreated' (*Mirror*, ii. f. 290). This use of beauty to justify rescue complicates further the balance of real and apparent power in the beauty topos. One woman is even saved from rape because her beauty is 'so piercing to [the giant], as he durst not awake her' (*Palmerin*, iii. f. 259v). Beauty only seems empowering until we recall that it was the excuse for rape in the first place. Pastora's beauty 'hath so much force, that it incouraged one shepheard to doe that which a thousand Knights durst not haue giuen the enterprise off' (*Mirror*, ii. f. 307), causing both the rape attempt and the successful rescue.

The beauty topos is a feature of the novellas as well as the chivalric romances. Sir John Harington makes a connection between beauty and virtue in his translation of *Orlando Furioso*. In his added 'Moral' to the eighth book, in which Angelica is threatened with rape, he notes 'how perilous a thing beautie is if it be not especially garded with the grace of God and with vertue of the mynde, being continually assayld with enemies spirituall and temporall' (p. 99). Virtue thus counterbalances the beauty which incites assault, and assures the woman's safety. This trope is instrumental in insinuating blame for the victims of rape.

The writer of *Amadis* is uncertain about the self-protective nature of virtue. God sends Amadis to end the giant Galpan's cruelty, but only after he has raped a great number of women (p. 39). In *Palmerin* a woman is saved by her virtue, 'the iust heauens, neuer permitting violence to that faire body, wherein so chaste a soule was enclosed' (iii. f. 66); but later, a wife is only saved from her husband – 'heauen beholding my intollerable iniuries' (f. 112v) – after he has beaten her and raped her sisters. Chivalric romances, however, tend not to pursue the implications of the virtue topos. It is the novellas which more extensively exploit the idea of the power of virtue.

In 'The Villainous Abbot', Parolina trusts God to 'defend her chastity against the malice of the wicked' (p. 272). When the abbot and his men ambush her, she steals the monk's sword and defeats them single-handed, but is then wounded and attempts to drown herself to avoid rape:

God, not willing as yet to deprive the world of so rare a mirror of virtue, gave her such force against the rage of the stream, that she kept breath till certain passengers ... recovered her. (p. 283)

The ostensible moral of this story is that if you are virtuous, you will not be raped, but the lengths to which Parolina goes to prove her virtue undermine this conclusion. Moreover, she is held up as a model not just for women in general but for 'unperfect and foolish women' (p. 283). The conclusion conflates rape with *all* illicit sexual behaviour, so that female readers are ordered to go to any lengths to remain chaste. The narrator orders the 'unperfect' women,

by studying to imitate her virtue, to leave no force unproved which may serve to guard the honour and renown of their name, and conquer the wanton delights of the frail flesh; assuring themselves that God imparts a wonderful strength and constancy of mind to such as be chaste in deed. (p. 283)

By conflating rape with 'whoredom' and 'wanton delights', Fenton figures the story of narrowly avoided violation as a story of 'virtue protected' which functions to regulate the sexual conduct of its female readers.

Another rape story in this collection, however, reaches a different conclusion about virtue. Read together, the two are profoundly contradictory about God's commitment to the virtuous. In the light of 'The Villainous Abbot', Julia's rape in 'A Modern Lucretia' should imply that she is insufficiently virtuous to merit his help. Indeed, after recording the rapist's decision to 'enjoy the first fruits and pleasant juice of the virginity of the chaste Julia', the narrator asks: 'But who is able to corrupt the chastity of her that hath her heart armed with assurance in virtue?' (p. 346). In the face of this assumption, Julia, like Lucrece, clearly has an ideological imperative to kill herself, as the only way (though, as we know, not a sure way) of proving her innocence and removing the stain of rape.

The writer prioritises female sexual conduct over male sexual violence in this story. When the rapist determines to 'corrupt [her] chastity', it is unclear whether the scenario is to be one of rape or of seduction. Going on to commend the 'pure and holy virgins in time past' who have been 'strongly assailed with semblable assaults', he describes how 'they have prevailed above the malice of them that undertook to rob them of the everlasting glory of their virginity' (pp.

346–7). While the words 'assaults' and 'rob' might indicate rape – particularly because of the etymological connection between theft and rape – it is quite possible to read the passage as an account of failed seductions rather than rapes. Fenton goes on to draw a strange equation: 'virtuous women have better means to resist the vain importunities of love than the wicked and evil disposed have reason to seek to seduce the honour of their chastity' (p. 347). Female virtue is stronger than male lust here: again, presupposing a seduction, rather than rape, situation. The definition of 'rape' becomes still more confused:

> he gives more argument of his fragility and weak resistance, who, at the first assault and motion of his wanton affections, doth yield himself prisoner to the appetite of his will ... than she that, resisting of long time the hot alarums of his vehement requests, is *driven* at last, unwillingly, to *resign* the keys of her fortress. (pp. 347–8; my emphasis)

The writer seems at first ready to define this situation as 'rape', that is, as a 'yielding rape', achieved through emotional force. However, the idea of a 'strong' woman who, however unwillingly, engages in sexual activity with a 'weak' man seems to be unacceptable, and he goes on to undermine his own exoneration of her:

> And yet cannot she escape the malice of suspicion, nor merit the name of perfect constancy, that is overcome with any enchantment, how strong soever it be, for that she cannot bear the title of true virtue unless she remain invincible to the end, weighing her honour and life in indifferent balance. (p. 348)

No degree of force can exonerate the raped woman not only from suspicion but from *being* unchaste or inconstant. But the writer's language is mystifying: does 'to the end' refer to death, or to the point where rape is achieved by force? Reading 'invincible' literally implies that she is not virtuous if she is raped under any circumstances. A similar ambivalence attends the description of Julia's self-defence: 'the more did she rampire herself in assurance of virtue, seeming valiant in the defence of a fort that was inexpugnable' (p. 348).

After the rape, it is not surprising that Julia believes that God '[doth] reward me this hard penance for the punishment of my faults passed' (p. 363). However, the writer concludes that God has saved Julia – not from rape, nor death, but from the crime and stain of giving in to the rapist. Her reward is immortality, though only on condition that she kill herself. Yielding is again conflated with illicit love, with the 'young ladies of England' ordered to 'resist the charms and sugared allurements of love' (p. 365). The tone of this conclusion is ambivalent. It reads as a warning to women of what could happen to them if they are not chaste; but as such it is invalid. Being chaste did not save Julia from rape or from death, although it saved her soul. The moral of the story is that death for women should be preferred to any kind of illicit sexual behaviour. The gruesome detail of the rape presumably serves to frighten the posited female reader into sexual decorum, while perhaps assuring the male reader that the tale's pornographic content has a moral purpose.

The representation of rape has a further purpose: to titillate. Rape scenarios are frequently accompanied by a wealth of otherwise superfluous physical detail, with an effect beyond simply measuring the power of the attacker. In chivalric romances, women are often tied naked to trees or rocks while the knightly combat takes place, or dragged naked by the hair while the attackers demand that they yield. When the rapist in 'A Modern Lucretia' looks forward to 'the first taste of the pleasant juices of love' (p. 358), for example, the erotic language suggests that the writer is identifying with the rapist, and appealing to his readers to appreciate the scene.

The tendency to eroticise ostensibly non-sexual threats to women confirms this function of rape. The sexualisation of violence against women is a marked phenomenon in romance. Scenes occur in which no rape is specifically threatened but which satisfy the sexual demands of a projected male reader or of the scene's narrative structure. Along with the beauty and virtue topoi, such scenes potentially work either for or against women. They allow female characters to escape rape without denying the reader the satisfaction of sexual action. However, they also denigrate and exploit the female body.

There are four types of symbolic or figurative rape. One occurs when rape is not mentioned but details suggest that it may lie behind the story. Women may be victims of abduction in which rape and marriage are not mentioned as goals, or of enchantments or non-sexual attacks. The semantic ambivalence of the words 'rape' and 'ravish' ensures that any abduction of a woman has some kind of sexual resonance. The obsession of the genre with sexual violence also makes it tempting to read all threats to women as implicitly sexual. The political significance behind many attacks (the power struggle between men) can, after all, coexist with their erotic component. Enchantment episodes may be particularly ambiguous. In *Palmendos* a woman is enchanted by the man she has refused to marry. She can appear only in the shape of a serpent to all but him, for whom she retains her human form; he imprisons her like this for five years and is referred to as her lover (f. 73).[21] The scenario implies that he has been raping her, but this is not explicitly stated. This interpretative problem shows the degree to which the portrayal of women in romance can never escape the sexual category; power issues related to women always have sexual connotations.

Second, in scenes which deploy the idea that rape is physically impossible, the attacker may make a sexually nuanced threat. In *Palmerin*, a knight 'made show to cut off [the woman's] head, if she refused to obey his lust' (ii. f. 107v). The sword may function as a phallic symbol, with a pun on 'head' for 'maidenhead'. This destabilises the idea of rape's impossibility at the same time as inscribing it.

The third type of 'symbolic' rape scene deploys the formulaic nature of the genre to set up the expectation of a rape where none in fact occurs, or is even threatened. *Palmerin* contains a scene with many features typical of rape narratives; the woman is being pursued, 'with her haire hanging about her shoulders, and tearing her faire visage with her nailes' (ii. f. 125). It turns out that the giant's goal is murder, not rape. The sexual threat has been created simply by the deployment of standard features of the rape narrative. In a similar scene in the *Mirror*, where the threat turns out to be murder, a sexual element is introduced because the woman has been 'bound . . . al naked vnto a tree' (ii. f. 294).

In the final category, an erotic substitute for rape occurs at the point demanded by the structure of the scene. The desire frustrated by the failure of the rape thus finds expression on a symbolic level. In the *Mirror* a woman avoids forcible marriage to a giant by falling on a sword (ii. f. 28v). While she escapes infamy, her suicide occurs at the structural point of rape and provides a symbolic and ironic substitute. This type of 'substitute rape' is a particular feature of native novellas.

While the translated novellas of the 1560s and 1570s (by Painter, Fenton and Pettie) treated rape stories with much sensationalism and graphic detail, native prose fiction of these years contained only a few examples either of rape or of such sensationalism.[22] In the 1580s and 1590s, however, the number of portrayals of rape increases, particularly in the works of Greene, Lodge and Nashe, and is accompanied by lurid description. In Lodge's *Robert of Normandy* the murder of Lady Beaumont is a response to her refusal to yield. The sexual language emphasises the function of the murder as an erotic climax demanded by the structure of the scene: 'seeing no meanes possible to accomplish his loose and vnbridled lust, he sheathed his sword in her entralls' (p. 24). In *Euphues Shadow* (1592) Servatia's suicide refigures her rape: 'snatching vp his weapon, the witnesse of his wickednesse, which through hast he had left behind, and through horror shee was bent to vse, she sheathed it in hir body' (p. 33).

While the incidence of rape increases in these works, the complex implications of the idea of inviolable virtue are submerged: implications which we have seen to have been available in Fenton's translations, earlier in the Elizabethan period. Greene's *Penelopes Web* (1587) and *Philomela* (1592) both feature women who are saved from rape by their own virtue. In the former, the inset story, 'Penelopes second tale' tells of the abduction of Cratyna by a nobleman. He eventually feels 'such a remorce' (p. 216) that he lets her go without raping her, and even rewards her financially, claiming that 'the vertuous and chast disposition of her mynd had made such a metamorphosis of his former thoughts, that...he was content to bridle his affections' (pp. 218–19). In *Philomela*, the heroine is in danger of rape by the captain of the ship on which she is travelling alone; when he hears her declaring her virtue and her intention of killing herself if ever threatened with rape, he too is 'metamorphosed' and reforms.[23] Virtue, then, is allowed to protect women in Greene's romances. The problematic implications of this equation of virtue and safety, however, are heightened in the context of the sexual violence of the other prose works of the time.

## RAPE AND COURTSHIP

> This was hee that rauisht *Helena* the first time, whose tender age might then well acquit her of the error.
>
> (*Mirror*, iii(3). sig. U)

This description of Theseus in the *Mirror of Knighthood* reveals the complex intersection of rape narratives with courtship. Theoretically, any attempt to woo has the potential to result in rape; conversely, any sexual threat may be met with consent. To underline this ambivalence, we have seen that the rhetoric of courtship frequently accompanies rape. In romance, rape and courtship intersect in two further ways.

In two scenes, one from native fiction, the other from chivalric romance, a woman is raped by a man who is or has been her accepted lover (though not necessarily in the fullest sense). In Gascoigne's *The Adventures of Master F.J.* (1573), Dame Elinor, a married woman who has enjoyed a sexual liaison with the hero, rejects his advances after an argument. F.J.'s response is clearly motivated by anger; where the novella had earlier played on the phallic imagery of the pen, here the more aggressive image of the sword takes over:

> having now forgotten all former courtesies, he drew upon his new-professed enemy and bare her up with such a violence against the bolster that, before she could prepare the ward, he thrust her through both hands and etc.; whereby the dame, swooning for fear, was constrained for a time to abandon her body to the enemy's courtesy. (p. 61)

As the repetition underlines, this is a marked inversion of the usual pattern where 'courtesy' is a euphemism for the mistress's granting of sexual favours. The comic effect of the military language and of the narrator's coy 'etc.' overshadows the woman's experience: her 'fear' is just punishment for her shrewish 'despiteful' words. After the event she is made to collude in this trivialisation: 'she found her hurt to be nothing dangerous' (pp. 61–2).

A scene in *Primaleon* demonstrates the complex interplay between the idea of love as justifying any male action, and the conflicting issues of female honour, desire and consent. Throughout the scene, the consummation of desire is presented as a male categorical imperative and as an expression of love, and the issue of the woman's consent is neatly side-stepped so as to avoid categorising the incident as a rape. The writer records Flerida's resistance, but at the point where knowledge of her volition is crucial to define the sexual act, he conflates her desire with the man's:

> after some few amorous ceremonies (in such cases vsed) he mooued the Argument, and shee (for a while) stood vpon absolute deniall: but in fine (after many nayes) *they made this conclusion*, that of a faire Maid, she was now become as faire a woman. (ii. 210–11; my emphasis)

Despite Flerida's subsequent description of the act as 'against my will' (p. 211), and the fact that she resolves on suicide, the writer claims that she regretted it only after the event: 'hauing a litle better considered on the matter'.

Although she accuses Edward of breaking 'faith and promise' with her (p. 211), Flerida concludes by blaming herself for the rape, because she in 'folly and lightnesse' (p. 212) had put herself in a compromising position. Once again, the woman's right to give or withhold consent is marginalised, and Flerida concludes that the fault is 'onely in my selfe' (p. 217). The writer suggests further that Edward's motivation is 'to be assured of her' (p. 210). The power he gains over her will deprive her of the commodity value which would enable her to look elsewhere, and make her dependent on him to restore her honour through marriage. Flerida is acutely aware of this position, as she makes clear at their reconciliation; when he falls to his knees she tells him, 'rise, and kneele not, for it beseemes not him who hath such power ouer me, to be thus on his knees' (p. 218).

Flerida's story demonstrates the politics of courtship, bringing together the courtship and rape narratives. It bears out Lucas's argument that 'the woman's response must always contain the knowledge that the man could, if he wished, take by force that which he pleads for by courtesy'.[24] The story also alerts us to the difficulty for women of articulating consent and the implications this has for the victims of unwanted sexual advances. Faced with an ideology that condemns women for allowing illicit sexual behaviour, a woman has an imperative to say 'no' even if she really means 'yes'. Although I read the story as one of rape, the privileged reading – that Flerida protested only to uphold her honour – is feasible in this context. The ambivalence of the tale demonstrates yet another way in which female consent is silenced or ignored.

Seduction, then, is a mystifying term capable of masking rape or, at the other end of the scale, of partially excusing female consent. The apocryphal story of Susanna and the Elders, as we know, exemplifies the thin dividing line between the two. Greene's version, *The Myrrour of Modestie* (1584), makes explicit the sexual threat in the Elders' proposition. After making clear their intention to 'haue [their] owne will', they plot 'to sucke the bloude of this innocent lambe, and with most detestable villanie to assaile the simple minde of this sillie *Susanna*'.[25] Their 'temptation' of Susanna involves images of force:

he is a cowarde that yeeldeth at the first shotte . . . : we haue the tree in our hande, and meane to enioie the fruite. (p. 25)

This version of the Susanna story makes it clear that what is categorised as a tale of attempted seduction can involve the threat of sexual violence. The position of the classical exemplar of chastity, Penelope, is equally anomalous. Greene's version of her story, *Penelopes Web* (1587), does not characterise her situation as one of threatened rape, but he does include an attempted rape narrative among the stories she and her women tell. He also compares Penelope's love for Ulysses to 'the loue of *Lucrece*' and has her voice a regret that the Romans 'grudge to erect an Image in the memorie of *Lucrece*' (pp. 157, 195). This suggests subtextually the nature of the pressure on Penelope.

Rape scenarios, then, intersect with and reflect on the representation of courtship in prose fiction. The power-dynamic on which they are based thus has a wider effect on the portrayal of gender-relations. I turn now to one of the most influential prose romances of the period, Sidney's *Arcadia*, in which an interrogation of the ambivalence surrounding the idea of 'ravishment' contributes to the work's portrayal of the close involvement between rape and courtship.

## PHILIP SIDNEY'S *ARCADIA*

. . . although he ravished her not from herself, yet he ravished her from him that owed her, which was her father.[26]

Philip Sidney's treatment of sexual conduct in *The Countess of Pembroke's Arcadia* changes dramatically in revision. The first version, *The Old Arcadia*, presents five distinct definitions of 'ravishment', which it both distinguishes and conflates. 'Ravishment' may be either rape, attempted rape, illicit (but consensual) intercourse, abduction or elopement. All these senses of the word appear in the trial, and all but one (rape itself) are staged. The trial, however, confuses the issues by either equating or conflating the different versions. Thus rape, attempted rape and illicit, consensual sex are conflated in Pyrocles's case, and his crime is equated with Musidorus's, which is presented as both abduction and elopement. In *The New Arcadia*, Pyrocles's and Musidorus's illicit sexual activities are eliminated and the rape impulse, we shall see, displaced and submerged. Much debate has surrounded the question of Sidney's participation in this revision. Some critics have attributed it entirely to Mary Sidney, using her gender as pretext for attributing the revision to prudishness.[27] It has been established, however, that these revisions were Philip Sidney's.[28]

The treatment of courtship and sexual conduct in the *Old Arcadia* pulls in two opposite directions. This is characteristic of the work, in which the unresolved tension between conflicting impulses is a central feature.[29] The narrator's attitude to the bed scene, and to Musidorus's rape attempt, is notoriously divided, and invites a similarly ambivalent response from the reader.[30]

The language of courtship itself problematises the work's complex engagement with the different categories of 'ravishment'. Militaristic imagery and the language of violence permeate courtship here. While we have seen such imagery deployed to ennoble or condone rape, here, conversely, we also find consensual sexual intercourse problematised by such language. The violence of love is a central trope in the work, as is that of the virtuous body or mind as a castle or fort. Musidorus thus 'assault[s]' Pamela's face by looking at it (p. 81), while Philoclea is 'oppressed' by the 'extreme and unresistible violence' of love (p. 111). Moreover, a fifth definition of ravishment as 'rapture' appears frequently; Philoclea is thus 'sweetly ravished' by Pyrocles's poem (p. 82). More problematically, initiation is defined as violence, eliminating the concept of female consent. The agreement between Pamela and Musidorus that they should not consummate their relationship before marriage appears as his 'vehement oath to offer no force unto her' (p. 172); this complicates Pyrocles's claim that he 'offered force' or 'violence' to Philoclea (pp. 394, 405), which is itself ambiguous.

The structure of the scenes treating the different versions of ravishment implies a progression which both parallels and contrasts the separate episodes. The elopement of Musidorus and Pamela is followed by his attempt to rape her (p. 202). This is interrupted by the arrival of the rebels, who abduct her (p. 308). This abduction is distinguishable from the elopement, since it is clearly enacted against Pamela's will; such carefully plotted distinctions are later ignored in the trial. At the end of Book III, the consummation scene between Pyrocles and Philoclea (pp. 228–43) then necessarily reflects back on the attempted rape, producing a contrast which again hinges on the woman's consent, although this contrast is simultaneously undermined. The wedding of Lalus and Kala in the Third Eclogues, a legitimate union, subsequently problematises the illicit premarital intercourse of Pyrocles and Philoclea.

Pyrocles and Musidorus are both formally accused of 'ravishment' (pp. 390, 406). Despite the difference both between the crimes with which each is charged and between those which we know each to have committed or attempted, the trial aligns them, equating their crimes and meting out equal punishments. For Musidorus, it is ironic that the name given to the crime he is tried for ('ravishment') also denotes the crime he attempted to commit, unbeknownst to the judge. In the public sphere of the trial, ravishment is defined as the theft of a woman from her father (and, in Pamela's case, from the state). In private, narrator and reader see Musidorus attempt another version of the crime, rape. The tension between Musidorus's official crime and his secret one both mirrors and heightens the tension between Euarchus's two definitions of ravishment.

The irony in Pyrocles's indictment for 'ravishment', by contrast, is based on the reader's knowledge that Philoclea consented to the sexual act. Yet the relationship between fact and fiction here is undercut on both the public and the private levels. In the trial, the issue of Philoclea's consent is side-stepped to protect her, by both Pyrocles and Euarchus. Pyrocles initially claims that he had attempted to seduce Philoclea, but that 'the excellency of her mind [made] her body impregnable' (p. 301). Later, he becomes more vague about whether his 'violence' was or was not successful. Although he calls Philoclea 'inviolate' (p. 393), he claims that he 'offered force to her' (p. 394), and provides a defence of rape which implies that his action was accomplished. Yet Euarchus does not pick up on this inconsistency, because it emerges that the woman's consent is irrelevant to the case. Consent or resistance does not affect her culpability; Euarchus's definition of 'ravishment' makes the female culpable whether or not she consents to the act: 'though both consent, much more is he whose wickedness so overflows as he will compel another to be wicked' (p. 406). Whether or not the act took place and whether it was consensual or not become irrelevant to the judgement. Euarchus thus conflates rape, attempted rape, and consensual but illicit sex.

Musidorus's rape attempt is prefigured by the consistent troping of his courtship of Pamela in terms of violence and power. His declaration of love gives 'alarum to her imaginations' (p. 106) and he sings to 'bring her to a dull yielding-over her forces' (p. 107); her glove is the 'fair spoils of [his] victory' (p. 169). The description of their elopement as 'the stealing her away' facilitates our acceptance of Euarchus's subsequent conflation of elopement with abduction. Pamela's consent to the elopement, while unambiguous, is thus marginalised. Similarly, her explicit refusal to consummate the relationship is formulated as a plea to Musidorus to refrain from 'force'. It is a short step from this marginalisation and disempowering of female consent to Musidorus's decision to rape Pamela while she sleeps.

With this narrowly avoided rape in mind, we might see the consummation scene between Pyrocles and Philoclea as entirely different, a consensual act as opposed to a constrained one. However, the scene contains several hints of a darker perspective. The complex relationship between the two scenes has been prefigured in the episode in which the princes rescue the princesses from wild animals. Here, the narrator explicitly compares Pyrocles to the lion, with Philoclea 'the prey [Cleophila] herself so much desired' (p. 47). Philoclea continues to run after the lion is killed:

> as Arethusa when she ran from Alpheus, her light nymphlike apparel being carried up with the wind, that much of those beauties she would at another time have willingly hidden were presented to the eye of the twice-wounded Cleophila; which made Cleophila not follow her over hastily lest she should too soon deprive herself of that pleasure. (pp. 47–8)

The allusion to Arethusa and Alpheus locates Philoclea in a tradition of women pursued by lustful men, a perspective heightened by Pyrocles's deliberate voyeurism.

Philoclea's rescue is simultaneous with Musidorus's rescue of Pamela from a bear. Where Philoclea's role in the event is comparatively active, Pamela's is passive – she faints where Philoclea had fled. Musidorus, unlike Pyrocles, is not explicitly compared to the bear; indeed, his destruction of the bear is presented in sexual terms:

> as she was ready to give him a mortal embracement, the shepherd Dorus, with a lusty strength and good fortune, thrust his knife so right into the heart of the beast that she fell down dead without ever being able to touch him. (p. 52)[31]

Musidorus follows up this victory by embracing the unconscious Pamela, prefiguring his later rape attempt. Just as he is later to blame Pamela's attractions for this act, he attributes his phallic destruction of the animal to 'the force of [Pamela's] beauty' (p. 52).

In the consummation scene as in the lion episode, the intimations of force are more subtle. Philoclea is connected to a second classical figure when Pyrocles arrives at her chamber. As she sings, she is called 'a solitary nightingale, bewailing her guiltless punishment and helpless misfortune' (p. 229). This recalls Philomela and her 'misfortune'. The account of the consummation itself balances the language of force against assertions of Philoclea's active participation and enjoyment:

> fighting against a weak resistance, which did strive to be over-come, he gives me occasion to leave him in so happy a plight, lest my pen might seem to grudge at the due bliss of those poor lovers whose loyalty had but small respite of their fiery agonies. (p. 243)

The central paradox here (Philoclea's 'weak resistance') imputes to her a strategy of 'coyness', which Catherine Bates has described as 'clichéd male wish-fulfilment'.[32] The 'happy ... plight' representing the sexual act is then defined as the man's, with Philoclea's attitude ignored. Finally, in a narratorial sleight of hand that recalls the *Primaleon* narrator's in describing Flerida's defloration, her perspective is merged into Pyrocles's as they become 'these poor lovers'. The moment illustrates the predicament of women and writers in expressing female desire: while the strategy allows Philoclea an unusual degree of sexual fulfilment, it also marginalises her perspective in a way that might call her volition into question.

Pyrocles's defence of his actions employs the standard topoi which we have found in rape narratives, topoi designed to excuse and trivialise rape. He attributes his action to the power of Philoclea's beauty, and to the inevitability of male desire: 'Let her beauty be compared to my years, and such effects will be found no miracles' (p. 394). His love is troped as a categorical imperative, 'whose violence wrought violent effects in me', and he argues that 'I offered force to her; love offered more force to me' (pp. 395, 394). Philoclea's collusion in this defence of the act of rape points to the location of blame with the woman in this rhetoric: 'alas, what hath he done that had not his original in me?' (p. 396). The confusion surrounding the lovers' presentation of their case – whether the act took place or not, and Philoclea's role in it – is increased with another common rape trope: the idea of invincible female virtue. Pyrocles claims that Philoclea cannot be violated: 'There needs no strength to be added to so inviolate chastity. The excellency of her mind makes her body impregnable' (p. 301).

Pyrocles's assertion of the inviolability of the virtuous female is belied not only by his own ambivalence about the success of his rape attempt (for which he offers recompense in marriage), but by his cousin's attempt to rape Pamela – an attempt frustrated not by her virtue but by interruption. Their cases share several features which align their actions. The two scenes treating their sexual activities are, of course, structurally parallel.[33] Both feature images of the penetration of the woman's body, and hypostasise it with the use of the blason: a device which, in cataloguing the female body, renders it vulnerable to rape.[34] Musidorus's lullaby ('Lock up, fair lids', p. 200) provides the image of penetration. His plea to sleep demands the sealing up of Pamela's body against the intrusion which he represents as a 'strange dream' that might 'make her fair body start'. However, he immediately personifies the dream, and appropriates it as his proxy:

> Then take my shape, and play a lover's part:
> Kiss her from me, and say unto her sprite,
> Till her eyes shine, I live in darkest night.
>
> (p. 201)

The blason of Pamela is not a poem, but the description of an actual physical act of contemplation or voyeurism. Like the lullaby, it includes images of containment, inviting penetration: 'Her fair lids ... seemed unto him sweet boxes of mother of pearl ... containing in them far richer jewels'; her breath issues from a 'well closed paradise' (p. 201). The imagery, moreover, is militaristic, with her forehead a 'field where all his fancies fought' and her teeth 'armed ranks' (p. 201). Such imagery not only places the relationship between the lovers on the level of a combat or power-struggle but, specifically, presents the sleeping woman as the powerful party, compelling response from the weaker male. Thus 'the roses of her lips ... now *by force* drew his sight to mark how prettily they lay one over the other' (my emphasis), and her teeth lie hidden 'as in ambush'. Her mouth 'did so tyrannize over Musidorus's affects that he was compelled to put his face as low to hers as he could'. As the blasonic impulse develops into rape, Musidorus appears as the victim of female beauty:

> all [her features] joined together did so draw his will into the nature of their confederacy that now his promise began to have

but a fainting force ... [;] so that rising softly from her, overmastered with the fury of delight ... he was bent to take the advantage of the weakness of the watch, and see whether at that season he could win the bulwark before timely help might come. (pp. 201–2)

Only at the final stage is Musidorus presented in the active role.

The blason's objectification of Pamela parallels her unconsciousness, both facilitating the rape; but the blason tropes her not merely as inviting but as compelling this rape. Philoclea's relationship to the blason is both more complex and more literary. In the poem which blasons her, she is penetrated by the male pen. The opening question,

> What tongue can her perfections tell
> In whose each part all pens may dwell?
> (p. 238)

is answered by the final couplet: 'No tongue ... ' (p. 242). To this claim the intervening lines give the lie, cataloguing the subject's body and 'dwelling' on every 'part'. As a literary act, the blason poem does not actually take place, for we are told: 'the only general fancy of it came into his mind, fixed upon the sense of that sweet subject' (p. 242). An interpolated poem rather than an experience, it is a substitute for the sexual act which takes place simultaneously with it. Philoclea is, of course, the 'sweet subject'. Yet she is distanced from the poem by the fact that it was written to celebrate another woman, Philisides's 'unkind mistress' (p. 238). While on the one hand the blason combines with other intimations of Philoclea's disempowerment, and with our knowledge of its function in Pamela's near rape, on the other hand, this distance between the poem's subject/object and Philoclea herself leaves space for her to consent to and participate fully in the sexual act.

Both the bed scene and the attempted rape scene partially implicate the women, albeit to different degrees. The contrast between Pamela's majesty and virtue and Philoclea's capacity for 'pity' points to their subsequent conduct. Philoclea's 'pity' – a word frequently used euphemistically for sexual favours – suggests the possibility of her surrender to Pyrocles. This combines with several instances of her failure to conceal her body, to suggest a 'contributory negligence' in her conduct. Pamela, by contrast, boasts a stricter virtue. Nevertheless, she receives some blame for eloping without '[looking] with perfect consideration into her own enterprise' (p. 196), and she becomes open to Musidorus's rape through sleep. Sleep, in *Arcadia* as elsewhere, often signifies negligence;[35] it would not have entirely exonerated Pamela if her lover had succeeded in raping her.

The details of the sexual exploits of Pyrocles and Musidorus, then, work both to align them and to distinguish between them. The process continues in the trial, which not only equates their confessed crimes, but suggests a darker connection between their hidden actions. While Euarchus equates the two forms of 'ravishment' which the cousins have perpetrated, Pyrocles's defence of the rape we know he did not commit echoes the rhetoric which surrounds Musidorus's actual attempt to commit this crime.

The *Old Arcadia*, then, both defines sexual behaviour according to the strict categories of rape, consensual sex, elopement and abduction, and simultaneously undermines such rigid distinctions. The narrator, who both condones his heroes' actions and condemns them, provides a model for the tensions in the work between competing moral and judgemental forces. It thus becomes a matter of perspective whether we read the consummation of Pyrocles and Philoclea as tainted by suggestions of rape implied by Musidorus's action, or as elevated by the comparison. In either case, the two women are implicated in the crimes against them, although to different degrees.

The *New Arcadia* takes further this shifting of responsibility to the women in courtship. Kalander claims:

> love played in Philoclea's eyes and threatened in Pamela's; methought Philoclea's beauty only persuaded – but so persuaded as all hearts must yield, Pamela's beauty used violence – and such violence as no heart could resist.[36]

This description fulfils the tendency of the *Old Arcadia*'s rhetoric to place the responsibility for male sexual conduct with the woman. There is a specific correspondence between the way each woman's beauty is troped as functioning and the way they are treated by their lovers in the original text. However, the *New Arcadia* renders rape solely the prerogative of villains.

The revised *Arcadia* shows a shift in the portrayal of rape. By displacing the rape impulses onto other characters and dissociating them from the heroes, it both disentangles and sidesteps the problems surrounding rape in the original text. The characters who attempt rape here are either outright villains (like Anaxius (pp. 459ff.) or Tiridates (pp. 205ff.)), or must themselves be distanced from the idea of rape. Sidney's definition of heroism has clearly altered since the *Old Arcadia*: even the anti-hero Amphialus is not allowed to condone rape, and must be distanced from such an impulse by the introduction of an evil female character.

Musidorus's attempt to rape Pamela is cut from the text; meanwhile, Pyrocles and Philoclea simply go to sleep in the bed scene, without consummating their love and without even the salacious influence of the blason, which is moved elsewhere. That these changes are authentic is suggested by the alteration of the wild animal scene in the first book. The explicit references to Philoclea as Pyrocles's 'prey' have been removed, although the voyeurism and allusion to Alpheus and Arethusa remain (p. 112). Musidorus's killing of the bear, with its sexual overtones, is omitted, along with his embrace of Pamela in her faint, for the episode is narrated by Pamela herself (pp. 114–16). However, although readers of the revised text would impute nothing more to Musidorus than Pamela does, readers of both might be aware that had he indeed touched her when unconscious, she would not know it. Sidney submerges Musidorus's transgressive actions, then, rather than eliminating them.

The captivity episode in the *New Arcadia* brings many features of rape narratives together, and condemns them by associating them with evil characters. The rhetoric justifying rape is given to Cecropia, the central tenet of whose argument is that a woman's 'no' means 'yes'. This idea is prominent in poetry and drama of this period, and is exemplified self-mockingly in Sidney's *Astrophil and Stella*, when Stella 'twice said "No, no"':

> For grammar says (O this, dear Stella, weigh) ...
> That in one speech two negatives affirm.
> (Sonnet 63, ll. 12–14)[37]

Cecropia argues '"No" is no negative in a woman's mouth' (p. 402), and rewrites classical mythology to prove it:

> Do you think Theseus should ever have gotten Antiope with sighing and crossing his arms? He ravished her ... But having ravished her, he got a child of her – and I say no more, but that, they say, is not gotten without consent of both sides. (p. 402)[38]

By rewriting classical examples, she hopes to give her son a precedent for the rape of Philoclea. To encourage him, she characterises the rape situation as the normative conduct of men and women:

> Think: she would not strive but that she means to try thy force. And, my Amphialus, know thyself a man; and show thyself a man – and believe me, upon my word, a woman is a woman. (p. 403)

Amphialus, however, asserts that 'lust may well be a tyrant, but true love, where it is indeed, it is a servant' (p. 401).

Cecropia voices another feature of rape rhetoric: the idea that beauty is its own protection. She tells Pamela that a beautiful woman 'need not seek offensive or defensive force, since her lips may stand for ten thousand shields, and ten thousand unevitable shot go from her eyes' (p. 356), invoking the blasonic military imagery which is itself associated with rape. The irony of her claim is apparent here. Amphialus, while distanced from his mother's justification of rape, is not altogether exonerated, since he does not free the princesses. His justification of his actions invokes the familiar beauty topos, blaming the woman for male desire and its consequences: 'it proceeds from their beauty to enforce love to offer this force' (p. 405).

The iconography of martyrdom, as Mary Ellen Lamb has pointed out, contributes much to the captivity episode, which includes the physical torture of the princesses. It redeems them from the potentially tainting sexuality of the *Old Arcadia*: 'through conquering the fear of death, [they] transcend not only sexual guilt, but all other desires of the flesh'.[39] Female desire is thus sublimated into heroic martyrdom, while the rhetoric justifying rape shifts from the heroes to the villains. Musidorus's anticipated rescue of the princesses (beyond the end of the text) will establish him as hero and rescuer, opposed to the forces associated with rape. Since he is in an emotional exile from Pamela at this point, as a result of his attempt to kiss her (p. 309), his reappearance would seem to contrast the position of the overreaching suitor with that of the prospective rapist.

However, the *New Arcadia* retains several elements which can be associated with female sexual danger, in particular the voyeurism of the lion episode, and the language of force or assault in the relations between the lovers. The blason of Philoclea ('What tongue can her perfections tell') is removed from the bed scene and becomes an actual performance, by Pyrocles, directly related to his voyeurism at

River Ladon (pp. 190ff.). The setting for this scene, moreover, has associations of male lust and female danger, in the story of Syrinx and Pan. The classical women whom Cecropia uses as examples to justify Philoclea's rape, moreover, are precisely those (Helen, Iole) with whom she is pictured when Pyrocles falls in love with her, in the summer house paintings – along with Diana as a victim of Actaeon's voyeurism (p. 15).

Although Musidorus's stolen kiss is removed (or submerged) in the lion episode, his 'assault' to Pamela's face is not, and the revised text adds much similar imagery. His forcible embracing of her and 'offering to kiss her' (p. 309) could be seen as the culmination of this pattern of imagery, a substitute for the stolen kiss or for the *Old Arcadia*'s attempted rape itself. As such, the scene shows on a smaller scale the likely consequences of the rape – whether it had been accomplished or whether Pamela had woken to realise Musidorus's intention. Musidorus's self-justification – like Pyrocles's in the original version and like the language describing the rape attempt – blames Pamela's beauty for his love, and thus for his assault. His poem 'Unto a caitiff wretch' (pp. 311–14) claims 'all my offence was love', and for this she is culpable: 'more fault in you to be lovely' (p. 312). Like a rape victim, or one seeking to avoid rape, Pamela should have torn her hair or face if she wanted to avoid such assaults. Although the inset story of Argalus and Parthenia renders this argument dubious by valuing love over beauty, Musidorus's stature as hero and lover partially obscures his reliance on a rhetoric which justifies rape and deprives the beloved of autonomy.

The reappearance of the image of Philomel in the revised text seems to mark a difference between the two versions. Where the image had lent dark implications to the consummation scene in the *Old Arcadia*, in the *New* it appears during the captivity episode, registering the princesses' abduction and the threat of rape. It is again Philoclea to whom the analogy is applied; this time she believes Pamela to be dead: 'so, like lamentable Philomela, complained she the horrible wrong done to her sister' (p. 427). The original image, of course, still appears in the composite *Arcadia*; we can only speculate whether Sidney intended to eliminate it.[40] Had he left it in place, it would have provided an echo of the captivity episode, perhaps suggesting dark implications that would not have been fulfilled. Had he removed it, it would underline the displacement of the rape impulse from the princes onto villainous characters whose morals could be wholeheartedly condemned.

The revision thus clashes with some remnants of Pyrocles's and Musidorus's dubious sexual conduct.[41] The revised text, then, works out some of the problems of the original, but in a 'safer' way: conveying sexual force in a stolen kiss rather than rape, for example, and eliminating the sexual consequences of voyeurism. Yet the relationship between the two texts is further problematised, for the reader of both, by Cecropia's speeches. Immediately after rewriting mythology to validate rape, she asks Amphialus:

> what can be more agreeable than upon force to lay the fault of desire, and in one instant to join a dear delight with a just excuse? (p. 402)

Cecropia's words recall the *Old Arcadia*'s strategy of excusing female sexual enjoyment with the rhetoric of rape. However, the fact that she is deploying this argument to advocate rape points to the easy reversibility of her terms. When 'upon force to lay the fault of desire' becomes 'upon desire to lay the fault of force', we have a scenario whereby the rapist excuses himself by invoking the inevitability of love, as Cecropia actually advocates. This scenario too takes place in the original text, albeit hypothetically, with Musidorus's foiled attempt and Pyrocles's defence of a rape he has not committed. In the revised text, Cecropia's remarks are irrelevant: Pyrocles is protecting his mistress without having seduced her, and Musidorus never attempts to rape Pamela. The irony which results from reading the actions of the *Old Arcadia*'s princes in the context of Cecropia's remarks points, at the very least, to the contrast between Sidney's conceptions of them in the two versions. Where other romances frequently express the rape impulse through various forms of 'substitute' or submerged rape scenario, Sidney submerges rape in the very process of revising the *Old Arcadia* into the *New*.

Where many fiction writers exploit the rape narrative to effect a warning against any form of illicit sexual activity for women, Sidney's deployment of the idea of rape, particularly in *The Old Arcadia*, can equally be seen as facilitating female sexual desire. That this coexists with darker implications – not least with the attempted rape of Pamela – is perhaps typical of the tension that characterises much thinking about rape in the early modern period. The conflict between the idea that it is physically impossible to rape a woman, and its opposite, the real possibility of rape, provides a key dynamic in many of these works. This tension finds a more subtle expression in *The Old Arcadia*'s negotiation of gender-relations. *The New Arcadia*, on the other hand, while associating the view that a woman's 'no' means 'yes' with specific, evil characters, still gives weight to the rhetorical topoi of the power of beauty and the power of chastity: ideas which we know to be involved in placing the responsibility for rape with the victim. The tension between seduction and rape, which this revised version submerges, we shall also find to inform poetic representations of female sexual shame.

# 3

# 'The subiect of his tyrannie': Women and Shame in Elizabethan Poetry

> Have I caught my heavenly jewel
> Teaching sleep most fair to be?
> Now will I teach her that she,
> When she wakes, is too too cruel.[1]

Sidney thus restages in the Second Song of *Astrophil and Stella* Musidorus's attempt to rape Pamela in her sleep. Here the lover is foiled by his fear of her anger, but chides himself 'for no more taking' (28). He again plays tricks on his female subject/object in the Fourth Song, in which the repetition of Stella's refusal, 'No, no, no, no, my dear, let be', is twisted – after the poet's rebuke for her 'striv[ing]' (43) against him – into implying a change of heart:

> Soon with my death I will please thee.
> 'No, no, no, no, my dear, let be.'
>
> (53–4)

The sonnet sequence rarely hints at rape. Yet its rhetorical manipulation of female 'subject' by male poet in a form so central to 'courtship' allows for an analogy with rape, which moments such as these underline.[2] Many poems of courtship hint at the possibility of the lover's sexual assertion, if not aggression. Sir William Alexander's *Aurora* (1604), for instance, uses the story of Daphne and Apollo to persuade his mistress into sexual compliance.[3] Sir Robert Ayton asserts in 'What others doth discourage' that 'women love best that does love least in show', adds that her denials increase his ardour, and concludes with a conventionally military image:

> Nor will I raise my siege nor leave my field
> Till I have made my valiant mistress yield.[4]

Barnabe Barnes's *Parthenophil and Parthenophe* (1593) goes further in contemplating the rape of the beloved. Barnes figuratively appropriates his mistress's body as he imagines himself as her necklace, 'that I might folde / About that louely necke, and her pappes tickle', and as the wine that 'runne[s] through her vaynes, and passe[s] by pleasures part' (Sonnet lxiii, ll. 9–10, 14).[5] Later, the echo structure of Sestine 4 (pp. 121–2) incites the poet to ignore any resistance:

> Then will I wrest out sighes, and wring forth teares when I do so?
> > *Eccho*, do so.
> But if she do refuse, then woe to th'attempter?
> > *Eccho*, attempt her.
> > > (14, 23)

The earlier Ode 8 (p. 104) similarly undermines the woman's denial, intimating her complicity by suggesting that she was 'willing displeas'd in the receauing' (36). Here the poet distances his fantasy of rape by staging it as a pastoral dream, enacted in the third person:

> Thence from his purpose neuer leauing
> He prest her further,
> She would cry murther,
> But somewhat was her breathe bereauing.
>
> At length he doth possesse her whoale,
> Her lippes, and all he would desier:
> Eft that chaunc'd which he did requier...
> > (37–45)

The ambiguity of 'her breath bereauing' – perhaps indicating she cannot breathe, perhaps suggesting she chooses not to cry out – is followed by the mystifying 'at length...', which evades the issue of resistance.

Such fantasies culminate in the final poem of the work (Sestine 5, pp. 127–30), which stages the consummation of the two in a setting of magic and May rites. Parthenophe is brought to the poet naked on the back of a goat (suggestive of magic and lechery), and images of violation – such as 'the *Cypresse* bowes be kindled, / This brimstone earth within her bowelles bare' (15–16) – compound the mystifying presentation of her as 'with loues outrage kindled' (24). Troped as the victim of love, in revenge for her cruelty to the poet, Parthenophe appears as the unwilling victim of Parthenophil's erotic violence, with repeated references to her tears. The eroticism of the poem, and of the consummation sequence at its end, is predicated on the asserted equivalence of her previous cruelty to Parthenophil to his or 'love's' cruelty to her now, as the final lines reiterate:

> For as she once with rage my bodie kindled,
> So in hers am I buried this night.
>
> (110–11)

The ambiguity surrounding women's volition is a defining feature of much of the material treated in this chapter. The idea that 'no means yes' may, as with *Astrophil and Stella* Sonnet 63, be voiced by a male character; in genres lacking the sonnet's identification of lover and poet, this strategy may or may not be obviously endorsed by the writer. Alternatively, a male narrator may voice the idea directly, or it may appear as a deliberate strategy deployed by a female character negotiating the ideological constraints on her sexual conduct. Inevitably, these situations often become indistinguishable.

The subsequent ambivalence of female desire in such situations may be seen as figuring a wider ambivalence about women's sexual conduct in the 'minor epic' poem and related sub-genres of the Elizabethan period. The 'minor epic' is commonly divided up as the 'complaint' and the 'epyllion'. As critics increasingly point out, however, any distinction between the two in terms of both material and treatment is an unstable one.[6] The term 'female complaint', more-over, usually designating the tradition growing from the *Mirror for Magistrates*, relates too to the 'laments' of women in the pastourelle tradition.

While the epyllion is characterised by its erotic content and by its proliferation of actively sexual women characters, the female com-plaint stages the woman as victim. Yet the complaint, along with poetic treatments of women's lives which do not share its formal characteristics, actually treats a range of female experiences, from rape followed by suicide (Lucrece), or suicide preventing rape (Matilda), to 'whoredom' (Helen, and other courtesans). Uniting these poems, then, is a fascination with female sexual shame. In some cases the woman actively avoids such shame, leading her to a laudable 'martyrdom' in the avoidance of rape. More commonly, it is the product of a sexual fall which is seen as tainting the character whether, like Lucrece, she resisted it or, like Markham's Paulina, embraced it.[7] Mediating these extremes, however, are the complaints of the mistresses of great men, Rosamond, Jane Shore and Elstride, which to differing degrees present the volition of the female narrator as ambiguous, sometimes bringing her closer to a rape scenario. This confusion over female sexual conduct, I shall argue, not only directly characterises some of the most prominent examples and most popular characters of the genre, but is also a principle of the genre as a whole, mirroring its attitude to the range of experiences it presents. The clash between the principles of 'shame' and 'guilt' which Lucrece's story and its interpretations exemplify, may lie behind this tension too. What unites the women of the complaints, then, is their 'shame'; it is the question of 'guilt' that unsettles that unity by insisting that the characters be categorised as 'innocent' or 'guilty'.[8]

The ambiguity of the female complaint deriving from the *Mirror for Magistrates* tradition is prefigured in the pastourelle-style laments so common in ballads and Tudor miscellanies. The ballads bear such titles as 'The Distressed Virgin: Or, The False Young Man, and the Constant Maid'.[9] Poems in miscellanies, by contrast, tend rather to display generic markers, as in 'A Lady Forsaken, Complayneth'. As these examples indicate, the primary concern in such poems is the predicament of the woman abandoned, often pregnant, rather than her volition in the sexual act which brought this about. The language of theft frequently used of defloration – as in Martin Parker's *The Desperate Damsells Tragedy*, for example – is as applicable to seduction as to rape.[10] It thus reflects the lover's subsequent base behaviour back onto the original sexual act, to underline the woman's present predicament.

Three poems stand out in their treatment of the woman's volition. In Howell's 'To her Louer, that made a conquest of her, and fled, leauing her with childe' the presentation of the 'conquest' is poised between seduction and coercion. The anonymous 'Complaint of a Woman Rauished, and Also Mortally Wounded', from Tottel's *Songs and Sonnettes* (1557), is exceptional in its categorical presentation of a violent rape. By contrast, a poem in the Arundel Harington Manuscript may by its ambiguity represent for us the confusion surrounding female volition as represented in such poems.

The speaker of Howell's poem tells her 'heauy hart' to 'ponder his fylthie deede, / that left his shame behinde', asking 'was euer boy so badde, / to vse a mayden so?' (p. 225).[11] Yet the extent to which she takes the sin upon herself makes it unclear whether he achieved his 'conquest' by force or persuasion, as the counterpart to this question

articulates: 'Was euer Mayde so madde, / that might her fayth forgo?'.
She continues:

> His teares did me beguyle,
>     and cleane opprest my powre,
> As doth the Crocodile,
>     in seeking to deuoure.
>
> Howe could I well denie,
>     when needes it must be so:
> Although a shamefull I,
>     should haue a shamelesse no.

Although the images of 'oppression' and devouring are suggestive
of rape, it is male tears, rather than male strength, which have had
this power. Similarly, the idea of inevitability might suggest force,
but the last two lines imply the woman's failure to resist – compounded by the pun on the man's 'shamefull [aye]' and the speaker's
'shamefull I'. The final stanza balances her former innocence not
only with sexual shame, but with the infamy of her decision to 'slay
thy silly childe':

> My daintie tamed wombe,
>     that to thy share befell:
> Shal finde no doubt a tombe,
>     amids the mayds in hell.
>                         (p. 226)

The ambivalence of this poem, like others of its genre, indicates
above all the victory of the issue of the speaker's abandonment over
that of her volition in the sexual fall. How much more striking, then,
is the 'Complaint of a Woman Rauished'. The speaker is categorical
in defining the 'rauish[ment]' of the title as forced intercourse:

> A Cruell Tiger all with teeth bebled,
> A bloody tirantes hand in eche degre,
> A lecher that by wretched lust was led,
> (Alas) deflowred my virginitee.
>                         (1–4)[12]

Where metaphorical violence (the force of pleas and tears) may
cover a subtext of male physical power, this complaint leaves no

doubt that the woman has been raped, and then murdered, by the 'lecher'. Moreover, the speaker's death, while it might be a figure for a mortal wound rather than indicating that she is a ghost, brings her poem closer to the genre of 'female complaint' subsequently to develop in the tradition of the *Mirror for Magistrates*.

The *Arundel Harington Manuscript* poem, 'A tale put in verse by M^r Grevell', is not a 'lament' or 'complaint'.[13] The woman's perspective is further confused because an inconsistency in the identification of the observer within the poem compounds the narrative distance from the central sexual act. In the heading, 'Grevell' claims that the story was told him by the '*Master* of the Rolles *that* nowe is and his ladye'. However, the poem opens 'A tale I once did heare a true man tell', and presents the 'true man' as observing a woman lying in a field and being encountered by another 'man' (19). The couple are observed in intercourse 'when as these frendes of myne came passing bye' (39): the friends who in the heading he claimed told him the story. This slippage between the 'true man' present from the beginning, and the married couple who enter in the middle of the story, is compounded by the woman's claim that, save for embarrassment, she would have called for help 'when *we* weare theare' (71; my emphasis).

This ambiguity over the narrative source for the poem draws attention to the voyeurism of narration even while confusing it. Clashing with the poem's deliberate claim to authenticity in the heading and opening lines, it parallels the ambiguity which surrounds the woman's conduct and expression. She is observed to be lying on the ground 'in wandrynge Muses' (13), her arms 'abrode as carlesse what befell' (11). A man sees her and lies on top of her, 'betweene her & the skyes' (23). The next stanza both asserts and undermines the idea that she resists him:

> As new awake yet in her fancye stronge
> she vpward moves as thoughe she fayne would flye
> from this base earthe to leve the starres amonge
> but that his downeward working dothe denye
>     And when she can of neyther syde escape
>     she clyppes him fast and would hav this a rape.
>                                             (25–30)

The introduction of an image of active female desire ('clyppes him fast') after this description of the woman's inability to move from under the man, is as striking as the inconsistency of the final line in itself. The poem pays no further attention to her attitude until the couple are summoned by 'these frendes of myne', to be charged with non-marital intercourse. Either, then, 'would hav this a rape' effects a jump in time to this later scene of the poem, or it hints at the woman's immediate attitude without amplifying.

In the later scene, the man claims 'her humble lyinge made him bolde' and that he 'woulde have ben full glad she had sayd naye' (64–6). This seems not to fit the narrative so far; yet the narrator ignores this interpretative problem by endorsing the claim as 'confess[ing] / the som*m*e of all as you hav hard it tolde' (61–2). The woman's speech then appears to be impeded by modesty:

> The woman lothe to speake as women be
> and when theie speake *to gentle to saye naye*
> for this tyme sware she ...
>    ... woulde have cryed for helpe when we weare theare
> but that she was afrayde least we should heare.
> (67–72; my emphasis)

Paradoxically, while the inconsistency of her statement undermines her claim of rape, the narrator's characterisation of female speech as unable to articulate resistance backs it up. The subsequent stanza implies that the idea of modesty has worked in her favour:

> Thus modestye whearwithe theyre seckes aboundes
> *per*swaded much to make her faulte the lesse
> And vppon him the greater payne redoundes
> bycause he tryumphes on her humblenes
>    she Could no lower go then to the grounde
>    and at the lowest on her he was founde.
> (73–8)

However, the final two paragraphs move from the competing contentions of the man and woman and again define them together as having 'the faulte ... not denyed' and as having obeyed 'theyre brutishe lust' (79, 89).

'Grevell''s poem exemplifies the problems of deducing female volition in the sexual act typical of the pastourelle genre, and stages the ambiguity surrounding her utterance. The 'laments' and 'complaints' of this tradition ventriloquise the female voice, but still fail to elucidate such matters. By contrast, this poem ventriloquises the woman's story by interpolating at least two possible intermediate narrators – and thus presents a male narrator explicitly confused by her. By bringing the central characters out of the pastoral setting into a courtroom situation, the poet effectively figures his interrogation of this stock situation, with all its ambiguities. That the poem's or court's conclusion is unsatisfactory, then, points to the difficulty of such a task.

The genre of 'female complaint' originating in the *Mirror for Magistrates*, as is well known, reaches its height in the 1590s. Royal mistresses are its most popular heroines, particularly Jane Shore, Rosamond de Clifford and Elstride.[14] With these figures of dubious chastity there are also a number of explicit 'whores' or courtesans.[15] Alongside these fallen women, however, are a number of 'martyrs' to chastity, beginning with Blenerhasset's Lady Ebbe (1578) and continuing with Drayton's *Matilda* (1594) and Barkstead's *Virginia's Death* (1617).[16] There is also interest in other exemplars of chastity, Penelope and Susanna. Colse's *Penelope's Complaint* (1596), more explicitly than Greene's *Penelopes Web*, emphasises the suitors' rapacity by presenting them both as forceful towards Penelope herself and as raping one of her maids.[17] Robert Roche's *Eustathia* (1599) and, later, Robert Aylett's *Susanna* (1622) present the Elders explicitly as threatening or prepared to rape Susanna, her cries causing them to slander her in their defence.[18] Shakespeare's *Lucrece* (1594) has been related to the complaint genre, and its story is reworked in Middleton's *The Ghost of Lucrece* (1601).[19]

The generic linking of works which praise women who commit suicide to avoid rape with those which show successful rape has, as we already know, problematic implications. Yet the coexistence of works which feature courtesans and those in which the woman's sexual conduct is uneasily poised between active and passive further complicates this juxtaposition. The poems are linked not just by generic markers, but by common concerns, such as the power of language and sexual conflicts between women and monarchs.[20] Thus the range of women presented across the genre does not serve simply to contrast Lucreces with Rosamonds or Helens, but also to align them.

Poems of the 'martyr' type, like Drayton's *Matilda*, may be explicitly didactic; his heroine is 'a mirror of so rare chastitie' (p. 210) and the 'glorious wonder of all woman-head' (l. 950). Richard Barnfield's *The*

*Complaint of Chastity* (1594) demonstrates the potential of such stories to be used against women. He uses Matilda's exemplary chastity to reflect unfavourably on contemporary women, and to support his diatribe against make-up or 'tincture':

> Then women were the same that men did deeme,
> But now they are the same they doo not seeme.[21]

This anxiety about the difficulty of knowing women underlies many of these poems. Yet it also perhaps contributes to the erotic fascination of writers with women like Jane Shore.

The complaints featuring Jane Shore, Rosamond and Elstride display varying degrees of ambivalence about female sexual volition, and consequently destabilise the boundary between seduction and rape. Like earlier poems, they sometimes deploy the language of male force and female vulnerability to imply the force of persuasion or temptation rather than physical force. Even were the initial sexual act clearly defined as a rape, however, the woman's status as a victim would be undermined by her living on as the man's mistress. Yet the complaint is predicated on the assumption that a reader may feel sympathy for the woman character, though 'fallen'.[22] This particular kind of sympathy, it seems, is produced by a fascination with the idea of woman's sexual shame, distress and dishonour.

In Churchyard's *Shores Wife*, Jane uses the language of force to describe her first sexual encounter with Edward: 'the strong did make the weake to bowe' (77). Yet she undermines this imagery by claiming that she 'agreed the fort he should assaulte' (84). The use of the military topos does not preclude the woman's taking or sharing responsibility. Here, as with the other 'mistress' poems, the language of power is further complicated by the man's royalty. Jane continues:

> Who can withstand a puissaunt kynges desyre?
> The stiffest stones are perced through with tooles,
> The wisest are with princes made but fooles.
>
> (89–91)

If the first image implies rape, the second implies rather seduction or deception. She continues to refer to herself as a willing prisoner, although she 'knew no way awaye to flee', and goes on to imply that she loved the king 'in whom was all my ioye' (161, 280).

In Lodge's *Elstred* the heroine's account to the poet and reader, which presents a story of reciprocal love, contrasts ironically with her claims to the king's wife that she 'sinn'd vnwilling and enforced' (p. 80):

> I was vnable to withstand inuasion:
>> For where the Conqueror crau'd, I knew full well
>> He could commaund, if so *I* should rebell.
>>> (p. 80)

Daniel's *Rosamond* shows the complexity and ambiguity of power-relations between the sexes when the man is not only physically but politically powerful:

> But what? he is my King and may constraine me,
> Whether I yeelde or not I liue defamed:
> The world will thinke authority did gaine me,
> I shal be iudg'd hys loue, and so be shamed:
> We see the fayre condemn'd, that neuer gamed.
>> And if I yeeld, tis honorable shame,
>> If not, I liue disgrac'd, yet thought the same.
>>> (337–43)

Is Rosamond concerned that people will think she has yielded to Edward even if she has succeeded in preserving her chastity, or that they will have the same opinion of her regardless of whether she is seduced or raped? Taking the first lines as a context facilitates the latter reading, implying that Edward will make her his mistress 'whether I yeelde or not'.

Rosamond's vulnerability to rape seems to be pointed to by the poem's allusion to classical rape stories. The casket sent to her before her 'defeature' (372) pictures Amymone's rape by Neptune and Io's by Jove – the former, though not the latter, explicitly portrayed as a rape. Rosamond first reacts that 'tis shame that men should vse poore maydens so' (385), and later looks back at them as 'presidents...Wherein the presage of my fall was showne' (407–8). Yet she also implies that they exemplify sin and blames herself:

> I sawe the sinne wherein my foote was entring...
> Yet had I not the powre for to defende it;
> So weake is sence when error hath condemn'd it.
>> (421–5)

Even here her sense of powerlessness is central, and the consummation is described in terms that show her distaste, as Rosamond 'felt
the hand of Lust most vndesired' (436).

That Daniel sets Rosamond's story against a backdrop of rape but
presents her as constrained into sin both by the king and by her own
'fraile flesh' (352) is a measure of the complexity of contemporary
attitudes to female involvement in any illicit sexual behaviour. It also
reveals the intersection of a taste for women as sexual victims with
an equally strong fascination with women as sexually erring. These
agendas also shape Drayton's versions of the stories of Rosamond and
Jane Shore. His Rosamond seems to state clearly that she was raped:

> For what my body was enforst to doe,
> (Heauen knowes) my soule did not consent vnto.
>
> (33–4)

Her distinction collapses, however, when she later declares that Henry
has made her 'a monster, both in body and in mind' (174). When her
maid asks her to identify the figure of Lucrece in a portrait, she is 'not
able then to tell the rest for shame' (100), privileging shame over issues
of volition and guilt. Like Daniel's casket pictures, this allusion prefigures Rosamond's fall. But where Daniel uses them to complicate
the issue of Rosamond's culpability, Drayton shows shame adhering
even to a figure whose position is less anomalous than Rosamond's.

His portrayal of Jane Shore achieves a different balance. Like
Lodge's Elstred, Jane argues that men have power over women:
'nature too well taught them to inuade vs' (86); she lists their weapons,
however, as tears, sighs and vows. Her defence is interesting in
blaming her marriage, as well as worldly temptation, for her adultery. This, with her final claim to love Edward, however, undermines the force of her attribution of blame to a male power that
might be physical or political:

> Thus still wee striue, yet ouer-come at length,
> For men want mercy, and poore women strength:
> Yet graunt, that we, could meaner men resist
> When Kings once come, they conquer as they list.
>
> (157–60)

These ambiguous figures, then, as well as the more clear-cut
whores and martyrs, provide a context in 1594 for Shakespeare's

presentation of Lucrece. It may be owing to the complaint poems immediately preceding it, with their problematic depiction of female sexual volition, that Shakespeare's _Lucrece_ intensely scrutinises its heroine's resistance.

Shakespeare significantly alters the account of the rape found in Livy, releasing Lucrece from the implication of complicity, even under duress. As we know, Painter, translating Livy, states that Lucrece, 'ouercame the puritie of her chast harte', and Ovid that she 'yielded, overcome by fear of scandal'.[23] Shakespeare departs from these sources to make it clear that Tarquin uses physical force to rape Lucrece:

> The wolf hath seiz'd his prey, the poor lamb cries,
>   Till with her own white fleece her voice controll'd
>   Entombs her outcry in her lips' sweet fold.
>
> For with the nightly linen that she wears
> He pens her piteous clamours in her head,
> Cooling his hot face in the chastest tears
> That ever modest eyes with sorrow shed.
> O that prone lust should stain so pure a bed!
>
> (677–84)

This account of the 'forced league' (689) fits in with Tarquin's determination to 'deflower' Lucrece (348) whatever she says or does, made evident earlier in the poem. It is also prefigured by several images of violation used to chart Tarquin's progress to Lucrece's bedroom – images, however, that maintain the ambiguity adhering to rape: 'each _unwilling_ portal _yields_ him way' (309) and the bedroom door has a 'yielding latch' (339), although the locks are 'each one by him _enforc'd_' (303; my emphases). While in this context 'yielding' must indicate a physical opening or giving way, the effect of this term on the imagery of violation is to set up a suggestion of ambiguity about whether to 'yield' is purely physical or not.

Shakespeare's account of the rape does not fit with the alternatives Tarquin had originally laid out for Lucrece: if she agreed, he would be her 'secret friend' (526), if she resisted, he would kill her after the rape and implicate her with the slave (512–17, 670–2). Given that she does resist him during the rape by crying out and weeping, and that the rape is not defined in terms of 'yielding', we are bound to ask why he leaves her alive. Shakespeare has altered his source to the point where, in order to fulfil the implications of Tarquin's threats and actions, he would have to alter the story completely. This may suggest that he found it hard to stomach a definition of rape as 'yielding under duress'. Carolyn D. Williams has argued that in the poem's 'slow-motion technique' it would be hard to portray compliance as anything other than 'indefensible', and this would indeed compound the problem.[24] Yet further evidence of Shakespeare's distaste for this definition of rape may be provided by his alteration of the plot of Whetstone's *Promos and Cassandra* (1578) when writing *Measure for Measure*. Whetstone's play contains no bed-trick: the heroine succumbs to a 'rape' achieved by blackmail. Shakespeare's bed-trick saves Isabella from the ambivalence of this situation, just as his portrayal of Lucrece's rape asserts her innocence.[25]

This and subsequent accounts of the rape create confusion about the definition of resistance. Lucrece blames her hand for 'yielding' (1036) by not scratching Tarquin; she also writes her verbal resistance out of her later narrative, claiming 'my bloody judge forbod my tongue to speak' (1648). Her ambiguous allusion to her body's 'accessory yieldings' (1658) might, like the 'yielding' of the portals, indicate merely the (involuntary) opening up of her body, but it might alternatively suggest sexual arousal during the rape: potentially implicating her further. Yet it is clear both that verbal resistance is the only kind open to her and that this resistance is ineffectual, not just because it is met with physical violence but because its effect on the rapist is erotically arousing. His claim that his 'uncontrolled tide / Turns not, but swells the higher by this let' (645–6) might figure the titillating effect of the eloquence of the complaint's sexually compromised heroines.

The complaint both privileges and circumscribes female speech. Lucrece's language in her own defence simply inflames her assailant; her denunciation of him is legitimised by her subsequent suicide. Lady Ebbe, Rosamond and Jane, comparably, provide the voices in their complaints, but are already dead and can only be empowered by their utterance to the extent of shaping their subsequent reputations. In presenting Lucrece as a 'pale swan in her wat'ry nest' (1611), Shakespeare foregrounds this issue. He images the rape as a silencing of utterance, as Tarquin 'entombs her outcry in her lips' sweet fold' (679); the trapping of her speech in her mouth figures the rapist's forcible invasion via the 'lips' of the vulva. The rape also begets utterance: but only the 'helpless smoke of words' (1027) of her curse and her 'swansong'. Her final speech, we know, has a significant political effect. The transition to political action is figured in a strikingly sexual image when Brutus, 'burying in Lucrece' wound his folly's show' (1810), moves into the foreground. Whether we read Lucrece's language as powerful, in its initiation of political action, or as circumscribed by its predication upon her subsequent suicide, is a moot point.

Shakespeare's allusion to 'Philomel' (1128) makes a further connection between rape and female language. Lucrece parallels her stabbing to Philomela's production of song by pressing her breast 'against a thorn' (1135): an image of rape engendering language. Middleton's *The Ghost of Lucrece* (1600) develops this analogy. His heroine compares herself to Philomela (395–6), and tells us, 'Philomela's choir / Is hush'd from prick-song' (535–6). She reveals that the complaint has been a symbolic letter written from her to Tarquin, or from Philomela to Tereus (532):

> Bleed no more lines, my heart! This knife (my pen),
> This blood (my ink), hath writ enough to Lust.
>
> (505–6)

Lucrece's knife both re-enacts the rape, destroys her and becomes her pen: liberating language just as Philomela's thorn produces song through its destruction and symbolic violation of her. Yet these images interpolate female action into the equation between rape and language, albeit within the parameters of swansong. The knife and thorn may be symbols of rape – action by the male – but they have been appropriated by the females, in order to write both their own deaths and their stories.

Issues of narrative control in relation to rape surface explicitly in John Trussell's *The First Rape of Faire Hellen* (1595). This poem displays the ideological problems thrown up by the range and diversity of the complaint genre. It encapsulates the clash between whores and martyrs as the subjects of the genre, particularly in the ways in which it fails to meet the genre's demands. Trussell takes a character famous for her adultery (her 'rape' in the sense of elopement/abduction), who more commonly features in complaints as a repentant whore, and attempts to portray her as a victim by having her tell the story of her rape by Theseus as a young girl.[26] He also chooses an obscure version of the story which makes this a rape in the modern sense, rather than the tale of abduction which was more common.[27] Yet the poet's attempt to cast the story as tragical complaint rather than erotic epyllion is compromised by his retention of much of the paraphernalia of the latter,[28] and by the poem's ending. Hellen first appears as a rape victim, with 'haires disheueld, eyes with tears besprent' (21), but the poem ends by looking towards her subsequent fall:

> Then heer I must abruptlie leaue to showe. [*sic*]
> my second cause of second detriment.
>
> $(889-90)$[29]

This attempt at closure is inadequate in explaining why Hellen's ghost should be lamenting the rape of her girlhood rather than her later fall. The poet-figure's ready sympathy clashes with the reader's awareness of this anomaly.

There is no ambiguity, however, about the nature of Theseus's possession of Hellen:

> He forc'd my flesh his fancie to fulfill.
> He hath his wish by force without my will.
>
> $(173-4)$

She thus becomes 'the subiect of his tyrannie' (162). Hellen's complaint is one of few spoken by a raped woman, in terms lacking the ambiguity of the Rosamonds and Jane Shores. Yet while the action of the poem defines the 'rape' of the title categorically as forced intercourse, the choice of Hellen as its 'subject' (or object) destabilises the victim's status this act should give her, by recalling her second 'rape'. The resultant tension in the work thus mirrors the tension within the genre as a whole.

The contrast between Hellen and Lucrece concerns the course of action taken by the raped woman. Hellen's marriage, in her view, 'covers' her rape, so that she is 'enfranchiz'd from all feare of shame' (874). Yet Schmitz has suggested that her concern with appearances brings Hellen in line with the courtesans whose complaints emphasise cosmetics.[30] Hellen's satisfaction at duping Menelaus could indeed be aligned with the later Paulina's warning to young men that 'our arts and falshood quickly will vndoe you' (p. 11). This emphasis on concealment thus signals an anxiety about the visibility or readability of rape as a crime.

Throughout the poem, the idea of concealment or covering clashes with that of disclosure in connection with both rape and narrative.

The word 'disclose' appears in the poem at least six times and Hellen associates it primarily with the shame of public knowledge:

> I curst the day, the enemy to blame,
>    for feare it would my rauishment disclose.
>
> (279–80)

Hellen's anxiety about the world's appropriation of her story is well founded. However, dis-closure and dis-covery figure the invasion not only of the woman's secret by the world but of her body by the rapist. Not only does Hellen accuse the sun of shining 'of purpose to discouer my disgrace' (214), but her rape is preceded by just such an image: 'His hearts il-tent [Theseus] openly discouered' (159). Jove's rape of Leda is represented in the same way, as he attempts to 'discouer [her]' (610):

> Now he discloseth that his feathered plumes;
>    are God in substance, though a Swan in showe.
>
> (625–6)

His disclosure of information is equivalent to the revelation of the godly 'substance' that effects Leda's rape.

Throughout the poem Hellen's moans and sighs, inarticulate 'woes interpreters' (187), contrast with her fear of such disclosure and with her relief when her rape is 'couered' (878) by her marriage at the end of the poem. The complaint itself she presents as uttered under duress, though perhaps emotional:

> That thing did chance which to my endlesse woe,
> I am enforst vnto the world to show.
>
> (53–4)

The duress of emotional compulsion here parallels that of narratorial compulsion. The poem's structure, with Hellen's speech framed by a few stanzas in the poet's voice at either end, highlights the proximity between the two, and between narratorial 'enforcement' and rape. The troping of rape as disclosure intensifies this proximity. As the 'subiect' of the poem as well as of Theseus's rape, Hellen is violated as much by the poet's exposure of her to the reader as she is by the rape; her language registers the voyeurism implicit in the experience of reading about rape. As the *object* of rape, she becomes the *subject* of the complaint poem, 'enforst' to publicise her tale of private, sexual shame.

Exposure by narrative, then, figures and is necessitated by the act of rape. This kind of literary self-consciousness extends to the manner in which rape stories are often treated. While Shakespeare was aware that Lucrece's story had become a 'theme for disputation' (822), Roche's elders warn Susanna: 'Contract thy tale, doe not at large debate' (sig. Fv). The principle of 'disputation' contributes to the tension in the presentation of these women, combined with the taste for publicised female sexual shame which the complaints supply.

The epyllion, which frequently overlaps with the complaint in subject matter and treatment, stages a comparable tension between female promiscuity and victimisation and questions the nature of sexual resistance. While the complaints open up cracks between different versions of a female character's behaviour, or stage her own confusion as to her situation and conduct, the epyllia destabilise the relation between desire and expression by asserting frequently that women say 'no' to mean 'yes', often deploying Ovidian examples.

Marlowe's *Hero and Leander*, probably written in or by 1593, presents Hero as deliberately deploying 'coyness' to convey her reciprocation of desire without compromising her honour:

> Heroes lookes yeelded, but her words made warre,
> Women are woon when they begin to jarre.
>  . . . .
>
> Yet evilly faining anger, strove she still,
> And would be thought to graunt against her will.
>
> (i. 331–6)[31]

Their courtship thus appears as a battle. She throws herself on him 'like light Salmacis' (ii. 46), but when he clasps her she 'fearing on the rushes to be flung, / Striv'd with redoubled strength' (66) – ironic, since her previous striving had been to win him. This time she 'sav'de her maydenhead' (76), but she loses the battle after he swims the Hellespont. The consummation is fraught with ambiguity, with Hero's coy manipulation, drawing Leander into her bed, balancing the language of male force and female resistance. It is 'gentle parlie' that wins her eventually (278), but the narrator's conclusion suggests that she would never have been allowed a choice:

> ... the truce was broke, and she alas,
> (Poore sillie maiden) at his mercie was.
> Love is not ful of pittie (as men say)
> But deaffe and cruell, where he meanes to pray.
>
> (285–8)

While *Hero and Leander* thus undermines female sexual denial by presenting coyness as an active strategy, Weaver's *Faunus and Melliflora* (1600) incapacitates it by asserting that a woman's 'no' always means 'yes'. When Faunus propositions a group of nymphs:

> ... some said nothing; these gave ful consent,
> And some said twice No, which affirmes content,
> And some said once No; these would grant and give:
> In womens mouths, No is no negative.
>
> (307–10)[32]

This provides the context for a rewriting of classical myth and history which claims that women enjoy rape (328–34). The speaker, however, is a woman who, like Salmacis in Beaumont's poem, is trying to seduce her male listener. Salmacis provocatively asks 'what Jove and Læda did, / When like a Swan the craftie god was hid' (723–4).[33] By writing out the rape, she turns the story into a titillating tale of illicit sex, and into an invitation to Hermaphroditus to take/ 'rape' her.

Salmacis's sexual assertiveness contextualises Weaver's ambiguous presentation of her attempted seduction by Bacchus. Bacchus 'forc't the lovely mayd to stay' (440); her wavering – 'faine she would have gone, but yet she staid' (456) – suggests either constraint or desire. He then throws her onto the ground and would have raped her ('stray'd beyond that lawful bound' (460)); her 'helplesse[ness]' (459) suggests that she is physically trapped, but connotes content. When Phoebus rescues her, the narrator claims she was actively desiring all along: 'gainst her will, he sav'd her maiden-head' (468). Like Trussell's Hellen, any resistance she puts up may be undermined by her subsequent behaviour; Thomas Peend even uses her sexual assertion to 'prove' the falseness of women who claim to be innocent.[34]

Such scenes seem to satisfy two conflicting impulses: the impulse to express male sexual aggression by staging rape, and the impulse to portray women as ever-desiring, non-chaste and coy. Hero desires, and is won by 'gentle parley', but before the consummation she

> [with] every lim did as a soldier stout,
> Defend the fort, and keep the foe-man out.
> (ii. 271–2)

The scene between Mercury and the country maid in this poem is even more ambivalent. He pins her on the ground and

> ... like an insolent commaunding lover,
> Boasting his parentage, would needs discover
> The way to new Elisium: but she,
> Whose only dower was her chastitie,
> Having striv'n in vaine, was now about to crie....
> (i. 409–13)

When he lets her go, the narrator comments:

> Maids are not woon by brutish force and might,
> But speeches full of pleasure and delight.
> (419–20)

This implies that the consummation is yet to come. Yet the possibility that he has already raped her is available in the phrase 'having striv'n in vain'.

As this episode shows, rape or attempted rape is not confined to the main plot of the epyllion. In fact, rape is part of the background to most of these poems. Venus in Lodge's *Scillas Metamorphosis* (1589) wears a robe decorated with rape stories, Jove propositions Salmacis in Beaumont's poem by reminding her of his rapes of other maidens (121–4), and Lamie in Thomas Edwards' *Cephalus and Procris* (1595) alludes to the rape of Leda.[35] It frequently takes place – or is threatened – in subsidiary action, as with the episode of Mercury and the country maid, or Bacchus and Salmacis in Beaumont's poem; Edwards' Procris is threatened with rape by a swain who finds her asleep, and this too is irrelevant to the main story.

While the high incidence of rape in the background to these poems creates a sense of its inevitability, several writers excuse it as the natural result of love. In Heywood's *Oenone and Paris* (1594) Paris blames Cupid for his 'rape' of Helen, referring to Jove's rapes: 'His scapes with fayre Europa shew loves might' (st. 110).[36] This blurs the two senses of 'rape', as forced coitus and abduction/seduction, both justified as responses to love's power. In *The Metamorphosis of Pygmalion's Image* (1598) Marston tells his female readers to 'thinke that they nere love you, / Who do not unto more than kissing move you' (st. 20, ll. 5–6).[37]

If these explicit attempts to justify rape relate to its proliferation in the genre, particularly in the poems' backgrounds, this should prepare us for its treatment in Spenser's *The Faerie Queene*.

## THE FAERIE QUEENE

> Ne may loue be compeld by maisterie;
> For soone as maisterie comes, sweet loue anone
> Taketh his nimble wings, and soone away is gone.
>                                                 (III.i.25)[38]

The threat of rape is extended to virtually every female character in *The Faerie Queene*. Britomart's claim that love cannot be compelled exists in uneasy relation to the action of the poem. It is predicated on the opposition between love and lust which Spenser is shortly to make in his own voice, when he tells the 'Faire Ladies':

> Let not [Malecasta's] fault your sweet affections marre . . .
> For this was not to loue, but lust inclind.
>
>                                                 (III.i.49)

This opposition facilitates his defence of the poem's erotic content in the Proem to Book IV, where he condemns those that cannot 'in their frosen hearts feele kindly flame' (IV. Proem 2). The Proem sets arousal and titillation against edification and instruction by asserting the heroic nature of love ('it of honor and all vertue is / The roote') in the epic, while acknowledging (and thus inscribing) the protests arising from the publication of its first three books.

This tension – the coexistence of arousal and edification or lust and love – mirrors a tension in the poem as a whole. Britomart's claim is validated by its immediate context (the attempt of six knights to make Redcrosse change in love); its proximity to the pursuit of Florimell by the Foster, however, pulls in two directions. While her claim is valid in this context too, as Florimell cannot be made to love her assailant, it raises the question of whether 'love' in a less rarefied sense *can* be compelled: that is, by rape. This question too seems to be answered by the fact that all the rape attempts that take place in the foreground of the poem fail. The impotence of force against love (the affection) thus seems to be mirrored in the triumph of the 'good' knights of the poem over the 'bad' characters who attempt rape. However, this failure of rape in the main action of the poem conflicts with the proliferation of rapes which form its background, many of them providing its foundational myths. Moreover, that the boundary between love and lust which the narrator posits may be less stable than he claims, is suggested by the fact that these rapes are not condemned, and are sometimes presented as 'love'.[39]

*The Faerie Queene*, then, displays a tension between condemning and inscribing rape. Susanne Lindgren Wofford has argued that 'the fiction of rape . . . allows the poet simultaneously to express and condemn' fantasies about women.[40] The inscription of rape is, we shall see, achieved both by writing rape into the history of the poem and by figuring 'legitimate' violence against female characters in terms which connote rape. The tension relates too to the ambivalence of the poem towards Elizabeth I. Not only is there a general conflict between praise and resentment or disapproval of the queen,[41] but the poem's deployment of rape narratives provides one expression of such resentment.[42] Thus Belphoebe, overtly a figure for the queen, is threatened with rape by Braggadocchio (II.iii.42); Mercilla, the 'mayden Queene' (V.viii.17), is faced with a threat both political and sexual, a threat which is represented by the attempted rape of her waiting woman (V.viii); and Florimell, the most 'chased' character in the poem, may represent an aspect of the other figure for Elizabeth, Britomart.[43]

The problems of reading rape in *The Faerie Queene* are exacerbated by the significance of allegory, which Maureen Quilligan has called 'a special kind of pleading for texts'.[44] 'Man the rapist' is thus 'an emblem of fallen humanity', while the rape victim's 'nature images the divine',[45] or Aemylia's imprisonment by Lust (IV.vii) is a psychological allegory for her own conduct (she is captured while awaiting her lover for a secret rendezvous). Yet such allegories depend on rape narratives: indeed, Wofford has argued that 'attempted rape becomes a primary figure in the text for the workings of allegorical representation'.[46] Sheila T. Cavanagh therefore advocates a literal reading, in order to foreground a 'female' perspective and to identify the poem's 'representational strategies' which work against such readings.[47]

*The Faerie Queene*'s vocabulary of rape registers such strategies. Spenser uses the word 'rape' only once or twice in the poem. He describes Lust as living 'all on rauin and on rape' (IV.vii.5), a context in which the modern sense of 'rape' is readily available. An Argument, however, defines 'rape' as abduction or seduction, when 'Paridell rapeth Hellenore' (III.x. Arg. 1). This episode also features the only use of 'ravish' in the work, which is used to mean sexual enforcement, but the impact of this definition is undermined by its context: it is while eloping with Paridell consensually that Hellenore tells her husband that he 'meant to rauish her' (III.x.13). 'Ravished' (used eleven times) or 'ravishment' (twice) refer, by contrast, to rapture.[48]

The word used most frequently for sexual forcing in *The Faerie Queene* is 'spoil', a word that also has a wider range of implications in the work. 'Spoil', 'spoils' and 'spoiled' appear 114 times in the poem, and about a third of the usages are unambiguously sexual. Moreover, the words often appear in clusters, so that sexual usages are not only found together but may be surrounded by non-sexual ones. For instance, Pastorella is Calidore's 'loues deare spoile' (VI.x.35) and later the 'spoile of theeues' (40); more ambiguously, the brigants live on 'spoile and booty' (39), and they also 'spoyld' houses and 'spoyld old *Melibee* of all he had' (39, 40).

This treatment highlights the proximity of the sexual sense (whereby a woman is a man's 'spoil' or is about to be 'spoiled') to the non-sexual senses of the 'spoils' or booty resulting from war or theft, or the gastronomic 'spoils' of animals. Ironically, Pastorella is Calidore's 'deare spoile' at the point where she is being pursued by a tiger, and the syntax potentially attributes her to either: he 'the beast saw ready now to rend / His loues deare spoile' (VI.x.35). Moreover, within the sexual usages, 'spoil' with its violent overtones inevitably creates a sense of sexual danger, and on nine occasions it is unambiguously used to indicate rape, as when Sansloy attempts to rape Una and 'win rich spoile of ransackt chastetee' (I.vi.5). This association is heightened by further examples where the context of the image is a scenario of attempted rape or potential rape, as when the False Florimell is Braggadocchio's 'spoile' (III.viii.13); his intention to 'reaue her honor' (14) puts this in a context of rape. The ideological and etymological connection between rape and abduction in the period may partially account for this phenomenon. 'Spoil' thus becomes strongly connotative of rape, so that some ostensibly non-rape encounters gain in significance.

The word 'spoil' gives particular nuance to the relationship between Scudamore and Amoret. Blandamour derides Scudamore for the 'fruitlesse end / Of thy vaine boast, and spoile of loue misgotten' (IV.i.51); the word becomes charged in retrospect, when the story of his forcible appropriation of Amoret comes out. As Scudamore relates how he claimed Amoret and refused to let her go despite her tears and entreaties (x.55–7), he images her as 'this peerelesse beauties spoile', 'so glorious spoyle' and 'that glorious spoyle of beautie' (x.3, 55, 58).[49] The image becomes increasingly loaded, particularly given the connotations the word has already acquired by this stage in the poem. The second image occurs when Amoret is 'with terror queld' (x.55); the third, after she has begged release and found that there is no way she can 'her wished freedome fro me wooe' (x.57). While 'spoil' in this context could signify abduction (already a sexually connotative action), the nuancing of the word elsewhere with implications of rape underlines Scudamore's ultimate goal of appropriating Amoret sexually in marriage.

Although the word 'spoil' is dominant in *The Faerie Queene*'s vocabulary of rape, it does not appear in any of the cases of successful rape in the poem. Such cases all take place in the past, and are either mythological or explain the genealogy of important characters. The genealogical rapes provide a backdrop to the poem. Yet although in most cases Spenser makes it clear that the encounter was rape, he does not use the word 'spoil' (let alone 'rape' or 'ravish'). Instead, he uses a variety of different epithets; a knight 'oppressed' Agape (IV.ii.45), while Blomius 'by force deflowr'd' Rheusa (IV.xi.42).

The marginalisation of the female perspective in these episodes may account for this absence of the vocabulary which elsewhere proves so potent in describing rape. Rape in these cases plays an important role as foundation myth, on the Ovidian model. Thyamis's rape by a satyr produces Satyrane (I.vi.22–3), Cymoent's rape by Dumarin produces Marinell (III.iv.19), Chrysogonee's produces Belphoebe and Amoret (III.vi.6–7), and Agape's produces Priamond, Dyamond and Triamond (IV.ii.45). Rheusa's rape by Blomius also produces sons (three rivers), but is primarily significant as an explanation of the history of the landscape (xi.42). Although the rapes of Thyamis, Agape and Rheusa are not 'written out' of the narratives, their production of sons is clearly more important than their experience of rape; Agape is congratulated as being 'full blessed' for having such sons and her assailant is called a 'noble' knight (IV.ii.43, 45). Cymoent's rape is conveyed in gentler language, for Dumarin 'by her closely lay' in her sleep (III.iv.19), while Chrysogonee, also asleep, is impregnated by the sun's rays (III.vi.7).

Chrysogonee's impregnation is a forcible, though gentle, possession of a non-consenting woman, represented in language which emphasises the penetration: 'The sunne-beames ... pierst into her wombe' (III.vi.7). Stevie Davies has called this a 'benign' 'rape', while Cavanagh argues that such an interpretation evades the scene's ideological implications.[50] The interpretative problem arises because the Chrysogonee episode pulls in two directions, one pagan and one Christian. Helen Hackett has pointed out the parallel between Chrysogonee's asexual conception and the Virgin Mary's.[51] Yet at the same time, Chrysogonee's place among the other raped mothers who proliferate in the poem's historical backdrop insinuates a definition of her experience as rape, albeit painless.

These cases avoid the issue of trauma and foreground history or genealogy as part of the epic's strategy of legitimating its heroes, establishing their chain of descent.[52] In Chrysogonee's case, moreover, it is the 'Legend of Chastity' which is built upon the myth of painless rape. Belphoebe, one of its exemplars, was conceived without pleasure; in a pagan rather than a Christian context, the only chaste conception possible (lacking female desire) is this gentle, 'natural' version of rape. Rape, then, legitimates and is legitimated by the interests of history and allegory. To image these reluctant mothers as 'spoil' would be to detract from the sense of their position in the poem's historical scheme.

Spenser's assertive distinction between love and lust in his address to his female readers ('this was not to loue, but lust inclind') follows a story not of male but of female lust, in the figure of Malecasta. Female characters tend to represent the extremes of sexuality in the poem, whether figures of sexual power (Acrasia, Venus, Argante) or figures habitually prone to rape (Florimell, Amoret).[53] Where the aggressor is female, the idea of rape inevitably functions differently from where it is male. In the case of Acrasia, the most prominent figure of female erotic power in the first half of the work, rape becomes a trope manipulated by the woman for her empowerment.

Acrasia subjugates men with her 'words and weedes of wondrous might' (II.i.52). The association of her craft with weaving – a craft traditionally linked with female discourse – underlines its simultaneously verbal nature. Acrasia's veil appears as a web:

> More subtile web *Arachne* cannot spin,
>   Nor the fine nets, which oft we wouen see
> Of scorched deaw, do not in th'aire more lightly flee.
>
> (II.xii.77)

Arachne's web recorded and exposed the rapes of mortal women by the gods; Acrasia's uses the idea of rape more insidiously to entice her male victims.[54]

The structure of the Bower of Bliss mirrors this web image, comprising concentric circles around a central scene. At its outermost edge we find a gate framed by a depiction of the story of Jason and Medea which emphasises Medea's power in 'mighty charmes' (xii.44). The 'spacious plaine' (50) beyond the gate is the subject of comparisons that bear witness to rape:

> More sweet and holesome, then the pleasaunt hill
>   Of *Rhodope*, on which the Nimphe, that bore
>   A gyaunt babe, her selfe for griefe did kill;
>   Or the Thessalian *Tempe*, where of yore
>   Faire *Daphne Phœbus* hart with love did gore.
>
> (xii.52)

The image of goring for Daphne's effect on Apollo simultaneously writes out and underlines the nature of his threat to her. The nymph's child was fathered by Neptune, and her suicide points to the likelihood of rape. However, Rhodope was also the mountain where Orpheus charmed the trees, and this is an apt image for the enchanting effect of Acrasia's art.[55]

Further in, Guyon finds two 'naked Damzelles' bathing, who 'ne car'd to hyde, / Their dainty parts from vew of any, which them eyde' (63):

> Sometimes the one would lift the other quight
>   Aboue the waters, and then down againe
>   Her plong, as ouer maistered by might, ...
>   The whiles their snowy limbes, as through a vele,
>   So through the Christall waues appeared plaine:
>   Then suddeinly both would themselues vnhele,
> And th'amarous sweet spoiles to greedy eyes reuele.
>
> (64)

Elsewhere in the work, voyeurism is associated with danger for the viewed female; here the nymphs invite it.[56] The emphasis on plunging may too be sexually connotative. The use of 'spoiles' as a euphemism for female parts implies that the nymphs are offering to play the role usually filled by *un*willing virgins, the objects of 'greedy [male] eyes' and vulnerable to rape: Serena, Pastorella or Amoret.

The continued emphasis on veiling and unveiling as the nymphs try to arouse Guyon anticipates Acrasia's presentation of herself and links their erotic strategy with hers. She is found at the centre of the landscape in the Bower itself, lying with her lover on the roses which her song recommends de-flowering (75):

> And was arayd, or rather disarayd,
> All in a vele of silke and siluer thin,
> That hid no whit her alablaster skin . . .
>
> (77)

In this carefully wrought illusion Acrasia plays both enchantress and victim. While the lover who is to be turned into a beast is the true victim, Acrasia tropes herself as the fulfilment of the male fantasy of rape aroused by the bathing nymphs, deploying the same language:

> Her snowy brest was bare to readie *spoyle*
> Of hungry eies, which n'ote therewith be fild,
> And yet through languour of her late sweet toyle,
> Few drops, more cleare then Nectar, forth distild.
>
> (78; my emphasis)

Acrasia's temptation lies in the balance she creates between imaging herself as the victim of male fantasy and as sexually active and powerful: a woman who has recently made love but is still open to violent appropriation.

If Acrasia stages the Bower of Bliss as a progression for the male intruder towards private, inner spaces, culminating in a paradoxical invitation to rape, it is possible that these significances hold good when Guyon destroys the Bower. The use of 'spoil' again may hint at this sense; he 'their arbers [did] spoyle, their Cabinets suppresse' (83), and his penetration of the Bower with the intention of destroying it has a violent, sexual resonance that Britomart's of the House of Busyrane in Book IV cannot have. By contrast, the punishment of Acrasia herself is devoid of sexual overtones; she is simply bound 'in chaines of adamant' (II.xii.82). As we shall see, the sexual nuancing of physical violence against women is to be a phenomenon of the second half of the poem.

Book III restages the Bower of Bliss in two different ways. The portrait of Venus in the Garden of Adonis recalls Acrasia's erotic power. Here, however, the goddess's power is protective too: the boar that in the myth destroys Adonis 'she firmely hath emprisoned for ay, / That her sweet loue his malice mote auoyd' (III.vi.48). Acrasia also finds a male counterpart in Busyrane.

Where Acrasia's power was already verbal, Busyrane's is more self-consciously literary. His house is structured in a way that recalls the Bower of Bliss, with his torture of Amoret contextualised by a series of layers: the outermost, analogous to the Bower's gate, his tapestry. This depicts the rapes of women by gods in a way that blurs the issue of consent. As such it is part of Busyrane's strategy to persuade or force Amoret to love him; yet our awareness of the rape dynamic alerts us to Amoret's imminent danger and prefigures the images of her symbolic rape.[57]

The tapestry's strategy is based on the love or beauty topos which tropes the male as weak and disempowered. It purports to show the massacre by Cupid of 'mighty kings and kesars, into thraldome brought' (III.xi.29). The majority of the encounters are portrayed simply as erotic unions, although some give slightly greater emphasis to the power-dynamic:

> In *Satyres* shape *Antiopa* [Jove] snatcht:
> And like a fire, when he *Aegin'* assayd:
> A shepheard, when *Mnemosyne* he catcht.
> (xi.35)

In Medusa's case, her description prefigures the metamorphosis which followed her rape:

> And like a winged horse [Neptune] tooke his flight,
> To *snaky-locke Medusa* to repayre,
> On whom he got faire *Pegasus*, that flitteth in the ayre.
> (xi.42; my emphasis)

Even the two unions more explicitly acknowledged as rape are fraught with ambiguity. Europa's fear is the central feature of her part of the tapestry, but it may relate as much to the sea as to the power and intent of its commander (ironically, her 'servant'):

> Ah, how the fearefull Ladies tender hart
> Did liuely seeme to tremble, when she saw
> The huge seas vnder her t'obay her seruaunts law.
>
> (xi.30)

The narrative of Leda and Jove, notoriously, at once establishes Leda's innocence (she is 'sleeping') and connotes the swan's use of force (he 'did her inuade') while undercutting both:

> She slept, yet twixt her eyelids closely spyde,
> How towards her he rusht, and smiled at his pryde.
>
> (xi.32)

The tapestry depicting the gods' rapes in the name of love thus provides a context for the masque of Cupid (thus giving us a key for interpreting some of its figures); the masque in turn bears along Amoret with her heart in a basin as its centrepiece; in a still deeper and more contextualised space, we find the 'actual' Amoret with Busyrane piercing and inscribing her heart. Susan Frye has argued that Amoret is symbolically raped three times: when she is figured in the masque, when she is tied up with her heart pierced and when she is subsequently rendered 'perfect hole' (III.xii.38), a moment which involves the most lurid and sexual description of her wound.[58]

Busyrane's tapestry thus has two functions. It firmly writes out the rapes it portrays, underlining one allegorical interpretation of the whole episode, which privileges the power of love; at the same time, it uses the residual rape connotations to anticipate and emphasise Amoret's symbolic rape.[59] It thus provides a warning about the possibility of rape, both for the woman at its centre and its female spectator, Britomart. For both Acrasia and Busyrane, enchantment is a substitute for physical force. The significance of this is inevitably gendered. While both pose a threat analogous to rape, Busyrane's strategy is enacted upon the victim while Acrasia's is a fashioning of herself. Acrasia seductively tropes herself as a willing rape victim contextualised by similarly appealing damsels; Busyrane's torture figures rape, and is contextualised by depictions of rape as love.

The alignment of Busyrane with the poem's narrator is heightened by a comparison of the tapestry's function and strategy to Spenser's. Its depiction of Leda has been read as revealing the complicity of the artist in representational strategies which disempower the female character.[60] The congruence between Busyrane and the narrator, however, extends beyond this moment. The tapestry, after all, is a backdrop in more senses than just the literal one. *The Faerie Queene*, as we know, has a similar backdrop. If we turn now to *Prothalamion*, published in the same year as books IV to VI (1596), the connection between the two becomes clearer.

The landscape in *Prothalamion* is the scene of numerous rapes, all but one completely submerged. As in Busyrane's tapestry, this rape is troped as a love story:

> The snow which doth the top of *Pindus* strew,
> Did neuer whiter shew,
> Nor *Ioue* himselfe when he a Swan would be
> For loue of *Leda*, whiter did appeare:
> Yet *Leda* was they say as white as he,
> Yet not so white as these, nor nothing neare.
>                                    (40–5)[61]

The rape allusion, submerged by the omission of the issue of consent, has a complex relation to the subject of the comparison: the two swans, who represent the two brides of the poem. The brides are compared to the rapist, Jove, as swan rather than to the victim; yet the final comparison indicates their potential identification with Leda too.

The other rapes in *Prothalamion* are identifiable only by external knowledge of myth. Pindus, in the passage above, was the site for the rape of Oenone/Liagore by Apollo, after which he told her the secrets of medicine. This is recorded in Book III, where once again the narrative depicts rape as 'love':

> (This *Liagore* whylome had learned skill
> In leaches craft, by great *Appolloes* lore,
> Sith her whylome vpon high *Pindus* hill,
> He loued, and at last her wombe did fill
> With heauenly seed, whereof wise *Pæan* sprong).
>                                    (III.iv.41)

The fifth stanza refers to 'pleasant *Tempes* shore' (79) where Apollo pursued Daphne, and where the *Epithalamion* tells us Jove 'tooke' Maia 'In Tempe, lying on the flowry gras, Twixt sleepe and wake' (307, 308–9).[62] The swans who figure the brides-to-be and relate to Leda, are thus set against a landscape whose history is one of rape.

This landscape backdrop to *Prothalamion* most obviously resembles the backdrop to *The Faerie Queene*; yet in terms of narrative strategy, the submerging and rewriting of rape in *Prothalamion* seems more akin to Busyrane's tapestry. The relationship between the House of Busyrane and *Prothalamion* is further strengthened by the role of marriage in the torture of Amoret. Several critics have argued that Busyrane's treatment of Amoret can be read as a continuation or symbolic figuring of Scudamore's appropriation of her, with its undertones of rape.[63] Bates reads Amoret against the bride in *Epithalamion*, whom we have seen compared to the raped Maia (above), and locates both in the context of Puttenham's description of the violence of the consummation.[64] Busyrane is thus inscribing Scudamore's imminent sexual claiming of her, just as Spenser is soon to inscribe it – whether in the cancelled stanzas at the end of the book or the explanation of the circumstances of the marriage in Book IV. To read Amoret's torture as figuring her forced marriage or its imminent consummation facilitates a comparison between Amoret and *Prothalamion*'s brides, with both encircled by contextualising forces that simultaneously signal and suppress rape.

Spenser's genealogical episodes are clearly analogous to Busyrane's tapestry in providing a backdrop or context. It follows that Busyrane's explicit motivation may suggest another agenda behind *The Faerie Queene*'s marginalising of every instance of actual rape in favour of the process of history. The congruence between Busyrane's tapestry and the backdrops to both *Prothalamion* and *The Faerie Queene* thus leads us to question the function of these backdrops in relation to the various rape dynamics in the poem.

Rape in the poem's main action is generally presented as a false or corrupted response to vision or female beauty, which Wofford calls 'false rapture'.[65] Yet some episodes implicitly define rape as good or valid. In the case of the genealogical episodes, the need to establish the legitimacy of the epic's heroes and heroines or their descent from the immortals validates the rapes. In books V and VI, the violent punishment of erring women is frequently figured in terms which imply rape; this suggests that rape may be a valid response to bad women.

This tension between these two definitions even contributes to an ambivalence in the portrayal of Florimell and Amoret, the two most prominent figures of the rape victim in the work. Florimell's pursuit of her love object is surrounded by some anxiety. Wandering alone in the woods renders her vulnerable to rape, but with its sexual connotations (for women) it also implicates her to some extent.[66] The monster who chases her is a dual figure for the threat of rape: he may take Florimell back to the witch's son, who desires her, or he may devour her; since he is like the hyena 'that feeds on womens flesh' (III.vii.22), this threat seems connotative of rape. Florimell would then be the 'spoile of greedinesse' (25) and, implicitly, this would constitute punishment for her rejection of the witch's son: the monster would devour 'her beauties scornefull grace' (23). In her flight, we are told:

> Not halfe so fast the wicked *Myrrha* fled
> From dread of her reuenging fathers hond:
> Not halfe so fast to saue her maidenhed,
> Fled fearefull *Daphne* on th'*Ægæan* strond,
> As *Florimell* fled from that Monster yond.
>
> (26)

Daphne's flight from sexual assault is clearly analogous to Florimell's, but Myrrha flies to escape just punishment for her own sexual transgression.[67] Although Florimell's speed, rather than her sexual conduct, is the focus of the analogy, the allusion to Myrrha in this context is disturbing.[68]

The same analogy is used of Amoret flying from the cave of Lust:

> More swift then *Myrrh'* or *Daphne* in her race,
> Or any of the Thracian Nimphes in saluage chase.
>
> (IV.vii.22)

The tension between the images of Myrrha and Daphne is intensified by the additional allusion to Thracian nymphs (Amazons); fleeing from rape she is imaged as an unnatural, aggressive woman in active 'chase'. Amoret too had been captured while wandering in the woods. Although, unlike Florimell, she was not pursuing an erotic goal, the shared allusion seems to signal a similar anxiety. This may be enhanced by her relationship to Aemylia, with whom she is imprisoned by Lust (IV.vii–viii). In Aemylia's case the psychological allegory is more straightforward, yet even so, Wofford has argued that it falls short, and that Lust's attack on Aemylia 'seems to represent rape'.[69] Again a gap opens up between psychological and literal levels, leaving space for a sense of rape as a punishment for active female desire. This may be authorised *by* allegory's 'special pleading'; Woffard argues that if we accept an allegorical reading of Lust here despite the strength of the representation of rape on the literal level, we would 'have to conclude that allegory could never represent rape as such'.[70] The same tension between interpretations affects the perception of Amoret in this episode.

Cavanagh suggests that Amoret may be suspect for her 'open resistance to Scudamour's attempt to claim her as bride'.[71] Resisting a sexual love sanctioned by Venus, marriage, and the text's insistence on Scudamore's rights, proves as unacceptable as actively seeking the love object. The parallel structure of the disclosure of these sources of suspicion about Florimell and Amoret strengthens this equivalence. We first see them as 'chased' (and chaste) and learn of the complicating factors later.

Several scenes later in the work more explicitly figure the punishment of erring females as rape. In the story of Flourdelis and Burbon, an inversion of the usual pattern of rape narratives effects the punishment of the female for sexual transgression. Flourdelis is seduced away from Burbon by the tyrant Grandtorto. Despite the claim that she despises her lover once Grandtorto has wooed her, the narrative blurs the boundary between rape and seduction. Grandtorto sends a 'troupe of villains' to fetch her 'by open force' (V.xi.51), and when Burbon and Artegall find her she is 'halfe dismayd . . . in doubtfull plight' (60). Although she is dressed in robes and jewels, 'those villens through their vsage bad / Them fouly rent, and shamefully defaced had' (60). The clothes thus attest both to her acceptance of Grandtorto's seduction and to implications of rape. Burbon's attempt to reclaim her is 'greedie' (61): an idea which is to gain rape connotations later in the work, when the blason of Serena captured by cannibals associates vision with both rape and cannibalism (VI.viii.38–43), and when Calidore views Pastorella with a 'hungry eye' (VI.ix.26). After rebuking her for inconstancy, Burbon again 'assay[s]' Flourdelis (V.xi.64) and carries her off, with no greater assent from her than silence. He is 'nor well nor ill apayd'; in the 'Legend of Justice' he has simply claimed his due. The phrase may apply equally to Flourdelis, who has received just punishment (in the form of a sexual reappropriation) for her 'foule disgrace' (62) of sexual wandering.

In other scenes such punishment is achieved with greater violence. Yet these scenes involve greater interpretative problems. At the very moments where the violence against women is both most extreme and most obviously justified, the sexual dimension tends to be symbolic or subtextual.

Male–female battles are one opportunity to employ sexual imagery with impunity. There is a striking closeness between the language used during Britomart's fight with Artegall and that used for their love. However, battles with female monsters best stage such anxieties. Cavanagh has argued that female characters portrayed as simultaneously beautiful and ugly are seen as the most evil;[72] the most extreme instances of this, when the characters are part-woman, part-monster, maximise the potential for expressing valid misogynistic aggression. Arthur's battle with one of these monsters, the Echidna's daughter, culminates in a 'combative perversion of a sexual act':[73]

> But as she prest on him with heauy sway,
>     Vnder her wombe his fatall sword he thrust,
> And for her entrailes made an open way,
>     To issue forth.
>
>                                   (V.xi.31)

The same overtones are found in several episodes associated with Artegall, the figure of Justice. Mirabella functions as a figure of pride, and is punished for her rejection of suitors. Accompanied by Infamie and Despight, she is seen in the typical pose of a rape victim, in 'foule array':

> ...And eeke that angry foole
> Which follow'd her, with cursed hands vncleane
> Whipping her horse, did with his smarting toole
> Oft whip her dainty selfe, and much augment her doole.
>
>                                   (VI.vii.39)

As Cavanagh argues, Mirabella gives her captors a 'sadistic sexual pleasure' as she is subjected to 'a twisted form of the sexual relationships she declined'.[74] Her treatment seems to bear out Susan Griffin's finding in relation to pornography, that 'the idea that a woman might reject a man seems to exist at the heart of culture's rage against women'.[75]

The problems of re-reading allegory are more extreme in the case of Munera, whose punishment allegorises the overthrow of avarice.[76] Yet Munera turns out to have points in common both with Mirabella and with the monsters whose sexually nuanced punishment the poem validates. Like them, she is 'full faire' as well as sinful (V.ii.10) and, like Mirabella, she rejects suitors out of 'great pride' (ii.10). The scene of her murder displays several characteristics of a rape narrative. Talus 'fowly did array' her, drags her 'by the faire lockes' (ii.25) and 'rudely hayld her forth without remorse' (26). He and Artegall successfully humiliate her, so that she becomes 'suppliant', 'kneeling at his feete submissiuely' (26). Before her death by drowning in 'durty mud' (27), which emphasises soiling, she is mutilated, with her hands and feet cut off. Nohrnberg argues that mutilation, like stripping, is used by Spenser as a form of 'symbolic obeisance, humiliation, or abasement', while the removal of her feet may add a sexual connotation to this violence.[77] Allegory's 'special pleading' makes of this episode a story of avarice destroyed and debased, and it is hard to read literally a description of golden hands and feet. Yet the extreme disjunction between allegorical and literal levels opens up questions rather than silencing them: questions as to why the destruction of a female figure, whether allegorical or not, must be figured in sexual terms.[78]

*The Faerie Queene* thus sets its victims of threatened rape against contextualising forces which simultaneously warn of rape, validate it and submerge it. The attempted rapes of Florimell and Amoret, along with numerous other female characters in the work, take place against a historical and topographical background which testifies to the feasibility of rape and its justification, and coexist with representations of 'legitimate' violence against female figures, cast as figurative rapes. Powerful female figures tend to receive these submerged rape impulses, which provide a response to the anxiety which such figures arouse.[79] The exceptions to this rule, however, point to the problems attendant on deploying rape to represent female, rather than male power.

The contrast between Busyrane's and Acrasia's deployments of the figure of rape, as we have noted, highlights the difference between male and female versions of sexual power in the poem. Thus, the figurative implications of Busyrane's enchantments make the woman the rape victim, while Acrasia's enchantment tropes her as the willing victim of her victim's 'rape'. Even when the idea of rape is functioning figuratively, then, 'symbolic rapes' of males by females turn out not to be presented (even 'symbolically') as forced sex.

The overthrow of a powerful female figure in Book V, Radigund, like that of Acrasia, lacks the imagery of rape adhering to that of the Echidna or Mirabella: perhaps because, like Acrasia, it is sex that she demands. Her story interrogates the idea that political and sexual power in women may be congruent. Radigund's power over her male captives is emasculating; she dresses them as women and makes them spin and sew, recalling Omphale and Hercules. The familiar image of spoiling may increase the sexual connotations, when she 'doth them of warlike armes despoile' (V.iv.31). When Artegall becomes her 'thrall' and 'vassall' (v.17, 18), she conceives a passion for him. However, her desire for her 'vassall' does not mirror her power over him as his captor, as is the case, say, with Busyrane or Lust and Amoret. Rather, to achieve her desire would invert the power-relation between them:

> Yet would she not thereto yeeld free accord,
>   To serue the lowly vassall of her might,
>   And of her seruant make her souerayne Lord.
>                              (27)

The disjunction between the symbolic equivalence of her emasculation of Artegall with rape and her actual inability to rape him underlines a significant difference between male and female versions of power.

Argante too must ultimately bully her victims, rather than force them, into sex. Although she intends to make the Squire of Dames the 'thrall of her desire' (III.vii.37), actual rape is an impossibility. In spite of the sexual horrors associated with her, she must give the male a choice: either 'in eternall bondage dye he must, / Or be the vassall of her pleasures vile' (50). This is an unenviable choice, of course, but it contrasts with the threat of rape extended to the female characters. The version of rape which defines it as a constrained 'yielding', then, applies in Spenser's epic to the sexual aggression of females against males.

The implications of Britomart's claim that love may not 'be compeld by maisterie' (III.i.25) prove true when the aggressor is female. The distinction between love and lust or between emotion and the sexual act which this claim necessitates and which Spenser posits in the Book IV Proem, thus pertains only to cases of male aggression.

In such cases, the love of the female victim cannot be compelled, but the idea that she cannot be forced into the sexual act is one which the poem repeatedly challenges. In claiming to condemn lust, in distinction from love, the fourth Proem thus clashes with the strong impulses towards rape which the poem both registers and manipulates.

Rape in Elizabethan poetry is something alluded to, threatened or attempted, rarely staged – except in the past of *The Faerie Queene*'s history. The ambiguous sexual act in the 'complaint' has taken place before the poem begins; in the epyllion, it takes place in the present-time of the poem, but its representation is confused by the prevalence of female coyness. The absence of actual occurrences of rape – with some notable exceptions – contributes to a destabilisation of the boundary between rape and seduction. It may also relate to the presence of Elizabeth on the throne, even if 1590s poetry often expresses resentment towards her in subtler ways. We shall see that after her death, the incidence of rape in literature increases dramatically. The tendency for epyllion writers to stage rape scenes while simultaneously undermining or transforming them by insinuations of female desire is analogous to *The Faerie Queene*'s simultaneous condemnation and inscription of rape. Both the resultant tensions, then, provide a way of negotiating courtly, sexual politics while satisfying the two conflicting impulses of staging rape and staging boundless female desire.

# 4

# 'Some women love to struggle': Rape in Renaissance Drama

I turn now to drama, a mode in which the absence of a narratorial presence and the importance of the visual both affect the presentation of rape. We shall see that ideas which were usually presented unproblematically in Elizabethan fiction, and often in poetry, come under scrutiny here by virtue of their necessary attribution to individual characters. After Elizabeth's death, rapes and attempted rapes become more prevalent in this, the genre in which rape is both more striking and more circumscribed: although there is an actual body upon which we imagine the rape will be enacted, this action cannot be represented on stage, but must be supposed to take place out of sight.

Drama of the 1590s, like poetry of the same period, tends not to present sexual violence directly. The anonymous *Edward III* (published 1595) features a failed attempt at seduction; Shakespeare's *Two Gentlemen of Verona* (1592) shows an attempted rape; and Heywood's *The Four Prentices of London* (1594) uses the threat of rape as a minor episode. The anonymous *Alphonsus Emperor of Germany* (1594) accomplishes rape without violence by means of a 'bed-trick'. In the 1575 play *Appius and Virginia* by R.B., the heroine dies before she can be raped; and in Whetstone's *Promos and Cassandra* (1578) the coercion involved is blackmail, not physical force. In fact, only *Titus Andronicus* (1594) and Peele's *The Love of King David and Fair Bethsabe* (1599) actually present violent rapes. As in the poetry, rape in Elizabethan drama mostly serves as an occasion for female suffering as spectacle.

The concerns of the 1590s female complaints featuring kings' mistresses also find dramatic expression in this period. In Shakespeare's *King John* a woman claims to have been forced into her adultery with the king. In Heywood's *Edward IV*, we find a more detailed analysis of the issues surrounding such adultery. Lady Faulconbridge in *King John* describes herself as having been 'seduc'd' by Richard's 'long and vehement suit'.[1] Ambiguously, she calls the act 'my dear offence, / Which was so strongly urg'd past my defence' (I.i.257–8), and her son concludes that 'your fault was not your folly' (262); it is specifically regal power which excuses her:

> Needs must you lay your heart at his dispose,
> Subjected tribute to commanding love ....
>
> (263–4)

Heywood's *Edward IV* presents Jane Shore in a sympathetic light.[2] A scene early in the play contextualises her appropriation by Edward by making clear the power of men to rape, particularly when enabled by political or military power. The rebel Faulconbridge, in confrontation with Shore, tells him, 'thy wife is mine, thats flat'.[3] Jane proves her chastity by vowing that she will kill herself 'ere force or flattery shall mine honour stain' (p. 24). When confronted with Edward claiming that his will 'may not, must not, shall not be withstood', she tells him:

> If you inforce me, I haue nought to say;
> But wish I had not liued to see this day.
>
> (p. 76)

Later, however, she tells her husband that she 'yeelded vp the fort', yet

> ... but to him that did assault the same,
> For euer it had been inuincible.
>
> (p. 84)

The king thus appears as the one qualification of the topos of invincible chastity.

The issues raised by these plays and the female complaints appear again much later in Middleton's *Women Beware Women* (*c.* 1621). Many critics have read Bianca as consenting to become the duke's mistress, whether through ambition or expedience.[4] Yet the text implies strongly that she is raped. She trembles and begs him:

> Make me not bold with death and deeds of ruin
> Because they fear not you; me they must fright.[5]

The Duke reminds her: 'I can command: / Think upon that' (364–5). However, although this makes rape a possibility for production, the neutrality of the stage direction is unhelpful, simply directing that the two characters exit, where directions in other plays often stipulate that the woman is 'dragged' by the man.[6]

For Bianca, questions of ambition or expedience arise only after the event. That she rejects the option of suicide for its only alternative, that of continuing to be the duke's mistress, damns her in the eyes of the contemporary audience and, it appears, some modern critics.[7] The possibility that she resisted is obliterated by her subsequent decision not to commit suicide. Yet she refers to suicide as a possible course of action (426–8), which strongly suggests that she regards the experience as rape. Bianca, like Jane and Lady Faulconbridge, cannot be exonerated from sin because despite the force with which she was initiated into a sexual relationship with a powerful man, her subsequent conduct implicates her in the crime. The extent to which an audience's sympathy for Bianca may be evoked is further undercut, as with Churchyard's Jane, by the growing evidence of her 'love' for the duke, her appreciation of social advancement and her harsh treatment of her husband.

The contrast between Bianca and Lady Faulconbridge or Heywood's Jane is symptomatic of the shift from late Elizabethan to Jacobean drama. Middleton's play is more violent both in its depiction of Bianca's coercion and in its portrayal of her potential for evil. Jacobean drama contrasts with late Elizabethan in its high incidence of rape and attempted rape, which Tennenhouse has argued begins as early as the year after Elizabeth's death.[8] Inevitably, then, the following discussion of rape and attempted rape will be focused primarily on Jacobean plays.

### 'HER MODESTY REQUIR'D A LITTLE VIOLENCE'

The prevalence of sexual violence in stage plays of the Jacobean period betrays a striking aggression towards women. Recent criticism has revealed the strong political (and sometimes religious) agendas of these plays.[9] This is a departure from earlier criticism, which tended to condemn the plays for sensationalism and titillation. The more recent trend, however, runs the risk of overlooking rape *as* rape. Political readings, though important, risk overlooking the extent to which scenes of sexual threat served to titillate the contemporary audience. It is necessary, then, to balance political readings of the plays against an awareness of the titillation provided by scenes of rape or attempted rape.[10]

Rape in early modern drama most commonly functions as a test. Rape may test men or women: the man's corruption or potential for reform, or the woman's chastity. The emphasis on testing means that we do not usually find in drama the strategies evident elsewhere for removing the responsibility for rape away from the perpetrators. For instance, the idea that rape is an understandable result of love (or at least, undeniable desire) is more often challenged, and love and rape are frequently opposed. The tendency to trope sexual assault as an heroic military encounter also largely vanishes. The imagery of female chastity as a fort and attempted rape/seduction as a siege is still prevalent, but its use no longer functions to glorify rape. It is often more politically charged, underlining a parallel between rape and war, as in *All's Lost by Lust*, where Iacinta's rape finds a context in the war fought in by her father in the service of the rapist.[11]

The emphasis on the testing of the ruler, however, remains problematic. The tradition in which sexual violence functions to bring about the downfall of a great man may image such men as the tragic victims of passion.[12] On the other hand, the chastity test, by placing the onus on women to resist rape, conflicts with a powerful subtext which conveys the physical power of men and the vulnerability of women to sexual violence or appropriation.

Jean Howard argues that 'the drama incorporated ideologically incompatible elements', showing 'traces of ideological struggle'.[13] As with poetry, this manifests itself strongly in the competition between seduction and rape – between the idea of female strength in virtue and that of male physical power.[14] Moreover, the tendency to hold up women such as Lucrece as exemplars is counterbalanced by an equally strong tendency to undermine them through subversive rewriting.

The ideology of chastity and the political agenda of such plays are inseparable from the erotic dynamics of the stage. The lurid descriptions of rape and the blasonic detailing of female nakedness which can be found in romance are replaced in drama with the physical actuality of actors on the stage. The relative degrees of titillation provided by detailed prose description and the presence of actors are, admittedly, difficult to establish. Nevertheless, stage plays inherently encourage a voyeurism which, paradoxically, may be heightened rather than modified by the transvestism of the boy actors, and which contributes to a problematising of the whole concept of the visual – the known and the unknown – in relation to rape.[15] This concern with the visual, which betrays an anxiety about female sexual conduct, relates, I shall argue, to the latent aggression towards women which simultaneously produces and denies a strong sense of male physical power and female vulnerability.

In the plays considered in this chapter, more than two-thirds of the rape attempts are unsuccessful. Raped women are, as in romance, most likely to be dead by the end of the play. They are conventionally aristocratic or noble, and most are either married or more or less formally betrothed; this suggests greater interest in the idea of marital fidelity than in virginal chastity, perhaps due to the emphasis placed on marriage by Protestantism. In half of the plays the assailant is the ruler; in all but six he is in some socially powerful position in relation to the victim, or belongs to an enemy faction. Where there is not this hierarchy of social or military power, the plays usually feature failed attempts.[16] *The Spanish Gypsy*, in which Clara is hijacked while travelling, abducted and raped, is the only play in which a rape is actually accomplished by a man without particular social or political power over the victim.

The narrative event of rape, as we know from romance in particular, has key structural significance. In most of the plays the rape or attempted rape is central to the plot, whether in initiating a train of events – often a revenge action – or as the culmination of the plotting of the perpetrator. Only a handful use rape as an episode, such as Fletcher's *The Faithful Shepherdess*, Massinger's *The Bashful Lover* and Heywood's myth plays, *The Golden Age, The Silver Age* and *The Brazen Age*. The position of the rape scene in the structure of the play varies. A few rapes take place before the beginning of the play.[17] Of the remaining plays the majority of rapes and attempts occur in the third or fourth act – a position of prominence which still allows for resultant action to develop.

In three plays, the anonymous *Edward III*, Dekker's *Match Me in London* and Beaumont and Fletcher's *The Humorous Lieutenant*, rape functions as a test of the ruler's capacity to reform. In the latter, the king Antigonus attempts to seduce/rape Celia, his son's chaste mistress. He is won over when she rejects the idea that she should submit because he is her king.[18] Yet if Antigonus has passed the test, he is surpassed by Celia. His hypocritical claim that he has 'made a full proofe of her vertue' (IV.viii.169) may reflect badly on him, but her triumph is assured.

We have seen that chastity is frequently proven in literature by exposure to a threat which is as likely to be rape as 'temptation' or seduction. Accordingly, most of the rapes and attempted rapes in the drama occur in scenarios which, initially, could evolve into rape *or* seduction, with any 'temptation' offered by the man usually having threatening undertones. Only in *The Spanish Gypsy* and *Hengist* does the man abduct and rape the woman without some kind of verbal exchange which gives her a chance to display her virtue by refusing to yield or persuading him of his folly. A belief in the power of seduction, after all, is responsible for such claims as that in Nathan Field's *Amends for Ladies* that 'if [Tarquin] had had any wit..., *Lucrece* had neuer been rauished, she would haue yeelded, ... & so will any woman'.[19]

The ideological confusion over rape and seduction, as we know, relates to the no-means-yes topos. This is frequently invoked in drama, often in the context of rape. In *The Womans Prize*, Sophocles suggests that Petruchio's wife may have rejected him in bed because

> Her modesty requir'd a little violence[.]
> Some women love to struggle.[20]

Heywood's *Rape of Lucrece* makes clear the connection between the no-means-yes topos and rape in a song that also provides a context for or warning of the impending rape:

> She that denies me, I would have,
> Who craves me, I despise.
>
> ...
>
> That crafty Girle shall please me best
> That No, for Yea, can say,
> And every wanton willing kisse
> Can season with a Nay.[21]

Valerius's song thus attempts to conflate two distinct cases: the 'crafty' woman who employs a 'coy' strategy to enjoy her desires while pretending to be modest, and the *un*desiring woman who is genuinely denying. The poet's claim that he despises a woman who 'craves' him is inconsistent with his enjoyment of the coy woman. His only concern is that a woman he desires should *seem* to resist him; he is not concerned with the veracity of her resistance. However, 'that crafty Girle' supersedes 'she that denies me', and the genuine resistance of the non-desiring woman is thus written out. The song is entirely appropriate to set the scene for a rape, in which the woman's resistance goes unheeded.

The concept of female sexual 'coyness', then, which at its most extreme is portrayed as a masochistic desire for violence, becomes closely connected with rape. This is made clear in some plays when the topos is invoked in specific justification of rape. In *The Maid in the Mill* Otrante abducts and threatens to rape Florimell. He is deterred by her denials and Gerasto tells him:

You should have taken her then, turn'd her, and tew'd her . . .
She would have lov'd ye infinitely.[22]

But it is Otrante, not Florimell, who is aroused by the idea of female resistance. Florimell saves herself by feigning wantonness; Otrante's horror – 'It is my part to wooe, not to be courted' (V.ii.35) – prevents him from touching her.

In Marston's *Sophonisba*, the heroine's use of the topos in order to gain time in which to escape exposes its fallacy.[23] Where it is voiced by a man attempting rape, too, as in *The Maid in the Mill*, the idea is shown to be both ludicrous and a strategy for justifying rape. Yet its prevalence in contexts which are not specifically connected with a rape or in which the connection is more subtle, as in *Rape of Lucrece*, suggests that it conforms to contemporary attitudes towards female sexuality.

Even the closure offered by suicide is often lost, through a tendency of these plays to rewrite even the most famous literary examples of rape in order to undermine them. These allusions are part of a wider literary self-consciousness in connection with rape narratives. Many characters allude to famous rape stories and read them as precedents for their conduct, female characters anticipating their own immortalisation. Yet such allusions, which are not all voiced by the victims and perpetrators, also function on a different level, to locate the plays in the tradition of rape stories and, frequently, to alert the audience to a forthcoming attack.

When Volpone attempts to rape Celia he describes her as 'like Europa now, and I like Jove'.[24] In Tourneur's *The Atheist's Tragedy*, D'Amville attempts to rape Castabella with the words 'Tereus-like /

Thus I will force my passage to –' before she is rescued.[25] Similarly, Iachimo in *Cymbeline* compares himself to Tarquin when approaching Imogen's bed.[26] In Fletcher's *The Tragedy of Valentinian*, the emperor sends one of his men to persuade Lucina to become his mistress and he reports:

> She pointed to a *Lucrece*, that hung by,
> And with an angry looke, that from her eyes
> Shot Vestall fire against me, she departed.[27]

After the rape she curses Valentinian: 'the sins of *Tarquin* be rememberd in thee' (III.i.91), defining his act as rape.

In *The Queen of Corinth*, Theanor's rape of Merione is described as '[acting] the Fable of *Proserpines* Rape'.[28] But again, it is Lucrece who is held up as role-model. After the rape, Theanor's friend claims that 'the woman is no *Lucrece*' (II.iii.22), hoping that she will not report it; she herself takes Lucrece's story as prescriptive of her conduct:

> . . . I have read
> Somewhere I am sure, of such an injury
> Done to a Lady: and now she durst dye.
>                    (III.ii.138–40)

Concern with literary record makes Celia, in *The Humorous Lieutenant*, ask 'what honourable tongue can sing my story?' (IV.v.51) if she is raped. Conversely, Sophonisba celebrates her chastity as she commits suicide rather than submit to Scipio's sexual demands (V.iii.103–4).

The frequency of such allusions establishes these mythological and classical stories as a significant background to the plays. But it is the subversive rewritings of stories like Lucrece's which constantly undermine the value systems encoded in them and, in so doing, point to an uncertainty in contemporary attitudes to rape. One of the daughters in *Bonduca* claims:

> . . . your great Saint *Lucrece*
> Di'd not for honour; *Tarquin* topt her well,
> And mad she could not hold him, bled.[29]

This rewriting is done in the spirit of competition, a common occurrence; characters are often keen to assert their or others' superiority over the more famous women of literary tradition. In *Edward III* the king gives up his attempt to rape the Countess of Salisbury, praising her above 'her whose ransackt treasurie hath taskt, / The vaine indeuor of so many pens'.[30] In *A Wife for a Month* a bawd tells Evanthe:

> ...do you think [Lucrece] yeelded not a little?
> And had a kinde of will to have been re-ravisht?[31]

All such analogies, of course, are made through the voice of a particular character: some with a clear motivation for subverting the familiar rape stories. Nevertheless, they destabilise any sense of certainty about female involvement in rape.

The frequent comparison of chaste with unchaste women in early modern drama intensifies the uncertainty surrounding female responsibility in illicit sexual encounters. Female sexual assertiveness is seen as the equivalent of – and analogous to – male (political and sexual) tyranny.[32] The opposition ostensibly serves to heighten the glory of the plays' heroines. However, it also establishes promiscuity as normative female behaviour. *The Second Maiden's Tragedy* polarises the two types, with the story of the Lady's suicide when faced with rape counterbalancing the Wife's adultery in the sub-plot. Other plays set one woman's chastity against a generalised female promiscuity. In *A Wife for a Month*, the king's sexual persecution of Evanthe contrasts with a widespread female corruption. One of the 'honest lords' claims that it is now 'honest'

> To ravish Matrons, and deflowre coy wenches,
> But here they are so willing, 'tis a complement.
> (I.ii.16–17)

By being the exception to the rule, the chaste Evanthe becomes a victim of the state's corruption.

Such a 'norm', set against the 'unique' qualities of the heroine, is the stock method of praising a chaste woman, and literary examples are commonly cited. In *The Womans Prize* it is Maria's refusal to consummate the marriage that elicits Sophocles's comparison:

> This woman is the first I ever read of,
> Refus'd a warranted occasion,
> And standing on so fair termes.
> (III.iii.16–18)

Elsewhere, chaste women under threat may be contrasted with promiscuous ones at the very moment of crisis. In *Valentinian* the emperor's men intercept Lucina's waiting-women so that she is left alone with him. After he has raped her, he tells her that her women have 'had some sport too, / But are more thankfull for it' (III.i.133–4). This conflates her rape with the 'sport' of the other women, while her distress registers ingratitude (for the emperor) or chastity (for the audience).[33] Such references function not only to differentiate between the heroine and all other women but, paradoxically, to bring them closer together. Since so many women enjoy illicit sex, they imply, there was a good chance that the rape scenarios might have evolved easily into scenarios of successful seduction: or, that a woman will eventually be grateful for verbal or physical 'persuasion'.

The function of rape as chastity test puts great emphasis on the female art of dissuasion. In spite of the numerous examples in which women are clearly powerless to prevent their rape, it is generally defined implicitly as a woman's failure of eloquence. While giving women a voice, this emphasis also implies that if a woman cannot dissuade a man from rape, her chastity is questionable. If she fails and is raped, suicide may redeem her, or alternatively, an impulse towards suicide followed by marriage to the rapist; in these cases her eloquence is often reserved for after the event. Preferably, however, she should succeed in protecting herself, usually to the wonder of her assailant.

*The Woman-Hater* strikingly exemplifies these problematic implications. Oriana is obliged to seek shelter at the house of Gondarino, who subsequently claims that he has 'whored' her. In order to prove her innocence, the Duke sets up an attempted 'seduction' by Arrigo, to be observed by himself. Oriana refuses to yield to Arrigo's persuasions and threats and is declared chaste, at which point the Duke asks her to marry him.[34] The voyeurism involved in this engineered rape attempt is itself disturbing, but the Duke's presence in the scene has further implications. If the scene is simply a test, Arrigo could cease to importune Oriana when he is convinced of her chastity, and then report back. Yet when the Duke intervenes, Arrigo's language of seduction has turned into the language of rape: 'I will injoy thee, though it be betweene the parting of thy soule and body' (V.iv.69–70). Although the Duke's presence is ostensibly justified by the need for a witness, his intervention at this point implies that without it, Arrigo might actually have raped Oriana. It certainly makes clear that had this been a real situation, Oriana's chastity could not have saved her from rape. In plays like *The Humorous Lieutenant* where a genuine attempted rape/seduction functions implicitly as a chastity test for the victim, her actual vulnerability remains a subtext. Ironically, it is in *The Woman-Hater* – where it is set up deliberately as a test – that her danger and powerlessness appear most clearly.

Where in *Measure for Measure* Isabella's participation in a strategy devised by the duke leaves her vulnerable to his sexual demands, in *The Woman-Hater* Oriana is put in the same position after a strategy in which she was not complicit and which actually endangered her. Where Shakespeare's duke uses his power as the ruler to oblige Isabella to marry him, this duke's offer also has behind it the fact that Oriana has just learnt a lesson about the physical capacity of men to disempower her, as her response makes clear:

> My Lord, I am your subject, you may command me ...
> I am no more mine owne.
> (V.iv.90–4)

The strong sense of sexual danger provided by both men here undermines the idea that virtue can protect a woman from rape.

Plays which virtually deny the possibility of rape by emphasising the power of female virtue might be seen as more ideologically problematic than those in which the irony of the virtue topos is made apparent. The *locus classicus* here, of course, is provided by a later work, Milton's *Comus*.[35] In all such plays, a powerful tension results from the clash between the ostensible theme and a subtext which registers male sexual power. This potential is fulfilled in the numerous plays which feature successful rapes.

In some plays, we are alerted to the danger of rape by allusions to classical rape stories. In *A Wife For a Month*, for instance, the bawd's reference to Lucrece, while functioning as persuasion, has a wider effect on the play as a whole, alerting us – even while attempting to rewrite the rape – to Evanthe's sexual peril. Some allusions make no reference to a rape which is implicit in the story. In *The Bashful Lover*, Matilda runs away in order to avoid rape by the duke, Lorenzo, and shortly before the attempted rape by Alonzo and Pisano she tells her companion, 'I can outstrip / *Daphne*'.[36] Ostensibly a reference to her swiftness, the allusion subtly locates Matilda in a long tradition of sexually threatened women and points forward to the next scene.

In *Volpone* the foreshadowing of rape is less subtle. When Celia refuses to offer herself to Volpone, her husband Corvino threatens to 'buy some slave / Whom I will kill, and bind thee to him, alive' (III.vii.100–1). The allusion to Tarquin's threat prefigures Volpone's attempted rape of Celia shortly afterwards. In *Valentinian* Lucina is entertained at court with bawdy songs, one of which features women who were raped, but whose stories are rewritten as love-stories:

> Heare ye Ladies that despise,
>   What the mighty love has done,
> Feare examples, and be wise:
>   Faire *Calisto* was a Nun;
> *Læda* sayling on the streame,
>   To deceive the hopes of man,
> Love accounting but a dream,
>   Doted on a silver Swan.
>                               (II.v.25–32)

The stories of these women raped by Jove are thus both rewritten as love stories and explicitly deployed as a warning to women who despise love that if they refuse a man's advances they may be raped. Being disempowered by love here becomes equivalent to being disempowered by a man.

The sexual vulnerability of these heroines is often brought out in connection with several attitudes which Renaissance plays share with prose romance. The rhetoric that attributes power to female beauty is prevalent, for example, in many cases clashing with actual male physical power. In many plays the power of female beauty is extolled in a context which shows, on the contrary, the power of men. In *Edward III*, for instance, the Countess is described as she 'whose beauty tyrants feare' (sig. B2v). The reference comes shortly after the Scottish King David has attempted to claim her as the spoils of war, and before Edward begins his attempt to seduce or rape her. Similarly, in the opening scene of *The Maid in the Mill* (which later features an attempted rape), Antonio tells Martin that Ismenia 'bears an eye more dreadful then your weapon' (I.i.65).

Several women in danger of rape threaten to disfigure themselves to prevent it, a threat predicated on a causal link between beauty and rape. In Dekker's *Match Me in London*, for example, Torniella swears to 'Drinke a Cup of poyson, which may blast / My inticing face, and make it leprous foule'.[37] Beauty may be more explicitly blamed for rape. In *Valentinian* the emperor tells Lucina:

> If I have done a sin, curse her that drew me,
> Curse the first cause, the witchcraft that abusd me.
>
> (III.i.54–5)

In Whetstone's *Promos and Cassandra*, Promos similarly claims that Cassandra's beauty 'lures'.[38] Yet where in romance the attribution of power (and blame) to female beauty was unproblematic, in drama it comes under a degree of scrutiny, particularly when it is voiced by the rapist. It can even be parodied, as we find in *Volpone*: when Celia is finally left alone in Volpone's bedroom, he leaps up, claiming that this is 'thy beauty's miracle' (III.vii.146).

The irony of the claim that women have power over men is brought out in *The Little French Lawyer*, in which Dinant supposedly teaches Lamira a lesson for her refusal to sleep with him by arranging for her and her friend Anabel to be abducted by strange men, who they think intend to rape them. He taunts her with

> The wit you bragd of, foold, that boasted honour,
> As you beleev'd compass'd with walls of brasse,
> To guard it sure, Subject to be o're throwne
> With the least blast of lust.[39]

The favours she denied him she must now 'yield up / To a licentious villaine' (IV.vii.50–1). One abductor tells Anabel:

> ... thinke how many for your maydenhead
> Have pin'd away, and be prepared to loose it
> With penitence.
>
> (82–4)

*The Little French Lawyer* also parodies the tendency for women to be under obligation to their rescuers. Cleremont rescues Anabel only on condition that she will marry him: 'if not I leave you, / And leave you to the mercy of these villaines' (V.i.103–4); Dinant rescues Lamira, but when she refuses to reward him with love, he threatens to rape her himself to make her 'feele the effects of abus'd love'

(232). Only when she has admitted her 'cruelty' does he claim that he intended only to teach her a lesson, and not to rape her.

To what extent would an audience have regarded rape as a legitimate punishment for female pride in this play? The play is, after all, a comedy. That Dinant remains the hero may be ensured by the audience's knowledge that he arranged the first attempted rape and by the revelation that his own attempt too was feigned. However, the fact that the whole thing is supposedly a joke does not lessen the sense of the physical power of men over women. While in tragedies like *Lucrece* or *Valentinian* the attribution of power to female beauty by rapists may be fairly transparent, here the comic plot minimises the problematic implications of such an attitude. Comedy, like political allegory, may marginalise the woman's perspective.

The idea that a woman is beholden to her rescuer is central to Massinger's *The Bondman*. In this play the 'hero' deploys the female fear of rape to achieve an ostensibly consensual appropriation of the heroine, and again the genre, centred on a trick, works to eliminate the dark implications this has for the woman. Cleora takes leave of Leosthenes, who goes to war terrified that she will be unfaithful to him. To prove her devotion, she vows to blindfold herself and remain silent until his return. In the absence of the men of the city, Pisander, in disguise, incites a revolt by the slaves in which he encourages them to rape their masters' wives and daughters. His sister, who is disguised as a slave to Cleora, tells her that Pisander intends to rape her; he then refrains from doing so and protects her from the rest of the slaves. Her gratitude for his 'worthiness' leads her to love him and, eventually, to choose him over Leosthenes, who has continued to wrong her with suspicion.

The ostensible contrast between Pisander and Leosthenes is easily dismantled. Leosthenes regards Cleora as his 'valours prize' for noble deeds in war, while Pisander is praised for his chivalrous protection of her.[40] Yet Pisander has manipulated Cleora more effectively than Leosthenes by instilling in her a terror of rape. Once again, the 'joke' – that the hero is only pretending to threaten the heroine – is supposed to eliminate the darker implications of the plot, but those implications remain. Cleora rejects Leosthenes on grounds that we know to be equally applicable to Pisander: 'Where crueltie raignes, / There dwels nor loue, nor honour' (V.i.61–2). Just as Lamira in *The Little French Lawyer* never realises that she was not to be raped by the men who abducted her, so Cleora is never told of Pisander's true role in the events. The 'joke' in these plays is not a joke that the women are allowed to share. Rather, it is an excuse to manipulate them into positions of humiliation and danger followed by capitulation to the 'hero' – and to do so without alienating the audience's sympathies.

Of the 12 actual rapes in the plays considered here, four of the women are killed, four commit suicide, and three marry the rapist. The one remaining play, Middleton's *Hengist*, is exceptional, as the rape of the heroine is carried out by her husband, in a version of the bed-trick which renders it – in the play's ideological terms – no rape at all.[41] The ideal course of action for a woman who has been raped is much debated in the plays, although the conclusion is usually the same. This debate involves the interrogation of three related issues: whether rape constitutes a loss of chastity, whether it necessitates death for the victim, and whether the mind or spirit and body are distinct.

*The Queen of Corinth* and *The Unnatural Combat* present rape as a loss of chastity, resolved in the first case by marriage to the rapist and in the second by the woman's death.[42] When the opposite is asserted, it is often by women who are being threatened with rape, who use the idea that their minds and souls are distinct from their bodies in order to defy their attackers. In *The Maid in the Mill*, Florimell tells Otrante: 'My body you may force, but my will never' (III.iii.77); in *Match Me in London* Torniella tells the king:

> Let me shake off the golden fetters you tye
> About my body, you inioy a body
> Without a soule, for I am now not heere.
>
> (III.iii.75–7)

The question of suicide often seems to be debated for the sake of debate. In Heywood's *The Rape of Lucrece*, Collatine tells Lucrece:

> I quit thy guilt, for what could *Lucrece* doe
> More then a woman? hadst thou dide polluted
> By this base scandall, hadst thou wrong'd thy fame:
> And hindred us of a most iust reuenge.
>
> (p. 237)

Collatine is certain of his power, as her husband, to purge her of the 'guilt' inherent in adultery. Lucrece, however, insists that 'Ile not debare my body punishment' (p. 238).

Lucina's husband Maximus in *Valentinian* takes the opposite course. He images her as a 'silver Swan' who should 'sing thine owne sad requiem' (III.i.159–60): an image which suggests that she should kill herself after bewailing her wrongs. He then bids her, 'if thou dar'st, out live this wrong' (161), an ambiguous comment which provokes the right response in Lucina: 'I dare not' (161). Aecius opposes suicide, partly by distinguishing mind and body: 'are those trees the worse we teare the fruits from?' (III.i.224). Maximus advocates death for fear of his wife producing a bastard (235–6); yet, conscious of literary record, he adds:

> ...when [people] read, she livd,
> Must they not aske how often she was ravishd,
> And make a doubt she lov'd that more than Wedlock?
>                                                    (242–4)

In the face of these arguments, Aecius's assertion that 'she must live, / To teach the world such deaths are superstitious' (245–6) can have no impact. While the playwright may be interested in presenting both viewpoints, there is no sense that the ultimate decision is the 'wrong' one.

*The Queen of Corinth* (1616–18) initiates a shift from the tragic to the tragi-comic genre in relation to rape, effecting a shift in morality. Suzanne Gossett relates this change to the atmosphere at the court at this time, where 'sexual vice was increasingly conspicuous'.[43] Previous rape plays – *Titus*, *The Revenger's Tragedy*, Heywood's *Lucrece* and *Valentinian* – had been tragedies, in which the 'constant and unambiguous' condemnation of rape related to the demand for the victim's death, despite sympathy for her.[44] The shift to tragi-comedy involves the new phenomena of the rape victim who does not die, and the rapist who is not punished.

In *The Queen of Corinth*, Merione's betrothed, Agenor, tells her that he is happy to marry her even though she has been raped, producing the familiar argument that 'the staine was forc'd upon ye' (II.iii.151); he even calls her 'more a Virgin yet then all her Sex' (III.ii.31). But Merione is not convinced, and only her eventual marriage to the rapist removes her 'stain'. Gossett argues that this resolution to the problem of rape is as problematic as the earlier stipulation that raped women must die. As a result of the tragi-comic treatment of rape, she argues, it becomes identified 'with all sexual impulse as it is treated in comedy', that is, as a 'natural' impulse to

be controlled by marriage. The resultant implication is that the rape
has been proof of the future husband's virility; by contrast, she
argues, the tragic ending 'at least implied that women have a personal integrity which cannot survive violation'.[45]

Rowley returns to the old tragic plot in *All's Lost By Lust* (1619),
but introduces new elements. After Iacinta's rape, both she and her
father seem to find it acceptable that she should continue to live and
to marry – even to marry someone other than the rapist. She is eventually killed by her own father, but in an accident engineered by the
Moor who had hoped to marry her.

The radical implications of Middleton's *The Spanish Gypsy* (1623)
are similarly subdued by its conclusion. The raped woman, Clara, is,
as Gossett points out, 'the first woman to be genuinely uncertain
that she is stained'; her description of herself as 'infected now / By
your soul-staining lust' condemns Roderigo's soul as readily as
hers.[46] She is then quick to believe that she has purged herself with
her tears (p. 376). For Clara, knowledge of her lack of complicity is
sufficient to ensure her right to live; she even refuses to rule out the
possibility that she will marry a man other than the rapist. Unfortunately, these implications are finally lost when she marries Roderigo.
Conventionally, she claims that she is now 'righted in noble satisfaction', and Roderigo's claim that he will 'redeem my fault' (p. 440)
enables the audience to assume a happy marriage for them and to
see him as the hero of the play.[47] The new pattern, then, in which
the heroine is allowed to survive rape, has problematic implications.
In any case, the trend ends with Massinger's rejection of the tragi-
comic solution in *The Unnatural Combat* (1621–5). No alternative to
death is entertained for Theocrine after her rape by Montreville, and
no explanation of her death is required:

> [He] [a]bus'd me sir by violence, and this told
> I cannot live to speake more . . . *She dies.*
> (V.ii.212–16)

### 'I AM NOW NOT HEERE': KNOWING WOMEN

The opposition of body and soul which Dekker's Torniella voices –
an important strategy for containing the crime of rape which, as we
know, goes back to Augustine – implicitly mystifies women, and in a
context crucially concerned with establishing chastity. It thus seems

likely to fuel a prevalent anxiety concerning the knowability of female sexuality. The implicit assertion of male power over women in these plays would seem to reflect such an anxiety. Kathleen McLuskie has explained how 'female chastity can only be affirmed by ocular proof, frustratingly unavailable'.[48] The problem goes beyond the mere practicality of catching a woman in the act of adultery, to the greater anxiety generated by the relative invisibility of the female genitals and female sexual pleasure. The unknowability of female sexuality or sexual status, which we have already seen to be of particular pertinence for the issue of rape, is strongly problematised by the dramatic mode. This anxiety is one cause of the confusion over rape and seduction; it also produces a self-consciousness about the single most striking respect in which drama differs from the other genres: the visual.

The concept of the visual must be read in the context of the erotics of the Elizabethan and Jacobean stage and, in particular, in the context of the cross-dressing of the boy actors. This transvestism has now been posited as 'central to the erotic dynamic of Renaissance drama'.[49] Particularly pertinent is Peter Stallybrass's discussion of audience (invited) speculation on the boy actor. He argues that 'the demand that the spectator *sees* is at its most intense in the undressing of the boy actor, at the very point when *what* is seen is most vexed'.[50] Stallybrass focuses on the breast as the part of the female body at once most displayed and most concealed. I would argue that attention is also drawn to and deflected away from the vagina, as the sexual status or history of women characters is speculated upon and controlled. In stage plays, the rapes that in prose fiction were often described in detail must take place off-stage, and therefore between scenes – a striking marginalisation of a dramatic event that is usually central to the plot. Paradoxically, as well as resolving the problem of staging, this may implicitly draw attention to the impossibility of raping the boy actor (in the heterosexual sense with which we are concerned here). Most women raped are lured or dragged from the stage; in Heywood's *Lucrece* this convention is most transparent, as the scene from which Lucrece is dragged is her own bedroom (p. 225) – the site where, according to all other versions, the rape took place.

A woman's sexual status or conduct is identified by the function of attempted rape as a chastity test (with her conduct after rape functioning in a similar way). At the same time, its knowability is also problematised by rape, which is an 'invisible' crime, without evidence. This anxiety about identifying a woman's sexual status replaces the visual tags associated with rape in other genres, which to a great extent disappear in drama. In particular, the motif of dishevelled hair, which in fiction and poetry had functioned as a sign of sexual assault (among other things), is no longer associated with rape in the drama.

Attention is drawn to the invisibility of the crime in two stage directions which describe a female character with the adjective 'ravished'. In *Titus Andronicus* the stage-direction to II.iv reads 'Enter the empress' sons, with *Lavinia*, her hands cut off, and her tongue cut out, and ravish'd'.[51] In *The Queen of Corinth*, Merione enters at II.i 'as newly ravished'. While visual markers such as blood stains may be used in production, both these descriptions work primarily for the reader, not the spectator, and the crimes need to be related by the victims in some way. While Merione's relation of the attack is unproblematic, Lavinia has been deprived of speech by her attackers, using Philomela as a precedent, and they exceed Ovid in cutting off her hands to pre-empt narration. She narrates her wrong not only by producing a copy of Ovid, but by enacting a visual equivalent of the rape, when she takes Marcus's staff in her mouth to write the names of her rapists.[52]

Despite Lavinia's attempts to narrate the crime, the rapists' brutal re-enactment of Ovid not only silences her but also obviates her need for language. Marcus recognises her tonguelessness as a signifier of rape:

> But, sure, some Tereus hath deflow'red thee,
> And, lest thou should'st detect him, cut thy tongue.
>
> (II.iv.26–7)

Lavinia's tonguelessness is thus the visual equivalent of the copy of Ovid which she later produces to relate her story to Titus. Not visible in the way that her handless arms are, it is represented both by her bloody mouth and by her silence. Visually, then, Lavinia's mutilation both displaces and represents her rape.

The problems of recognising a woman's dishonour, particularly as resulting from rape, are also connected to the idea of such dishonour being 'written' in the face. The prevalence of images of branding or scarring women with their shame suggests a preoccupation with the ways in which female sexual conduct can be evidenced or identified. While some images of branding or scarring may be purely metaphorical or, more rarely, purely physical, a great number have both physical and spiritual connotations.[53] Melantius threatens Evanthe in *The Maid's Tragedy*:

> This sword shall be thy lover ...
> That on thy branded flesh the world may reade
> Thy blacke shame and my justice.[54]

Her flesh will be branded both metaphorically by her crime and physically by the physical and symbolic re-enactment of that crime by his sword.

This preoccupation with the visual relates to the anxiety about literary record displayed by many characters, as images of reading convey. In *All's Lost* Iulianus tells Iacinta that 'in thy sullied eyes / I reade a Tragicke story' (IV.i.103–4), while in *Hengist* Castiza fears that Vortiger 'may read my shame, / Now in my blush' (III.iii.307–8). To have a woman's sexual status identifiable, her past conduct 'written' on her body, helps to establish her as a figure either of shame or of chastity. This preoccupation suggests a profound anxiety about the *un*knowability of women.

The idea that the female body registers its own sexual conduct – the inadequacy of which idea the *un*readability of its signifiers makes uncomfortably clear – thus paradoxically reinforces the conception of female sexuality as *un*knowable. The crime of rape shows this situation at its most extreme, for the blushes which may correctly identify shame do not differentiate between guilt and innocence, between voluntary and involuntary stain. It is appropriate, then, that non-visibility or mis-identification should be the basis for a common dramatic strategy, the 'bed-trick', which has a complex relationship to rape.

Recent criticism has suggested that, far from being an unproblematic dramatic convention, the bed-trick has darker implications which would not have escaped a contemporary audience.[55] In early examples of the bed-trick, from the 1590s, it is the male partner who is substituted, so that the sexual act constitutes rape, although not necessarily accomplished with force. In later examples, it is the female partner who is substituted, ostensibly negating any rape. In my final example, *Hengist*, the bed-trick is radically inverted.

In Shakespeare's *Two Gentlemen of Verona* (1592–3), the attempted rape of the heroine by her beloved's friend has its source in a bed-trick story from Boccaccio and, then, Sir Thomas Elyot's *The boke named The gouernour* (1531). In these sources, Gisippus marries Sophronia, but discovers that his friend Titus loves her, and arranges for Titus to take his place in the marriage bed after the ceremony, resulting in an effective marriage between Sophronia and Titus.[56] Shakespeare's version makes the rape in this story explicit. Proteus's rescue of Sylvia from outlaws under Valentine's leadership is already a theft from her betrothed and presages his attempt to rape her (IV.iv). Although Valentine prevents the rape, he then offers Sylvia to Proteus in friendship, an action only averted by the intervention of another woman. Shakespeare thus conveys both elements of the source; he stages the willingness of one lover to give his mistress to his friend, and makes it clear that Proteus's sexual appropriation of Sylvia, with or without his friend's permission, would be rape.

In *Alphonsus Emperor of Germany* (1594), the tyrant Alphonsus incites his page Alexander to substitute himself in the bridal bed of Edward Prince of Wales and Hedewick, the daughter of the Duke of Saxony, thus jeopardizing the alliance between the two men.[57] This version of the bed-trick is facilitated by the custom whereby German brides avoid consummating their marriages until the second night. Hedewick escapes from her husband by sinking through a trapdoor when he gets into bed with her. Alexander finds her concealed in an inner chamber, to which Alphonsus has directed him:

> ... there shalt thou find
> The danty [*sic*] trembling bride coutcht in her Bed ...
> Taking her farewel of Virginity.
>
> (p. 38)

He then plays the part of Edward, who Hedewick thinks is consummating their marriage after all. Hedewick's rape is thus set in a framework which suggests the reluctance of women to give up their virginity. This reluctance, however, operates only as a traditional wedding rite: as a ritual mimicking of coyness which has no weight as an expression of her own volition. Once she has delayed the consummation she is expected to yield without complaint.

The fact that this rape is accomplished without violence and without raising the issue of consent, defines rape as dishonour. It dishonours both Hedewick and her father and husband; the definition of rape as a male crime against other men thus becomes prominent.

They are solely concerned with lineage; thus Edward cannot forgive Hedewick:

> ...Were I not a Prince of so high blood,
> And Bastards have no scepter-bearing hands,
> I would in silence smother up this blot.
>
> (p. 55)

The male victims of the rape are here more important than the female, and they give remarkably little thought to the question of her volition. Although Saxony asks, 'what think'st thou her a whore?' (p. 46), Edward's curse on 'the damned villanous adulterer, / That with so fowl a blot divorc'd our love' (p. 54) reflects the prevailing feeling that the act committed upon Hedewick is of greater significance than her attitude to it; the label 'whore' denotes her new sexual status, more than her complicity.

Hedewick's dishonour necessitates her death; killing her, her father compares them to Virginius and Virginia: 'like *Virginius* will I kill my Child' (p. 54). The analogy, however, is imprecise: Virginius killed his daughter to *prevent* her rape; moreover, Saxony's decision seems to be motivated by revenge on Edward rather than as the only solution. However, her death satisfies the convention that a raped woman should not outlive her shame. That the possibility of a 'bed-trick' has never occured to Saxony is made clear by his surprise and anguish when it is finally revealed. At this point the implications of disregarding the question of the woman's volition are made manifest. Yet the father's grief, implying as it does that the 'bed-trick' exonerates Hedewick, is out of step with the logic of the play. It is clear that no other course of action could have been taken in terms of the play's ideology. Hedewick's rape has made her a 'Whore' and 'strumpet' (p. 56) and her child a bastard.

The visual proves an important category in this play too. Female distress is seen in terms of spectacle throughout the play; this, as we know, is typical of the function of rape in the 1590s. Alphonsus falsely accuses his wife Isabella of adultery, and although she does plead verbally, there is far greater emphasis on the 'silent Oratorie of her chastest tears' (p. 61). Edward describes her as a spectacle of female distress, 'with blubberd cheeks, Torn bloody Garments, and disheveld hair' (p. 45). More strikingly, Hedewick speaks mostly in German, and speaks less and less as the play goes on. Seeing her dead body, Alexander calls her a 'piteous spectacle' (p. 57). Hedewick's body thus registers the play's central crime: first in pregnancy (not explicitly referred to), then with her child, and finally in death. The problem does not arise from a lack of visual evidence of the rape, but from the difficulty of identifying those signs with either legitimate or illegitimate sexual behaviour, in the absence of any consideration of female volition.

When the substituted party is the female, the implications of the bed-trick are no less complex. One factor distinguishes the two examples in Shakespeare's *Measure for Measure* (1604) and *All's Well that Ends Well* (1603–4): that the sexual act to be transformed in the latter is consensual, but in the former is akin to rape. One source for the play, Whetstone's *Promos and Cassandra* (1578), defines the heroine's capitulation to the Angelo character unproblematically as rape.[58] In *Measure for Measure*, however, this virtual rape is transformed into consensual sex by the substitution of a desiring for an undesiring female.

*The Queen of Corinth* further problematises the complex implications of Mariana's substitution for Isabella in *Measure for Measure*. Before the play starts, the queen's son Theanor has been betrothed to Merione, but his mother has broken the betrothal in order to make a political match between Merione and Agenor, the prince of Argos. Enraged, Theanor has Merione abducted and (disguised or concealed by darkness, so unidentifiable) rapes her. Merione believes that the rape has rendered her unfit for the proposed marriage. However, when Theanor tells his friend Crates that he plans to rape Beliza, Crates' indignation leads him to betray Theanor to the queen. Merione then substitutes herself for Beliza and endures a 'second Ravishment' (V.iv.110), after which Theanor is brought to trial. Both women are now entitled to demand punishment; while Beliza demands that he be beheaded, Merione demands marriage.[59] Eventually the bed-trick is revealed and the situation is resolved by the marriage of Merione and Theanor.

*The Queen of Corinth* thus displays several significant contemporary attitudes towards rape, particularly in its dependence on the marriage resolution. It is acknowledged, however, that this is problematic. Beliza begs Merione to consider

> What joyes thou canst expect from such a husband,
> To whom thy first, and what's more, forc'd embraces,
> Which men say heighten pleasure, were distastefull.
>
> (V.iv.96–8)

Merione, however, now claims that the first experience was distasteful simply because it was unlawful. The trauma of which ample evidence was given at the time is marginalised in favour of a model whereby rape becomes a valid consummation of marriage. Crates explains:

> She was his Wife before the face of Heaven,
> Although some Ceremonious formes were wanting,
> Committed the first Rape, and brought her to him,
> Which broke the Marriage.
>
> (V.iv.196–9)

This conflation of rape with consensual pre-marital sex writes out the woman's trauma.[60]

Theanor's first rape thus functions as an inverted version of the bed-trick, and has the effect of consummating the marriage that had originally been planned between himself and Merione. Where darkness usually conceals the substitution of an alien party for the selected partner, here it conceals the fact that the supposed alien party is actually the (previously) desired partner. It is the revelation of the rapist's identity that reveals the rape as a transformed consummation.[61]

The second 'rape' further problematises the bed-trick and the issue of consent. Where the first had transformed consummation into rape, Merione's substitution of herself for Beliza transforms rape into consensual sex. This results in the paradox indicated by descriptions of Merione as being 'again (but willingly) surpriz'd' and enduring a 'second Ravishment' (V.iv.208, 110). Just as the trauma of the first rape is marginalised in the final act of the play, so the issue of violence in the second 'rape' is completely avoided.

In *Alphonsus* the issue of Hedewick's consent had been marginalised from the beginning of the play, with her right to say 'no' confined to the first occasion alone; in *The Queen of Corinth*, Merione's denial of consent is subsequently forgotten in a dénouement which ties her to the man who raped her. If Hedewick's claim to autonomy is quashed after a single refusal, Merione obliterates hers by submitting to a charade of rape in order to restore her 'honour'. *The Queen of Corinth* implies an analogy between the bed-trick and rape for cases when the substituted party is the female, even if its effect is to marginalise the idea of rape as trauma.

In the latest play of the period to feature a bed-trick, Middleton's *Hengist* (1617–20), an inversion of the convention renders its implications still more complex. Vortiger decides to put aside his wife Castiza in order to marry again. This he can justify only if he can prove that Castiza has been unfaithful. Hersus suggests that he abduct her, 'makeing a rape of honor without wordes' (III.i.187). Such an act is 'too [common]...to be so little knowne... / [T]will be never perceiud' (194–7). The backdrop to the play is thus one in which women are in constant danger of rape. When Castiza is attacked by Hersus and Vortiger in disguise, her first reaction is to cry 'Treason' (III.ii.29); as the king's wife, an attack upon her is, by statute, a crime against him. She then asks 'Whats my sin' and is told 'Contempt of man' (39, 40). Hersus tells her that because she considers him and his companion 'vnworthy to be Loude [loved]' (44) she deserves rape. Vortiger then substitutes himself for Hersus (who does all the talking) as the rapist.

Despite Castiza's emphasised Christianity, she regards rape as 'an eternall act of death in lust' (81). It is presumably her faith, however, that prevents her from killing herself. When challenged about her fidelity by Vortiger she confesses the 'Constraind [sin]' (IV.ii.188). When the trick is eventually revealed, the problem of what course of action Castiza should take is solved, since she was not technically 'raped' at all. She is supposed to be delighted by this revelation: both the sense of pollution and the horror of her rape wiped out. Hersus had anticipated this moment:

> ... never was poore Ladye
> So mockt into false terror: *with* what anguish
> She lyes with her owne Lord.
>
> (III.ii.117–19)

Despite the evident brutality of the rape, the trauma for the victim is written out in favour of a definition of rape as forcible *adultery*. At the end of the play, Aurelius concludes that Castiza's distress is invalid; she

> Liues firme in hono<sup>r</sup>, neither by Consent
> Or act of violence staind, as her greife judges.
>
> (V.ii.261–2)

Either Castiza was not stained by the act of violence she underwent, or she did not experience any act of violence. The semantic ambiguity here functions to write out the trauma and violence of the experience.

In *Alphonsus* the substitution of the male partner had transformed a legitimate consummation into rape. Conversely, the substitution of a desiring female for an undesiring one in a rape situation can render it no rape, although not unproblematically, as in *The Queen of Corinth*. In *Hengist*, the substituted partner is again male, but this is supposed to transform rape into marital sex – an act which, according to contemporary law and ideology, cannot constitute rape. Again the knowability of the woman in this play hinges on the knowability of the rapist, since the final revelation transforms her from a rape victim or adulteress into a chaste wife.

The development of the bed-trick through the period is illustrative of a shift in attitudes to rape which may reflect wider legal and semantic issues. In the 1590s play *Alphonsus*, the party substituted by the bed-trick is the male. This reflects the fact, borne out by the rest of the play, that the woman functions as male property here: it is her appropriation, not her volition, which is significant. The same is true of the basic plot of *The Two Gentlemen of Verona* (which we recall comes from a much earlier source), although we have seen that the play is self-conscious about the ideological significance of the transformed bed-trick here. When the substituted party is female, however, this implies that the woman's volition is of greater weight. *The Queen of Corinth* plays with both types of bed-trick and, while the ideological implications of both are certainly vexed, the mental state of the raped woman is significant, while female desire proves to have some agency in resolving the play's tangles.

This play clearly bears some resemblance to *Measure for Measure*, which is in turn based on Whetstone's *Promos and Cassandra* of 1578. In the latter, the sexual possession of the heroine by means of blackmail is described, without quibble, as 'rape'. Rather than being radical, this reflects, again, the privileging of women's function as male property (and thus their virginity as a an economic bargaining-chip) over their volition. Any kind of fraud or pressure which results in the loss or theft of virginity, as here, constitutes 'rape'. But where this was unchallenged in the 1578 play, by the 1590s and early 1600s Shakespeare, at least, is troubled by it. We have seen that in *The Rape of Lucrece* he alters the story to remove from Lucrece the possible stain of having 'yielded'; when he comes to use the Whetstone story in *Measure for Measure* (1604), he uses the bed-trick to remove from his heroine any implication of complicity, despite the blackmail involved.

In 1594, then, *Alphonsus* depicts rape as a property crime, while in the same year Shakespeare's *Lucrece* is self-conscious about both this definition and the newer definition of rape as a crime against a woman's volition. Laura Levine has argued that *A Midsummer Night's Dream* too is 'caught in a dynamic between these two views of rape'.[62] She argues further that the play represents rape as a condition of existence, dooming to failure Theseus's attempt to transform an originary rape into legitimate marriage. Once again, the transformability of rape, to which the bed-trick testifies, becomes apparent. Levine argues, however, that the play represents theatre as incapable of achieving such a transformation because of its own resemblance to rape.[63] Rape thus becomes a condition of theatre.

The shift in the definition of rape implied in drama relates too to the shift we have seen in attitudes to suicide following rape. We have seen that Clara in *The Spanish Gypsy* challenges the idea that she is stained by rape: her volition clearly has weight here, although the marriage solution eventually undermines it. Yet such progressions are also counterbalanced by the ease with which actions like suicide become standard dramatic devices, as in *The Unnatural Combat*.

*Hengist* might seem like a 'throw-back' to the old pattern where the male party deploys the bed-trick and the woman's volition is insignificant. The play seems self-conscious, however, about its problematic implications, and we should also note that Castiza does not even consider suicide. While using an older pattern, Middleton has also inverted it and brought it into radical conjunction with the question of marriage. *Hengist* actually makes available another reading of rape: a reading which undermines its definition as theft from the husband. By this reading, Vortiger's rape of Castiza becomes an emblem of the marriage itself. When the play begins the two characters are betrothed, but Castiza refuses to marry Vortiger after choosing celibacy. Vortiger is furious, already regarding her as his possession. When he has gained the crown, he marries Castiza, who is seen in dumb show 'brought in vnwillingly' (II. Dumb Show ii. 17) and who accompanies him with 'a kind of / Constrained Consent' (19–20). The equation of this forced marriage with rape is heightened by Castiza's soliloquy, which she delivers just before she is ambushed. Displaying the contentment with her lot for which we are meant to admire her, she expresses her relief that God has sent her

> ... a Contented Blesedness
> In this of marriage *which* I euer doubted:
> ... thoug in greate feare
> At first I was *inforced* to venture ont.
> (III.ii.17–22; my emphasis)

The radicalism of *Hengist* thus lies both in its use of the bed-trick to pose the question of whether a man can rape his own wife, and in its implicit equation of that rape with 'constrained' marriage.[64] These issues, we shall see, prove pertinent to an earlier closet drama, Elizabeth Cary's *Mariam*, and are raised later in Mary Wroth's prose romance, *Urania*.

# Part II
# Writing Women

# 5

# 'Here the leaf's turn'd down': Women Reading and Writing Rape

> ... Lavinia, shall I read?
> This is the tragic tale of Philomel,
> And treats of Tereus' treason and his rape.
> (*Titus Andronicus*, IV.i.46–8)

> ... She hath been reading late,
> The tale of Tereus, here the leaf's turn'd down
> Where Philomel gave up.
> (*Cymbeline*, II.ii.44–6)

Lavinia and Imogen provide two distinct models of women reading about rape. In *Titus Andronicus*, the act of reading is two-fold. It is first Lavinia's experience, off-stage, and presumably prior to the rape. It then becomes a method of communication: by obliging Titus to read, Lavinia herself defines and articulates her own experience. The emphasis in this scene is on reading *as* writing or speech, rather than as reading *per se*; this is followed up when Lavinia writes in the sand with the staff she holds in her mouth (S.D. l. 76).

The image in *Cymbeline*, by contrast, uses the spectacle of a woman reading about rape as the final detail in a catalogue of her attractions. Imogen is here entirely passive; the act of reading has no connotations of writing, and has in any case taken place in the past. Imogen's sleeping, which has interrupted her act of reading at the crucial point in the story, heightens the stasis implied by the act of description. This description, moreover, is part of an explicit analogy between Imogen and Philomela or Lucrece. Iachimo's intention is to catalogue Imogen in such a way as to render credible his tale of 'enjoying' her; his reference to Tarquin's rape (u. 12–14) reinforces the overtones of rape which adhere to his own plan. The reference to Philomela not only functions as a warning of a potential rape situation, as is common in drama of the period; it is also presented as the final piece of evidence ('I have enough', he concludes after this (46)) that will destroy Imogen's reputation – itself a form of violation.

Where Lavinia is an active agent in the communication of her experience through reading, Imogen is as passive in her reading as she would be in a rape: as she *is* in Iachimo's violation of her privacy and reputation. Yet Posthumus's later commendation of her chastity subtly recalls the resistance which is also part of Philomela's story. It is a measure of Imogen's chastity that she 'restrain'd' him of his 'lawful pleasure' (II.iv.161). Her resistance of lawful intercourse – a sight that would 'have warm'd old Saturn' (l. 164) – parallels the resistance of rape with which her reading associates her; and both are erotic for the observer. Iachimo's voyeurism, with all its connotations of rape, suggests that the spectacle of a woman reading about rape (an act which takes place in her bed, in this case) may be sexually titillating. For the spectator, the fact that Imogen is reading a rape story enhances the attractions that have already been catalogued.

Shakespeare's second model of women reading rape, then, denies female agency and ignores its own implicit question: how does a woman respond to a story about rape?

'The tragic tale of Philomel' provides an originary myth for women's discourse, of which a woman writing about rape – or writing at all – is likely to have been aware. Her story shows both the silencing of female utterance – specifically, protest at rape – and the emergence of the woman from that silence into a discourse of resistance.[1] This emergence takes two forms: Philomela's narration by means of weaving, and her metamorphosis into a nightingale (the acquisition of song). It is the former that facilitates her rescue and revenge; like swansong, the nightingale's song does not empower her.[2] However, the tradition by which the nightingale produces song by impaling her breast on a thorn makes available an image of violent penetration which maintains a memory of the rape of the original story.[3]

To use the nightingale as a figure for the poet was conventional. In many cases, the rape of the story is entirely suppressed; even where it is not, as Lamb points out, it engenders a grieving, rather than an angry response, ignoring the vengeance of the women in the story.[4] Yet while this appropriation of a female voice by male poets thus frequently writes out the story behind it, the use of Philomela as a model of authorship can accommodate the gender of a woman writer. Several women writers use the model, some explicitly negotiating its attendant complexities. Aemilia Lanyer, for instance, 'allegorizes the difficulty of female speech' in her comparison of herself to 'a bird that wants a wing, / And cannot fly, but warbles forth her pain'.[5] Like Lanyer, Mary Wroth inscribes Philomela's pain ('her former luckles payning') as she too uses the mythical figure to express the problems of women's authorship.[6] Moreover, Lamb's analysis of three newly discovered poems by another female member of the Sidney family, shows the poet using the nightingale to write unproblematically of love, and self-consciously eradicating the rape in order to '[elicit] an awareness' of it.[7]

While Philomela's metamorphosed form provides one figure for women's utterance, her weaving provides another, and one explicitly associated with resistance. Arachne too weaves stories of rape – the rapes perpetrated on mortals by the gods.[8] For both women, weaving is equivalent to writing.[9] This coincides with the use of weaving (traditionally *the* female industry) as an image of writing; the word 'text' derives from the Latin word for weaving, *texere*.[10] While weaving as an image of writing is not always gendered female (Mary Sidney uses it as an image of male–female collaboration), it is frequently associated specifically with female language.[11] The image also recalls two other classical figures, Penelope and Helen. Penelope's weaving is a means of resisting the advances of her suitors.[12] Helen weaves the story of the war which results from her 'rape' – in the more ambivalent sense of abduction or elopement; her weaving/language can thus connote promiscuity, balancing the other myths in which language or weaving is a resistance of male tyranny. Another association of the web, however, is with witchcraft. This alternative female art too associates itself with language. The coexistence of these different associations reflects the cultural ambivalence towards women's discourse.

Women's writing of this period shows a negotiation with the subject of rape which is surprising given the ideological impediments which worked against women writing at all. Setting out to read rape in women's writing, however, necessitates several caveats. Female writers just as much as male may manipulate conventions or topics for reasons other than simply to convey opinion. Where references to rape are part of proto-feminist polemic, or where its use is typical of the genre, we must be cautious of attributing each instance to a gender-specific 'attitude'.[13] Conversely, some women writers use the stock paragons of chastity from rape stories. Elizabeth Jocelin's *The Mothers Legacie* cites Susanna as an example of female worthiness; Whitney uses Lucrece as a model of chastity, and refers to the 'rape' of Helen in a conventional way.[14] That Whitney also warns her female readers against trusting men does not necessarily affect our reading of these moments. It is perhaps significant that the one poem of this period by a female writer which purports to refer to the writer's own experience of rape, comes from the pen of a woman whose writings have caused centuries of controversy: Mary, Queen of Scots. Her 'casket' sonnet 'For him what countless tears', along with her other writings, has been scrutinised and exploited for its political and biographical significance, including its claim that Boswell 'made himself my body's lord / Before he had my heart' (ll. 2–3).[15]

Despite such potential interpretative pitfalls, women writers' treatment of rape in many cases differs significantly from the conventions. Rape material can be found in texts by women from a variety of genres, fictive and non-fictive. Their focus is often on seduction rather than rape as such: perhaps a particularly emotive topic because a seduced woman is perceived as receiving society's condemnation, rather than sympathy.

The proto-feminist pamphlet, *Jane Anger her Protection for Women* (1589), condemns seduction; within her argument exists a warning about rape. She argues:

> The tiger is robbed of her young ones when she is ranging abroad, but men rob women of their honour undeservedly under their noses. The viper stormeth when his tail is trodden on, and may not we fret when all our body is a foot-stool to their vile lust?[16]

The emphasis on force in this description is more suggestive of rape than seduction, as is her claim that men 'bring care ... and continual fear to women' (p. 37). Later, when she catalogues lustful men, her list includes two rapists, one condemned for 'violent ravishings' (p. 43). Having lamented the impotence of Roman law to prevent sexual offences, she adds: 'there are terrible laws allotted in England to the offenders [in "lechery"], all which will not serve to restrain man' (p. 43). Anger's arguments are to some extent dictated by the purpose of her pamphlet, which is a response to the misogynist *Book: his Surfeit in Love* (registered 1588). The extremity of her language when condemning male behaviour is clearly designed to portray all women as innocent, all men as predators. Nevertheless, the sense of male violence – physical as well as verbal – suggests that Anger has a message to convey about rape.

Elizabeth Grymeston condemns seduction in her conduct book, *Miscelanea, Meditations, Memoratives* (1604), deploying the conventional imagery of besieged city and 'guilefull' serpent.[17] Aemilia Lanyer's *Salve Deus Rex Judaeorum* (1611) is less conventional in its engagement with the subject. Lanyer extols female virtue, partly as a validation of her own writing.[18] While arguing that virtue must accompany beauty, which is an enemy to women, she conveys the dangers of male lust. Women's beauty, she argues, 'draw[s] but dangers and disgrace' (l. 196), and it is the women themselves who suffer from it:

> When men do seek, attempt, plot and devise
> How they may overthrow the chastest dame
> Whose beauty is the white whereat they aim.
> (205–8)

Lanyer's first example, Helen, is ambiguous, although Helen's role is presented as passive (209–10). Her next is Lucrece, and she presents Tarquin indirectly as a murderer:

> 'Twas beauty made chaste Lucrece lose her life,
> For which proud Tarquin's fact was so abhorred.
> (211–12)

Not all her examples concern rape, however. She goes on to discuss Cleopatra and Rosamond, whom she presents as 'betrayed' by beauty into social aspiration (227). Finally, she praises Matilda for resisting John to the point of death. Her beauty works against her chastity, which 'sought folly to prevent' (236).

Lanyer sacrifices her praise of women's resistance, however, to her need to flatter her dedicatee. When she comes to Susanna, she compares her unfavourably to Margaret Clifford, Dowager Duchess of Cumberland:

> For she opposed against old doting lust,
> Who with life's danger she did fear to trust . . .
> No fear of death, or dread of open shame,
> Hinders your perfect heart to give consent.
> (1543–4, 1561–2)

In criticising Susanna's resistance for being motivated by the fear of death or defamation, Lanyer invokes the idea that resistance of an undesired male does not qualify as perfect virtue.[19] This charge clearly disregards the power-dynamic in the story. Moreover, fear of death or defamation is not what 'hinders' Susanna from consenting to the Elders; it is in the face of such threats that she refuses them. The implication that such threats are insufficient excuse for 'yielding' does not fit the story. Lanyer's discussion becomes conventionally focused on the polarity chastity/unchastity, at the expense of gendered power-relations.

In 1615 the 'woman controversy' intensified with the publication of Joseph Swetnam's *Arraignment of Lewd, idle, froward and unconstant women* and the pamphlets answering it by Rachel Speght, 'Ester Sowernam' and 'Constantia Munda', all published in 1617.[20] Speght challenges the deployment of paradigms to prove the wickedness of women. She argues that both men and women may be good or bad, and that 'I may as well say Barabbas was a murderer' as that 'the noble city of Troy [was] sacked and spoiled by the fair Helena'.[21] 'Munda' counters Swetnam's story of a prostitute called Theodora with that of the Theodora who dissuaded a soldier intent on raping her (p. 146).

'Sowernam''s pamphlet takes up the attack on seduction, defining it as abusive and arguing that men 'with violence . . . seek and sue after women' (p. 101). She attacks the double standard which condones male but condemns female promiscuity; moreover, she clearly sees the man as to blame: 'if a man abuse a maid and get her with child, no matter is made of it – but as a trick of youth; but it is made so heinous an offence in the maid that she is disparaged and utterly undone by it' (p. 103). However, she goes on to argue that this double standard is justified in order to 'prove that women in their creation are the most excellent creatures' (p. 103). 'Sowernam' details the ways in which men tempt and pressure women into bed, comparing them to the serpent with Eve. The seduced woman is a victim on two counts: she is 'the unhappy subject to a lustful body and the shameful stall of a lascivious tongue' (p. 113). 'Sowernam' thus conveys the violation experienced by women whose reputations are destroyed, and defines their sexual experience as subjection.

'Sowernam' challenges the idea of beauty as being responsible for male sexual conduct. Rather than women provoking men, men reveal their sinfulness by responding lustfully (p. 110). She overturns the conventional attribution of blame to women, telling Swetnam not to 'rail at women to be the cause of men's overthrow, when the original root and cause is in yourselves' (p. 110). It is men who provoke women to unchaste behaviour, and who devote all their energies to making women unchaste (pp. 113–14). 'Sowernam''s attack on seduction and rape, however, finds a wider context as performance. Her arguments, as Diane Purkiss points out, may be undercut by the theatricality of her medium and, perhaps ironically, by its combination with the very knowledgeability which enables her to voice such matters.[22]

The polemicists may deal with rape tangentially, but they concentrate on seduction as the chief signifier of male subjection of women. It is, perhaps surprisingly, in an advice book, Dorothy Leigh's *The Mothers Blessing* (1616), that we find a more thorough engagement with the issue of rape.[23] In the context of a definite, albeit sometimes inconsistent, assertion of women's equality, and a validation of female learning and her own writing, Leigh argues for both the emotional rights of women in marriage and their right to freedom from rape and seduction. She also engages with the complex issue of the chastity of the rape victim, defining her as innocent and showing an awareness of the psychological impact of rape.

The 'mother's advice book' was a popular genre, and one which reproduced the problematic conditions surrounding female eloquence in the complaint genre. Its existence tends to be justified by two topoi: the writer's concern for her children's well-being, and her lack of involvement in publication. The two coincide when she has written in the fear that death will prevent her passing on her maternal wisdom orally to the child, as in the case of Jocelin's *Mothers Legacie*: the author's imminent death validates this exhortatory swansong. Just as female complaints are mediated by the (male) poet, 'mother's advice' books tend to be mediated by a male printer, in a way which distances and protects the woman from the 'stain' of publication. Leigh defines her work according to this model, claiming that 'the care of Parents for their children' was the occasion of her writing (p. 1), and excusing her unconventionality in writing with a note of defiance:

> Therefore let no man blame a mother, though she something exceede in writing to her children, since . . . the loue of a mother to her children, is hardly contained within the bounds of reason. (pp. 11–12)

Leigh's work, however, markets itself carefully for posterity, with a dedicatory epistle to Princess Elizabeth by the author, rather than the preface by a male printer recording her death and innocence of publication, as in Grymeston's case (sig. A2). Moreover, Leigh wavers in her projection of the specific readership as her sons. Having defined the 'third cause' of writing as 'to moue women to bee carefull of their children' (p. 16), a female readership hovers thereafter behind her ambiguous subsequent references to 'them'.

Leigh's discussion of rape appears in a chapter the title of which not only defines it as part of her maternal project, but gives no indication of its chief subject-matter: 'The seuenth cause [of writing] is, that they should giue their children good names' (p. 27). The most highly recommended name is Susanna. By portraying her story as one of sexual threat, Leigh defines chastity as involving caution and wariness, rather than as its own protection:

> wee women may now say, that men lye in waite euery where to deceiue vs, as the Elders did to deceiue *Susanna*. Wherefore let vs bee, as she was, chaest, watchfull, and wary. (p. 33)

She claims:

> now men, like *Iudas*, betray their Mistresses with a kisse &, repent it not: but laugh and reioyce, that they haue brought sinne and shame to her that trusted them. (p. 33)

Leigh's reference to the kiss seems consciously understated; the malice attributed to the men, and the woman's 'shame', are suggestive of a more extreme sexual coercion. In that she is positing a scene between a lover and his 'mistress', she seems to be defining seduction as violent or coercive. However, she concludes from this that the only way to avoid such an eventuality is 'to be chaste with *Susanna*' (p. 33) and, like 'Sowernam', goes on to condemn unchaste women as the cause of countless 'mischiefes' (p. 34). Yet this sits uneasily with her earlier emphasis on male force, suggesting that her arguments about coercion are being wrapped up in more conventional diatribes against unchaste female conduct.

Leigh's subsequent more explicit discussion of rape seems to confirm that this was the subtext of the earlier passage. To prove the chastity of many 'heathen women', she asserts:

> many of them before they would be defiled, haue been carelesse of their liues, and so haue endured all those torments, that men

would deuise to inflict vpon them, rather then they would lose the name of a modest mayd, or a chaste Matrone. (p. 38)

Again she conveys the sadistic power of the male torturers. Although this passage follows her commendation of wifely subjection to the husband, she undermines the relationship between marital chastity and resistance to rape by referring to maids as well as matrons. By thus separating out the issue of uxorial submission and women's sexual torture, she gives equal weight to the latter.

Leigh argues that rape does not undermine a woman's chastity:

so farre they haue beene from consenting to any immodestie, that if at any time they haue been rauished, they haue either made away themselues, or at least haue separated themselues from company, not thinking themselues worthy of any society, after they haue once bin deflowred, though against their wils. (pp. 38–9)

Leigh is categorical that shame signifies innocence, ignoring the worries of Augustine and others that it might suggest consent to or even enjoyment of the sexual act. In including suicide unproblematically in this argument, moreover, she ignores its sinful nature and the age-old controversy surrounding the implications of suicide pre-empting or following rape. Yet she disingenuously enlists in support of her argument the very scholarship which had problematised the issue: clerics 'were oftentimes constrained to make diuers Sermons …to disswade [women] from that crueltie, which they inflicted vpon themselues, rather then they would suffer themselues to be deflowred' (pp. 40–1). Disregarding again the sinful nature of suicide which was the Church's chief concern, she implies that the clerics unproblematically support her contention that rape does not render a woman impure.

Leigh then challenges the idea that is a 'disgrace…to haue but one spot of vncleannesse' (p. 41). This seems to admit of degrees of pollution, undermining the rigid opposition of chaste and unchaste/polluted women. This may reflect the 'real-life' genre in which she writes, displaying an unconventional pragmatism. Read alongside her condemnation of suicide, it implies that a raped woman should live as proof of her innocence. In joining the long-standing debate over the necessity of suicide, and by discussing it in terms of pollution (producing shame without implying guilt), Leigh thus attempts to disentangle sexual ideology from the psychological impact of rape.

Leigh's suggestion that there are different degrees or types of pollution might seem to contradict an earlier interruption to the argument about rape: 'wherefore the woman that is infected with the sin of vncleannesse, is worse then a beast' (p. 39). Such conventionalities as these seem an unfortunate distraction from the substance of Leigh's argument. Yet they may thus function to validate her less conventional discussion, providing reassurance, in this case, that her sympathy for raped women does not imply condonation of unchaste women. Her awareness of the gender politics of writing undoubtedly contributes to this strategy. Not only has she defended her project in the first place, but she also frequently emphasises that her anecdotes or references to ideological points come from male writings: men 'haue written' of women's chastity and 'some of the Fathers haue written' that women must be and seem chaste (pp. 30, 39).

Leigh's emphasis on male language ('the vaine words of men' (p. 31)) as a tool of seduction, with the references to male learning, underlines the significance of language and knowledge in the battle between the sexes. Just as Leigh must defend her writing against the men who think it inappropriate, so women must use reading not just to signify their chastity but as a defence against threat. Because the chaste are free from the sin of idleness, 'who so is truly chaste, is ... alwaies either reading, meditating, or practising some good thing which she hath learned in the Scripture' (pp. 30–1). Leigh's advocacy of female learning is validated, conventionally, by its religious nature, but the woman's reading becomes a substitute for listening to male persuasion. This is itself a model of seduction which portrays the female as the less culpable party. It is idleness, not wickedness, which leaves her open to male suggestion:

> The vaine words of the man, and the idle eares of the woman, beget vnchaste thoughts oftentimes in the one, which may bring forth much wickednesse in them both. (p. 32)

Even when she attributes wickedness to the woman, then, Leigh portrays the man as the active party. To protect themselves, women should cultivate learning. The popularity of *The Mothers Blessing* suggests that there was a market for such advice.[24]

Leigh shares with the pamphleteers, with Whitney and with Lanyer, an awareness of the threat posed to women by male language. Whitney and Lanyer argue that it is written language, as well as speech, which works against women.[25] Attacks on male language may be inevitable in the pamphlets which are written in answer to specific misogynist works. Yet their equation of verbal seduction with misogynistic writing has a wider relevance; as Anger argues:

> [men's] glozing tongues... [are] the preface to the execution of their vile minds; and their pens, the bloody executioners of their barbarous manners.[26]

The cumulative effect of these pamphlets and advice books, then, is to imply an analogy between defending women from slander and defending them from rape. This has a wider connotation: that men's language, whether spoken or written, is a key weapon in their control or subjection of women. For women, writing becomes an appropriate means of resisting this male domination.

The four writers featured in the following chapters find different ways of negotiating the constraints on women's mental and sexual autonomy. For all four, this involves an engagement with existing texts as well as with the ideology of gender. Two of the writers, Jane Lumley and Mary Sidney, are translating their texts; the third, Elizabeth Cary, rewrites an episode from Josephus's *Antiquities of the Jewes* in *Mariam*, and in *The History of Edward II* engages with and rewrites the histories of that period. In my final chapter, Mary Wroth works in the romance tradition in her *Urania* and specifically engages with Philip Sidney's *Arcadia*. All four are thus engaging with and responding to existing works by male writers; the oppositional nature of these texts will be implicit in the rest of this study.

These four writers, it will be clear, come from a higher social class than the majority of the writers discussed so far. Sidney, Cary and Wroth, to varying degrees, were patronesses or at least dedicatees of literature: 'muses', whose assumptions of the authorial voice reversed the expectation created by this role.[27] Mary Sidney and Mary Wroth, as aunt and niece, are both, of course, part of the 'Sidney circle'.[28] Elizabeth Cary's closet drama *Mariam* has been associated with the work of the Countess's literary milieu on the basis of its genre, although there is no evidence to associate her personally with either Sidney or Wroth.[29] Indeed, all four writers can be linked by their production of closet dramas.[30]

Cary and Wroth both fell from favour in ways which illustrate the interdependence of sexual, political and, in Cary's case, spiritual issues. For her conversion to Catholicism in the late 1620s, Cary was abandoned by her husband to penury; this also effected her alienation from the court. For her sexual impropriety in bearing two illegitimate children Wroth lost Queen Anne's favour and left the court.[31] Both writers did some of their writing from these socially marginalised positions: Cary's *Edward II* was probably written in the late 1620s, while *Urania* was certainly begun in Wroth's widowhood and its sequel begun after her fall from grace.

These writers are now well on their way either to joining the 'canon' or, more probably, to forming an alternative 'canon' of women's writing for this period. This is both laudable and problematic; at such a point, it is clearly important to emphasise their engagements with and participation in their literary contexts, as well as any divergences from such contexts. Much of the criticism of their works has focused on 'difference', as the titles of, for example, Beilin's *Redeeming Eve* or Krontiris's *Oppositional Voices* make clear. More recently, however, Danielle Clarke has brought into the picture the continuities between their works and their literary and political contexts, arguing that they participate more fully than has been realised in the public, rather than the private, 'feminine', sphere.[32]

Like the writers discussed in this chapter, Lumley, Sidney, Cary and Wroth specifically negotiate and recast the contingencies attendant upon women's utterance within their texts. In each case, it will be apparent, the circumscriptions contingent upon the writer's own ideological position find a reflection in these fictional situations as she presents them.

That parallels arise between the female complaint and several of these women's texts should be no surprise. By the time Sidney and Cary were writing, it had become a prominent model of female utterance. Like the use of Philomela as a model, it is logical that it should be engaged with by women taking up the pen. This is not to say that the 'complaint' or the 'swansong' modes are the only means by which women writers may find a voice in this period, or that their inherent constrictions necessarily disempower those voices. On the contrary, both Sidney and Cary take issue with the complaint's circumscription of female eloquence, and later, Mary Wroth's character Antissia explicitly rejects 'complaining' in favour of an alternative (revenge) that precipitates her characterisation as 'mad'.[33]

These writers, then, find a new context here. The prominence of rape in the portrayal of gender-relations and the rhetoric of courtship is already a suggestive context for works by women writers, particularly those which articulate concern with female sexual conduct. We have also seen the ways in which the 'discourses' of rape reflect contemporary attitudes to women's utterance, as well as to their sexuality. Female eloquence may be simultaneously licensed and disempowered: whether through the function of rape as a chastity test, or a cue for male chivalry, or through the various situations which I have characterised as 'swansong'. Moreover, an anxiety about the relationship between body and mind, which we have seen to be heightened by rape narratives, is implicit in the injunction to women to be 'chaste, silent and obedient'. I shall be focusing on the equation between women's sexual autonomy and their autonomy in writing. In each case, however, the ways in which the writers negotiate or engage with the subject of rape prove an intrinsic part of their treatment of the subjects of women's sexual autonomy and agency, and their political or linguistic power.

# 6

# Translation and Intervention: Jane Lumley and Mary Sidney

> The inuention ... is wholy another mans, my part none therin but the translation, as it were onely in giuing entertainment to a straunger.
>
> Margaret Tyler[1]

Tyler's image of the female translator as hostess seeks to trope the translation process as a 'passive, nonthreatening activity appropriate to women', in order to ensure her work's acceptability.[2] However, studies of women translators have shown that it could be a form of 'intellectual self-assertion'.[3] Not only was translation an important part of the humanistic education programme, but the very idea of original as opposed to secondary writing had little weight in this period.[4] For women, moreover, translation provided a way of evading the polarities circumscribing female authorship: public versus private, speech versus silence. Yet Tyler's defence of translation as a woman's activity does not entirely escape these terms. Her 'giuing entertainment to a straunger', with its possible sexual connotations, suggests the potential of translation to empower the woman writer. Translation enables the writer to engage with the text both through her choice and her treatment of it. Ostensibly a mediation or ventriloquizing of another (male) voice, translation can enable intervention and resistance.[5]

The works of Lady Jane Lumley (1536–76/7) and Mary Sidney Herbert, Countess of Pembroke (1561–1621) exemplify opposite methods of translation. In her translation of Euripides' *Iphigenia at Aulis* Lumley abridges and alters the text freely, conveying an interest in certain aspects of the story and her interpretation of its central theme. In Sidney's case, her concerns and interpretation are implied by her selection of texts.[6] In this chapter, I shall focus on her translations of Robert Garnier's closet drama *Marc Antoine* (1578) and Petrarch's fourteenth-century poem *Trionfo della Morte*.

Both writers have been criticised for their methods: Lumley for altering her text so radically, Sidney for the 'conservatism' of her translations, the one read as incompetence, the other as self-effacement.[7] Yet if they differ in their methods, they share an interest in female virtue and heroism; Lumley's Iphigenia and Sidney's Cleopatra and Laura all display heroism in 'dying well'.[8] Both writers, too, highlight female speech – an issue pertinent to their own writing. Lumley emphasises Iphigenia's intelligence as part of her heroism and links it to the circumscription of female knowledge which is central to the play. Her adaptation intensifies the equation between women's access to knowledge and their sexual autonomy, which is already central to the plot. Sidney, in *The Triumph of Death*, presents a heroine whose speech is privileged but legitimised by her being a ghost, contrasting with her silence during life; her choice of this text has implications for Cleopatra in *Antonius*, whose speech relates problematically to her power.

Both writers engage with the subject of rape in different ways. Lumley chooses a text which has the 'rape' story of Helen of Troy as its background and in which the equation of heroic female sacrifice with rape is implicit. Her negotiation of this context to the play, and of references to rape within it, is poised suggestively between avoidance and engagement, perhaps reflecting the constrictions on her own writing. Sidney's exploration of the problematic relationship between female discourse and virtue finds a context in the poetic taste for female characters whose eloquence is often yoked to sexual shame or rape.

## 'TO SPEKE THOS THINGES': LADY JANE LUMLEY'S *IPHIGENEIA*

Lady Lumley's *The Tragedie of Euripides called Iphigeneia*, which was not published until 1909, is apparently the first translation of a Greek drama into English. The manuscript, which was probably her commonplace book, also contains orations by Isocrates in her autograph, apparently translated by her from Greek into Latin, some accompanied by Latin missives to her father.[9]

The date of Lumley's translation is unknown. From the little evidence we have, it could have been written at any time between her marriage in 1549 and her death in 1576 or 1577. Harold H. Child assumes that she was working in conjunction with her husband, who translated Erasmus's *Institution of a Christian Prince* in 1550.[10]

The fact that *Iphigenia* was a work also associated with Erasmus, while interesting, is insufficient premise for this contention, which makes Jane Lumley 13 or 14 at the time of translation. Unfortunately, in the absence of any evidence to disprove this tenuous hypothesis, critics have used the idea of her extreme youth to deprecate her work.[11] More recently, however, Diane Purkiss has pointed out that if Lumley used the Greek original at all, she cannot have begun the translation until 1553.[12] It seems more plausible, in view of the consistency and focus with which she adapts the text, that it is a work of her adulthood, written in the 1560s or even the 1570s.

*Iphigenia* was a popular work in the early sixteenth century, both in Greek and in Erasmus's Latin translation.[13] Where Erasmus was concerned with linguistic training for the public sphere, Lumley's interest is in the content of the play. There are several reasons why the story of Agamemnon's sacrifice of his daughter for the good of Greece might have appealed to her. Her father, Henry Fitzalan, twelfth Earl of Arundel, was associated with the plot to put Lady Jane Grey, Jane Lumley's cousin, on the throne in 1553 (for which she was executed) and, in 1569, was arrested for his involvement in the plan to marry Mary, Queen of Scots to Norfolk. His daughter's interest in the story of the sacrifice of a young woman to further male goals gains significance in this context.[14] This might suggest that her *Iphigeneia* is likely to have been written later than 1569, or at least after 1553.[15]

Lumley's *Iphigeneia* is an adaptation rather than a literal translation. Her alterations strongly suggest an overriding concern with questions of female autonomy and the ideological constraints circumscribing that autonomy. The intelligence of her heroine adds irony and pathos to the central theme of her rewriting – the limits on what women may say, do and know. Lumley's version characterises female heroism as a quality of mind, brings out the gender-specificity of the predicament of the women characters, and focuses on the rules constraining female conduct, particularly those concerning speech and knowledge.

Rape figures not only in the background to Iphigenia's story but in its main plot. The suppression of knowledge in the play facilitates a parallel between marriage and sacrificial murder which brings out the implicit violence in such transactions involving women. Lorraine Helms has read the play in the context of Lynda E. Boose's work on the sacrifice of daughters by fathers, and has argued that 'in consenting to her own sacrificial death, the daughter transforms murder into martyrdom and incestuous rape into symbolic marriage'.[16] Moreover, Clytemnestra reveals that her own marriage began with rape: that is, rape by the same figure who arranges Iphigenia's marriage/sacrifice. Lumley's negotiation of rape as originary myth, as symbol and as the experience of one of her characters, is intriguingly poised between elimination and engagement.

Details of Lumley's rendition suggest that she worked from both the original text and Erasmus's Latin translation; the Isocrates translations evidence her knowledge of both languages. Her 'Argument of the Tragadie' is translated from Erasmus;[17] she also follows him in translating the name 'Artemis' as 'Diana', and 'πρεσβιτης' as 'Senex' rather than 'old man', throughout. While David H. Greene has identified several places where she follows Erasmus in distorting or enlarging the original,[18] there is also at least one place where she retains the original line-order in preference to Erasmus's rearrangement.[19] Her spelling 'Iphigeneia' (or 'Iphigeneya'), rather than 'Iphigenia', also suggests a knowledge of the Greek.[20]

The prose *Iphigeneia* is considerably shorter than the original, and Lumley's concern was patently not to 'produce an accurate, complete, poetic account of the play'.[21] She omits the choral odes and significantly abridges the whole play in a consistent and detailed fashion. She condenses or summarises long speeches, and rearranges dialogues to cut out interjections and merge short speeches. The consistency of her pruning belies any charge of incompetence, since she frequently makes alterations to compensate for earlier omissions. The omissions, moreover, fall into several marked patterns; she tends to omit mythological and genealogical detail, for instance, so that such details do not distract from the progression of the plot, and also cuts most references to the baby Orestes. The patterns, however, do not account for every detail, which suggests that abridgement was an aim in itself.

Lumley's adaptation intensifies and redefines the heroism of the women in the play. This heroism she defines as a quality of mind. Her translation of the Nuntius's praise of Iphigenia's *'good courage and virtue'* (1562) as 'the stoutenes of her minde' (1355)[22] typifies her version's concern with the heroine's mind. In an exchange about the 'marriage' which is a cover for her planned sacrifice, this concern surfaces:

*Aga.* Trulye daughter the more wittely you speake, the more you troble me.

> *Iphi.* If it be so father, then will I studie to seme more folisshe that
> you may be delited.
> *Aga.* Suerly I am constrained to praise gretlye your witte, for I do
> delite moch in it. (608–14)

Agamemnon's last speech does not appear in the original. Lumley
may well have been inspired by Erasmus's addition at this point:
'Collaudo uero te, proboque filia' ('I do indeed praise you highly
and approve of you, daughter', f. 53). Yet her version emphasises
Iphigenia's intelligence, not only focusing Agamemnon's praise on his
daughter's 'wit', but also suggesting that her intelligence is habitual.

Patience and joy in suffering – qualities both Christian and feminine – become the dominant features of this heroic virtue, emphasised
by three specific changes. In a discussion between Iphigenia and
Clytemnestra, Lumley adds a line to Iphigenia's speech: 'I wolde
counsell you therfore to suffer this troble paciently' (1170–1). Later,
she has the Chorus comment: 'Suerlie you are happie O Iphigeneya,
that you can suffer so pacientlye all this troble' (1210–11), rather than
describing her as playing a 'Noble ... part' (1402). In a subsequent
Chorus speech, which she has largely summarised, she adds: 'Yet
happie arte thou, O Iphigeneya, that withe thy deathe, thou shalte
purchase unto the grecians a quiet passage' (1323–6).[23]

Agamemnon commends Iphigenia's intelligence at the very moment
that he withholds information from her. The denial of information
to the play's female characters is already the source of much of its
drama. Lumley's translation heightens this tension by focusing on
the limits the rules of decorum place on female knowledge. She
amplifies Agamemnon's injunction – 'Enough! It fits not maidens know
such things' (671) – so that it prohibits knowledge to any woman:
'Leaue to enquier of suche thinges, for it is not lawfull that women
shulde knowe them' (636–8).[24] Her rendering of a later exchange
focuses on this restriction of women's knowledge. In the original, when
Clytemnestra reveals her knowledge of his plan, Agamemnon reacts
with indignation: 'A hideous question! foul suspicion this' (1132). In
Lumley's version, he blames his wife for breaking the rules governing
female speech and thought: 'you haue spoken thos thinges, whiche
you oughte neither to saye, nor yet to thinke' (935–7). They continue:

> *Aga.* It is not lawfull for me to answer you to thos thinges, which
> you ought not to knowe.

*Clit.* I haue not enquired of any thinge that dothe not becomme me: but take you hede rather, leste you make suche an answer as you ought not. (940–6)

This is strikingly different from the original:

*AG.* To question fair fair answer shalt thou hear.
*CL.* Nought else I ask, thou answer me nought else. (1134–5)

Erasmus may have pointed Lumley in this direction. His translation, here as elsewhere, emphasises what is 'fitting' rather than what is 'fair' by using the word 'decet' (f. 66v). Lumley's version, however, brings out the constraints placed on women's knowledge by ideological 'law', and the debate comes to focus on the competition between a woman's decorum and her speech and access to information. In the additional lines Clytemnestra shifts the ground of the argument to imply that she is fulfilling her maternal duty while Agamemnon is failing in his duty as a father. She thus answers Agamemnon's rebuke about decorum by substituting parental for female conduct as the subject of contention.

Lumley underlines Clytemnestra's disempowerment when she pleads with Achilles for help, adding: 'Besides this yf you do not helpe us, we can bi no meanes auoide this mischefe: for I alone beinge a woman can not perswade Agamemnon' (826–9).[25] That she is powerless to influence her husband is the basis on which the original plea to Achilles is predicated, but Lumley has her state this explicitly, and identifies the problem as a gender issue. Later in the same scene, Lumley again shifts the language from the particular to the general, to emphasise that a woman's position is circumscribed not only by her sex but by her role as wife. Her Clytemnestra tells Agamemnon:

Wherfore if you will not be moued withe pitie, take hede leste you compelle me to speke thos thinges, that do not become a good wife. (992–5)

The emphasis on the role of the 'good wife' is not in the original,[26] while there is again an emphasis on decorum in Erasmus's rendition that may have inspired Lumley, but is less specific than hers.[27] Lumley thus suggests that female language is a measure of social/sexual decorum. This ideological model replaces the more conventional one found elsewhere in the original speech, in a section she omits. Here, Clytemnestra describes herself as a 'blameless wife . . . Chaste in desires' (1158–9).[28] A model of wifehood that links marital and linguistic decorum thus replaces one that categorises her on the basis of sexual chastity.

Lumley extends the implicit injunction against female knowledge and speech to the Chorus. By twice rendering 'alien women' simply as 'women', she focuses on gender at the expense of nationality. The Chorus comment:

> We also lamente your chaunce, so moche as it becommethe women to lamente the miserie of princes. (480–2)[29]

It is not their foreignness but their sex that denies the Chorus the right to sympathise with Agamemnon and to express such an emotion. Agamemnon himself commands their silence, again addressing them as women rather than as foreigners.[30] Lumley also adds an original line, in which they demand of Clytemnestra: 'after what fassion shall we lament, seinge we may not shewe any token of sadnes at the sacrafice' (1307–9).[31] The Chorus's awareness of the constraints on their utterance is fitting for this adaptation, which omits all the choral odes. While Lumley may have had other reasons for the omission, such as abridgement, it does allow her to align the Chorus with the female protagonists in terms of their verbal autonomy.

The emotions of the women in the play, then, are as much under scrutiny as their words. Iphigenia's warning to her mother not to be angry with Agamemnon, as Lumley writes it, focuses on the rules of female conduct. Where in the original she tells her, 'against thine husband I behold thee anger-stirred / Causelessly' (1369–70), Lumley's version reads: 'I perceiue you are angrie withe your husband, whiche you may not do. for you can not obtaine your purpose by that meanes' (1163–6). She thus emphasises both the transgressive nature and the ineffectuality of wifely anger.[32] Later in the scene she makes a similar adjustment. As Iphigenia departs to be sacrificed, in the original, she tells Clytemnestra not to accompany her because it is 'better so' (1461). Lumley's Iphigenia is more concerned with her mother's decorum and her own role in moderating it: 'Take hede I praye you leste you happen to do that whiche shall not become you: Wherfore O Mother I praye you folowe my councell and tarie heare still' (1281–4).[33]

Under scrutiny for their actions as well as their words, Lumley's female characters are obliged to negotiate the problematic boundary between the public and private spheres. When Clytemnestra offers to bring Iphigenia out to beg for Achilles's help, he warns against risking 'the reproach of fools' (999). Lumley renders this:

No trulie I thinke it not mete, that she shulde come abrode, for suerly men wolde iudge euell of hir, if she shulde come moche amongste companie. (871–4)[34]

By altering 'fools' to 'men', and by making Iphigenia the sole object of the projected slander, Lumley makes the problem gender-specific.

Such concern with female knowledge and expression seems to inform Lumley's adaptation generally, affecting her criteria in abridging the play. Although Helen retains her role in the story, Lumley omits at least nine references to her as a 'whore', or to her adultery, and this seems consistent with her more general tendency to eliminate details which might be thought unsuitable for a female pen.[35] She cuts Agamemnon's allusion to things which are unsuitable for young virgins to hear, and his description of Iphigenia's hair and bosom, as well as a line by Iphigenia which might show her as indiscreet.[36] Finally, when Iphigenia offers to give herself for Greece, Lumley adjusts her line to remove the focus on the woman's body. '*I resign my body to Hellas*' (1397) becomes 'I will offer my selfe willingly to deathe, for my countrie' (1201–2).[37] This editing suggests a concern with the ideological constraints which inevitably adhere to her project. Her circumspection in adapting the text necessarily reflects the concern she displays within it with women's mental and linguistic autonomy.

Such circumspection may account for an apparent inconsistency in the work, whereby Lumley shows her concern with women's autonomy in language and conduct, but omits most of the available references to their sexual disempowerment through rape. Whether concern for decorum or a wish not to portray women as sexually compromised is her motive, she cuts Agamemnon's line which imagines Iphigenia being raped by Hades after her death, and omits an allusion to the rape of Leda.[38] She also cuts three allusions to Greek wives being ravished.[39] On the other hand, as Purkiss points out, she sexualises the imagery concerning Iphigenia's sacrifice, emphasising the violation of her 'bewtifull face and faire bodi' which will be 'defiled withe hir owne blode' (1321–3).[40]

That Lumley thus underlines the symbolic connection between the sacrifice of a virgin and rape, despite omitting several more explicit references to rape, should prepare us for her complex negotiation of Clytemnestra's revelation of the start of her marriage. The original states that Agamemnon *'married me, unwilling, and took me by force'* (1149).[41] This makes abduction and rape congruent: both the violent removal and the sexual force are conveyed by 'took' in this context. Erasmus's rendition reproduces this, so that the idea of 'raptus' signifies at once abduction and rape, with Clytemnestra's unwillingness made clear.[42] Lumley's rendition, 'takinge me awaye withe stronge hande' (964–5), seems to suppress the sexual dimension, by translating the original as though it signified only physical removal, without the duality that also conveys sexual appropriation. The line, however, comes from a passage which Lumley has substantially pruned, so that her retention of the reference to the rape, however oblique in her rendition, seems the more striking.[43] Lumley adds that this action was 'withe out the good will of all my frindes' (963–4), which underlines the transgressive nature of Agamemnon's act. This perhaps provides a way of emphasising that the marriage was against Clytemnestra's will without foregrounding the sexual component of forced marriage, rape. She retains the account of how Clytemnestra's father prevented her brothers killing Agamemnon in revenge and permitted the marriage; this retrospectively separates the 'takinge me awaye . . .' from the marriage itself, making clear that they are two distinct acts. However, she then omits a crucial line, in which Clytemnestra describes herself as 'reconciled to thee' (1157): Lumley's Clytemnestra simply continues, 'who after I was maried . . .' (972). While the idea of being 'reconciled' to the idea of marriage is hardly very positive, Lumley's omission eradicates even this concession on Clytemnestra's part, portraying her as the passive victim of Agamemnon's sexual appropriation and her father's mediation.

Moreover, Lumley's wording inevitably recalls the etymology of 'rape', so that the sexual violence attendant on the forced marriage remains available in the claim that Agamemnon '[took] me awaye withe stronge hande'. This wording has actually appeared twice before. It occurs when the Senex complains that Menelaus has stolen the letter he was delivering from Agamemnon to Clytemnestra. Here, 'hath snatched / By violence thy letter from my hand' (314–15) becomes 'withe stronge hande, he hath taken awaie your letter'

(236–8).[44] Agamemnon's relation of Paris's elopement with Helen uses a similar formulation, rendering 'ἐξαναρπάσας' ('*snatched her away*', l. 75) as 'takinge hir priuelye awaye' (95–6).[45] The wording of the three phrases thus aligns violent, non-sexual theft (the letter) with the connotative theft of Helen (physically removed and sexually appropriated) and with the theft *and* rape of Clytemnestra. The closeness of the phrases suggests a degree of thought by Lumley about the related ideas of violent theft and sexual force. This proximity between rape, elopement and theft is particularly fitting in a play in which the action is brought about by a 'rape' which is both a sexual theft and a 'wanton' act by its object, and in which the volition of the woman is irrelevant to its political impact.

Lumley's formula allows her to relegate Clytemnestra's rape to the subtext of the story. Yet as a subtext it feeds into the symbolic equivalence between marriage and sacrifice in the play, and into its originary 'rape'. She may not directly 'speke thos thinges', but they remain inherent in her *Iphigeneia*.

## MARY SIDNEY'S *ANTONIUS* AND *THE TRIUMPH OF DEATH*

Lumley's free adaptation of her text contrasts strikingly with Mary Sidney's approach. It is ironic, then, that in her role as editor of Philip Sidney's *Arcadia*, Mary Sidney has till recently been portrayed as a ruthless bowdlerizer. Her alleged responsibility for the elimination of its sex or 'rape' scenes might be comparable to some of Lumley's editing.[46] Yet her approach to the texts she translates is markedly different. Her literary project is effected primarily through the selection, rather than alteration, of these texts.

Sidney's choice of Garnier's and Petrarch's works implies an interest in the portrayal of female virtue and heroism; yet reading them together is problematic. The double nature of 'ventriloquism' here is particularly clear. Where Cleopatra speaks in *Antonius* (1592), and where Laura addresses the poet in the second half of *The Triumph of Death* (probably written in the late 1590s), Sidney presents a female voice, authored by a male writer but translated by a woman.[47] In Laura's case, the poem's form and literary context legitimise her speaking position. That Cleopatra's voice is less easily validated is one source of conflict in the relationship between them.

Cleopatra's control of language is central in this play, in which she, rather than the titular hero, is the central figure. It is at once a source

of her power and of anxiety about her. Diomede's blason identifies
this linguistic power as both sexual and political; her beauty is

> ...nothing [to] th'e'nchaunting skilles
> Of her cælestiall Sp'rite, hir training speache,
> Her grace, hir Maiestie, and forcing voice.
> (sig. I2)

Cleopatra's control of language brings about Antony's downfall; her
message claiming she has died causes his suicide. Yet while, usually
off-stage, her language controls and destroys Antony, she uses it in
our hearing to declare and elevate her faithful love for him.

The love Cleopatra expresses is at once ennobling and self-
effacing. Her assertion of her 'self' as lover is simultaneously a sub-
mersion of her self and life into Antony's, as an exchange with
Charmian articulates:

> *Ch.*  Our first affection to our self is due.
> *Cl.*  He is my selfe.
> (sig. H3v)

Despite Charmian's exhorting her twice not to 'loose your selfe'
(532, 549), Cleopatra defines love as self-negation:

> Dead and aliue, *Antonie*, thou shalt see
> Thy princesse follow thee...
> (sig. H3)

The tension between Cleopatra's self-effacement and her power is
at the centre of the tension in the work between positive and negative
images of her. This itself facilitates a debate about identity which is a
prominent theme of the play. Sidney's translation underlines this
theme, by translating different French phrases into the single English word 'self' in this scene. 'To loose your selfe', 'to ourselfe is due'
and 'he is my selfe' (sigs H3, H3v) come from French phrases using
'mesme'.[48] However, another 'to loose your selfe' and 'Outrage our
selues' (sigs H3, H4) correspond to reflexive verbs, while 'you selfe-
cruell are', 'Selfe-cruell him from crueltie to spare' and 'to hir selfe
vnkinde' (sigs H3v, H4) correspond to neither.[49]

Cleopatra's definition of herself as a lover clashes with Charmian's representation of her as a mother and a queen. Although she

gains sympathy as a mother when she bids her children farewell before dying, she has rejected motherhood in favour of sexual love, declaring Antony's love 'more deare then ... children' (sig. H), and rejecting Charmian's appeal to her maternal duty:

> *Ch.* Liue for your sonnes. Cl. Nay for their father die.
> *Ch.* Hardhearted mother! Cl. Wife kindhearted I.
>
> (sig. H3)

It is Cleopatra's self-definition as a wife, then, that validates her identity as a lover over alternative roles. Yet this too the play undermines. Krontiris has argued that it legitimises the lovers' relationship by deploying the vocabulary of marriage, and Lamb claims that Cleopatra appears as a 'faithful wife'.[50] Yet comments by other characters, and the off-stage presence of Antony's wife, work against this impression. Octavia provides an alternative model of female virtue in the play; she is chaste and silent, and the Argument (Sidney's own) associates her with her 'excellent Children' (sig. F). Antony contrasts the two women:

> In wanton loue a woman thee misleades
> Sunke in foule sinke: meane while respecting nought
> Thy wife *Octauia* and her tender babes ...
>
> (sig. F4)

It is only Cleopatra who images herself as a wife. Charmian tells her:

> And you for some respect of wiuelie loue,
> (Albee scarce wiuelie) loose your natiue land,
> Your children, frends, and (which is more) your life.
>
> (sigs H3v–H4)

By emphasising Cleopatra's roles as wife and mother, but portraying them as mutually exclusive, Sidney thus both elevates and undermines her.

The ennobling effect of Cleopatra's love should not lead us to believe, along with earlier critics of the play, that Garnier or Sidney completely desexualises her.[51] Cleopatra's descriptions of herself again conflict with other representations in the play. She has only a few clearly erotic lines, which are delivered over Antony's dead body:

My bodie ioynde with thine, my mouth with thine,
My mouth, whose moisture burning sighes haue dried
To be in one selfe tombe, and one selfe chest,
And wrapt with thee in one selfe sheete to rest.

(sig. O2)

While the confinement of erotic language to this speech may 'purify' and elevate her, it clashes with the characterisation of Cleopatra in terms of erotic linguistic control with which we began, and also conflicts with Antony's descriptions of her. Yet the consistency with which he characterises her as sexual, whether praising or condemning her, suggests that no representation of Cleopatra is likely to escape this category. She is his 'faire, entising foe' (sig. K4v) even when he declares her 'more deare then life to me' (sig. I4v), and his desire for the 'Image [which] haunts my minde' (sig. K) repeats the terms used when he attacks her as his 'Idoll' (sig. F3).

Sidney's selection of vocabulary, however, allows Cleopatra to anticipate a charge of sexual misconduct. In contrasting Caesar's definition of Cleopatra's conduct with Cleopatra's own, Sidney again translates two French words as one. Caesar defines the relationship between the lovers as a sharing of 'leud delights' (sig. L4v). Cleopatra, however, had defined 'lewdness' as infidelity, and from such lewdness she firmly dissociates herself. She refuses to live on as Antony's widow because it might be said that

... in hard estate
I for another did him lewdlie leaue.

(sig. H4v)[52]

Cleopatra's definition and repudiation of immorality thus ennobles her and answers Caesar. Yet elsewhere she partially capitulates to the images imposed on her by others. Although she had denied 'ensnar[ing]' him (sig. G4v), she finally calls Antony 'deare husband, whome my snares entrap'd' (sig. N3v). Her definition of their relationship as a marriage here proves compatible with an awareness of her dangerous sexual power.

Cleopatra's attitude to her political role displays a similar ambivalence. She rejects the idea of her duty to her country, and this in itself is problematised by Diomede and Philostratus, who lament the destructive effect of her love on her people.[53] Diomede, moreover, advocates a sexual/political strategy which he sees as essential for Egypt:

> . . . if hir teares
> She would conuert into hir louing charmes,
> To make a conquest of the conqueror,
> (As well shee might, would she hir force imploie)
> She should vs saftie from these ills procure.
>
> (sig. I2)

Although Cleopatra rejects the explicit deployment of sexuality for political ends, it remains possible to attribute political motivation to her actions. Caesar refers to Antony's gift to her of Syria, Arabia, Lydia and Cyprus (sig. Mv), while Antony claims:

> . . . Too wise a head she weare [*sic*]
> Too much enflam'd with greatnes, euermore
> Gaping for our great Empires gouernment.
>
> (sig. I4v)

Cleopatra herself emphasises her royalty, referring to her 'royall hart' (sig. G4v) and reminding her children they 'were borne / Of such a Princelie race' (sig. N4v). The defeat at Actium suggests, moreover, that all her actions have a political effect regardless of her motivation. As the play underlines, the sexual and the political are inevitably congruent; Antony (her 'Lord, my King' (sig. G4v)) imagines himself 'vnarm'de' by Cleopatra and 'yeelded to *Cæsar* naked of defence' (sig. F2v).

The characterisation of Cleopatra as 'princely' is a feature specific to Sidney's translation. As well as this reminder to her children (above), Lucilius asserts, 'too high a heart she beares, / Too Princelie thoughts' (sig. L4v); in neither case is the word 'princely' Garnier's.[54] Not only ennobling in itself, this term also recalls Elizabeth's use of the term for herself, in preference to 'queen' or 'princess'.[55] Any implied parallel is likely to elevate Cleopatra, rather than denigrate Elizabeth: a wise strategy considering Fulke Greville's claim to have burned his version of the story for fear of offending her.[56]

While I have dwelt on the problems inherent in reading Cleopatra as virtuous and heroic, there is no doubt that despite the tensions surrounding her, she is presented in a comparatively sympathetic light.[57] Yet, as a notorious *femme fatale*, she inevitably relates to the sexually powerful females who proliferate in contemporary literature. The taste for such female characters is manifested in the 1590s in both drama and poetry, particularly the epyllion.[58] However, the balance or tension which characterises Cleopatra's portrayal – between denigrating and elevating, or between sexualising and purifying – more specifically recalls the complex balance of sympathy and horror integral to the 'female complaint'.

Sidney's translation of *The Triumph of Death* intersects strikingly with this genre. As we know, the female complaint manifests a taste for female characters both fallen and sympathetic. *The Second Chapter of the Triumph of death* participates in this vogue by presenting an eloquent female spirit who addresses her lover with a freedom she would not have had during her lifetime.[59] Her speech occupies most of this section of the poem and she marginalises the poet's voice by telling him they have no time for his response:

> [Aurora] to my sorrowe, calles me hence awaie,
>   Therfore thy words in times short limits binde,
>   And saie in-brief, if more thow haue to saie.
> (ii. 181–3)[60]

Laura's linguistic power, like that of complaint women, is a 'swansong' validated by death, so that it does not suggest self-assertion. However, in this genre, rape or some other form of sexual shame figures largely. Yet, unlike Rosamond or Jane Shore, Laura is a chaste heroine, and not a fallen woman; and unlike Matilda or Lucrece she did not commit suicide, and defended her chastity against both her lover's passion and her own. Sidney's translation of the work thus interpolates into the poetry of the 1590s a heroine who delivers a long speech as a spirit, but who lacks the sexual taint of most of this genre's heroines. Moreover, she is not a victim of male aggression, but of death, over which the poem celebrates her 'triumph'. The common pattern of rape leading to suicide (or death at another's hands) finds an inversion here as the successful preservation of chastity followed by the defeat of death.

The beginning of the poem pictures Laura defeating Death:

> ... not with sword, with speare or bowe,
>   But with chaste heart, faire visage, upright thought,
>   wise speache, which did with honor linked goe.
> (i. 7–9)

This emphasis on speech fits her role in the second half of the *Triumph*, but contrasts with her characterisation of herself. The poet's connection of Laura's eloquence with honour or virtue would imply that she used her speech moderately in order to maintain her chastity. In her account, however, spoken language plays no significant part. Even when she counterfeited anger to deter her lover, her strategy was visual rather than verbal:

> A thousand times wrath in my face did flame,
> My heart meane-while with loue did inlie burne.
> (ii. 100–1)

Laura used silence and dissembling to control her lover's passion and her own, and contrasts his volubility with her restraint:

> In equale flames our louing hearts were tryde,
>     At leaste when once thy loue had notice gott,
>     But one to shewe, the other sought to hyde.
> Thow didst for mercie calle with wearie throte
>     In feare and shame, I did in silence goe,
>     So much desire became of little note.
> (139–44)

Laura's description of her desire also points to the conventions of courtly poetry, which foreground the male poet's desire at the expense of the woman's.

Whereas Lucrece and Matilda, threatened with rape, find that words only inflame their assailants further, Laura's concealment of her desire is effective in protecting her chastity. Laura thus shares with the women of the complaints an eloquence which is licensed by her death, but contrasts with them in her uncompromised purity.

*Antonius* and *The Triumph of Death*, then, intersect to different degrees with the literary trends of the 1590s. Lamb has located Cleopatra and Laura in the tradition of works in which death exonerates the heroine from sexual guilt; yet this connection on its own is unsatisfactory since, as Clarke points out, Laura does not commit suicide and neither woman is threatened with rape.[61] It is, specifically, the connection with the circumscribed female eloquence of the minor epic which provides a context for these works. The portrait of Cleopatra in *Antonius* answers a demand for heroines who are both 'fallen' and presented sympathetically. The tension between positive and negative impressions of her in the play thus aligns her with other such female characters popular at the time. Petrarch's poem licenses its heroine's speech in a way that recalls the complaint, but this heroine voices an explication of her own behavioural strategies instead of a lament. Sidney's translation thus provides a chaste speaking heroine, rather than a sexually compromised one. The result is a more positive female role-model than the complaints provide, although it shares with them its dependence on the woman's death.

That Sidney would be aware of these literary relationships is suggested by her involvement in literary culture as a patron. Daniel, whose *Rosamond* was a prominent example of the complaint genre, was a poet closely associated with her. *Rosamond*, moreover, was in 1594 published with his closet drama *Cleopatra*, a work apparently written at Sidney's request to match her own play, and which continues the process of elevating Cleopatra.[62] This pairing would seem to set a precedent for Sidney's following her translation of Garnier with the Petrarch poem later in the decade, although her *Triumph* was never published. The *Antonius*, with its simultaneously elevated yet transgressive heroine, is thus followed by the poem with its eloquent, spirit heroine. These are, of course, not the only significances of Sidney's translations, and there is no doubt that through them she also participates in political discourse of the time, as well as in these literary tastes.[63] The associations are inevitably submerged: the titles of the works do not announce, as Daniel's and other 1590s writers' do, the centrality of the female characters to them. Yet Sidney's choice of these texts at a time both when female characters were so popular and when the conditions for their eloquence and conduct were so limiting, suggests an awareness of how they would participate in this literary climate.[64]

The possibility that Cleopatra and Laura are different responses to a set of literary conventions and preferences surrounding the presentation of women in the 1590s may be one cause of the complex relationship between them. Paradoxically, the congruities between the two women both reinforce and minimise their differences. The theme of female heroism and virtue links the two women, and the prominence of their deaths strengthens this connection. Just as the emphasis on motherhood and wifeliness in the play both strengthens and undermines the elevation of Cleopatra, with Octavia's existence implicitly calling Cleopatra's claims to virtue into question, the congruences between her and Laura similarly cut both ways.[65] While both display a heroism which is seen as specifically female, the differences between them work against any simple definition of such heroism. Unlike Cleopatra, after all, Laura accepts death passively and chastely tempers her lover's ardour.

Despite the unavoidable opposition between them, however, Sidney seems to suggest a similarity between Laura and Cleopatra. Cleopatra's claim that her duty is founded on 'vertue' is matched by Laura's description of

> Our concord such in euerie thing beside,
> As when united loue and vertue be.
>
> (137–8)

More strongly, Sidney images both women as 'martyrs', by again translating different words or phrases consistently into a single word. Laura tells the poet that 'the crosse / Preceeding death, extreemelie martireth' (ii. 46–7); a description of Cleopatra is rendered, 'selfe cruell she still martireth with blowes', while Cleopatra herself tells her women, 'Martir your breasts with multiplied blowes' (sigs I2, O2v).[66] In so rendering these phrases, Sidney not only aligns the two heroines, but locates them in the line of female martyrs, sanitising their desire with this image, which we have seen to have such an effect also on women whose sexual status has been rendered problematic by rape.

The centrality of female desire provides in fact the most striking connection between the two works. Both women experience love actively, despite the obvious contrast in their conduct. The fire imagery which both Petrarch and Garnier use to characterise love helps bring out this congruity. Laura's passion is active, and a central force in the *Triumph*. Although it associates her with reason ('onelie thy flame I tempred with my cheere', l. 90), she asserts that her passion equals the poet's: 'In equale flames our louing hearts were tryde' (139). Liberated by the conventions of the genre, it is she who articulates desire. In *Antonius*, however, fire imagery signifies the peril of Cleopatra's and Antony's love. Philostratus laments that it 'hath ashes made our townes' (sig. G2v), and Diomede characterises it as a 'firebrand' which 'Laies waste the trophes of *Phillippi* fieldes' (sig. Iv). The shared emphasis on passion and its imagery thus brings Laura and Cleopatra closer together.

The two also share the eloquence which empowers them; yet their relationship to language underlines the difference between them. Cleopatra exerts political and erotic power through her eloquence. Laura uses hers, to some extent, to maintain her chastity in life; after her death, she commands it to justify her earlier conduct. Clarke argues, moreover, that Laura's manipulation of erotic discourse recalls Elizabeth, giving it a political resonance.[67] Both voices have different functions 'on-stage' and 'off', Cleopatra's power being conveyed chiefly by other characters' descriptions, and Laura's moderate use of speech in life contrasting with her volubility as a spirit. However, her voice is, as we know, validated by its 'swansong' status, a status Cleopatra's more dangerous voice lacks. A comparison of the two works, then, both strengthens and undermines Cleopatra's claims to heroic virtue. The intersection of these works in the literary taste of the 1590s partially accounts for the complex relationship between the two. At the same time, Sidney's translations – and her selection of the texts – bring the two characters into conjunction, with conflicting implications.

Lumley and Sidney both foreground the idea of female heroism and virtue, and foreground the themes of women's knowledge and discourse in ways that reflect on their own literary activities. Each negotiates a context for her works in which female sexual shame is prominent: in Lumley's case, the 'rapes' of Clytemnestra and Helen which lie behind the story, in Sidney's the taste for sexually debased or fallen women. Their negotiation of these contexts, along with the conditions circumscribing their own writing, impacts upon their portrayals of women's eloquence and desire.

# 7

# 'Vnbridled Speech': Elizabeth Cary and the Politics of Marriage

> But what sweet tune did this faire dying Swan
> Afford thine eare . . . [1]

The works of Elizabeth Cary (1585/86–1639), her closet drama *The Tragedie of Mariam* (1613) and her *History of the Life, Reign and Death of Edward II* (published in 1680 but apparently written around 1627) place women's sexual and discursive self-determination at centre-stage.[2] The issues of female sexual autonomy and linguistic power take on new meanings in the context of marriage which these works provide. Writing original works rather than translating, Cary goes further than Sidney in her engagement with her female protagonists and treats with unprecedented sympathy two characters whose portrayal in contemporary texts was far from favourable. Mariam's story was known in England primarily through the works of Josephus, translated by Lodge in 1602.[3] She argues with her husband Herod over his murder of her grandfather and brother (to secure his usurped crown) and his insistence that she should be killed in the event of his own death; for this defiance, and incited by his sister Salome, he accuses her of infidelity and executes her. Josephus's portrayal of the character (Mariamme) is largely unsympathetic, and this is a feature of other versions too.[4] The story of Edward II's neglect of his wife and her adultery and deposition of him was treated by numerous historians and poets, who generally portray Isabel as an unnatural, transgressive woman, even if they simultaneously deny her power.[5]

Having selected these unsympathetic characters, Cary rewrites their stories in two apparently contradictory ways. She heightens the transgressive nature of their conduct, but at the same time accords to each an unprecedented sympathy: the clash between these practices is a strength of the works. In both cases, the contrast between Cary's and previous versions, and – as with *Antonius* – the degree of sympathy in the portrayal, threatens to obscure such important ambivalences.[6] Yet, in *Mariam*'s case in particular, this tendency to simplify the ideological positions of the characters is largely due to the discursive strategy given to the heroine herself.

In this chapter, I argue that Cary posits the potential for rape as central to the power-relationship between the sexes, in a sourceless, interpolated scene. She also focuses on the sexual agenda of the play to inscribe Mariam's deployment of sexual resistance as a weapon in her struggle with Herod. Mariam's 'vnbridled speech' (1186) is a prominent feature of the play, and has been the prime focus of critical attention. I suggest that her discourse self-consciously reveals the erotic, political and linguistic power which it seeks to disclaim. Moreover, Mariam employs a rhetoric of chastity which conceals the transgressive nature of her conduct: a rhetoric which the Choruses repeatedly challenge. Through this reading, I argue that Cary radically destabilises the ideological opposition between chaste and transgressive women. This extends both to her portrayal of Isabel in *Edward II*, and to the relationship between Mariam and Isabel.

Herod's image of Mariam as a swan (above) seeks to impose upon her an acceptable definition of female language. Her 'swansong' would constitute little threat, unlike the 'vnbridled speech' (1186) and 'publike voyce' (1) with which she is earlier associated. Unlike the heroine-speakers of poetic 'complaints', however, Mariam's utterance characterises and determines her life, while her brief 'swansong' is reported rather than staged. The competition to define Mariam according to opposed female models finds a counterpart in Cary's treatment of Isabel. Where *Mariam* asks how a woman is to define herself publicly without thereby problematising that definition, Isabel even more self-consciously fashions images of herself, provoking anxiety in the male characters. In both texts Cary interrogates the relationship between language, sexuality and power for women.

Mariam's drama is played out against two competing contexts: an awareness of female sexual vulnerability, that is, the political and physical male power which facilitates sexual tyranny, and an alternative model of dangerous female sexuality. This complexity is intensified in the later *Edward II*. Here, the competition to define Isabel according to opposing roles is enacted both by the characters and in the text's characterisation of her. On the resultant tension is based the sympathy for Isabel which characterises her portrayal until her invasion of England. With success (which is not Mariam's lot) Isabel forfeits such sympathy; this is the price Cary pays for portraying her as powerful and self-determining.

*Mariam* and *Edward II* are poised generically between the public and the private, the one a published closet drama, the other a prose history with substantial portions in dramatic verse, published only posthumously. Ambivalent themselves, these texts also stage the clash between the private and public realms for their protagonists: a tension which modern criticism of Cary, much of which has been biographically based, tends to reflect.[7] Recent criticism of *Mariam*, however, has suggested that its dramatic colour brings it closer to public drama than most 'closet' plays, and that this may reflect the influence of Cary's recorded enthusiasm for theatre-going.[8] We shall see that *Mariam* contains echoes of Shakespeare's *Othello*, while both Cary's works share much imagery with another 'public' dramatist, Webster.[9] Textual as well as thematic associations thus locate them in a complex relationship with the public domain and highlight their ambivalent status: a published closet drama and an unpublished verse and prose history. This interplay between the public and private is analogous to the simultaneous connection and tension between the public and private in the lives of Cary's women protagonists.

*Mariam* in fact reworks tensions that characterise many stage plays. Plays that present rape or attempted rape, as we know, display a tension between troping chastity as powerful and conveying male physical power; they also present individual chaste women as exceptions to a general female promiscuity. In *Mariam*, the competition between chastity and male physical power is equally important, but works differently. The idea of rape, we shall see, functions tangentially: its possibility provides a model of power-relations between the sexes which reflects on Cary's portrayal of Mariam's relationship to virtue. The play thus also dismantles the polarity between female 'types' which it ostensibly sets up. This interrogation of the opposition between good and transgressive women is equally a feature of *Edward II*. Moreover, the interplay between female protagonists which characterises the relationship between Sidney's Cleopatra and Laura proves significant here too, as Cary interrogates the relationship between women's utterance and their sexual autonomy.

Both works engage tangentially with the period's preoccupation with women rulers. Cary wrote *Mariam* comparatively soon after the death of Elizabeth I.[10] Like Mary Sidney, she uses Elizabeth's term 'prince' three times of Mariam, and Mariam, like Elizabeth, deploys the idea of chastity as a means of self-empowerment.[11] In this play the compatibility of power with virtue becomes the subject of debate – a debate which intensifies in *Edward II*, where the possible roles open to a royal female come under scrutiny.

The anxiety which adheres to these concerns intersects with another contemporary preoccupation: the possibility of adulterous wives murdering their husbands.[12] A few well-documented cases of husband-murder triggered a spate of literary versions, and conduct literature reflects an anxiety related to these notorious events.[13] This provides a backdrop to Cary's works. If Herod wrongfully suspects Mariam of plotting his death, Isabel's key role in the deposition and murder of her husband suggests retrospectively the validity of his anxiety.

## 'PURE AT MY REQUEST': *THE TRAGEDIE OF MARIAM*

> You haue preserued me pure at my request,
> Though you so weake a vassaile might constraine
> To yeeld to your high will . . .
>
> (606–8)

The gratitude of the lowly handmaid Graphina towards her lover Pheroras, Herod's brother, reflects the power-relationship between men and women in and beyond the world of Cary's play. Far from the passive creature critics have made of her,[14] Graphina displays a command of language which she uses on-stage to praise her lover, but off-stage to articulate her resistance to his sexual advances, as the passage above indicates. The model she posits here is one which admits the possibility or even likelihood of rape, particularly of a lower-class woman by the man who is her 'Lord' (590) socially as well as emotionally. For Graphina, literally Pheroras's 'hand-maid' (604), the phrase 'so weake a vassaile' is poised between a sense of physical weakness and one of social inferiority, and both render her vulnerable to rape.

While Graphina is not as radical in her speaking as Mariam, whose 'vnbridled speech' is blamed for her downfall, she is far from conforming to the model of passive feminine silence. Her dialogue with Pheroras debates the functions and impact of women's utterance. Her speech follows his exhortation:

> Why speaks thou not faire creature? moue thy tongue,
> For Silence is a signe of discontent.
>
> (586–7)

Graphina's speech is thus a direct, though licensed, assertion of her right to express herself. She even echoes Pheroras by referring to her 'mouing tongue' (598). Pheroras's opposition between silence/discontent and (presumably) speech/contentment is a problematic one. Graphina is in fact the only woman in either work who uses speech to voice happiness rather than dissent or resistance. Moreover, her claim to have 'request[ed]' celibacy suggests that her speech too has been used to express resistance. By Pheroras's model, however, female language can express only satisfaction: specifically, with the male lover and his conduct.[15] Graphina's gratitude for his encouragement and his sexual restraint implies that both her verbal and her sexual autonomy are dependent on male good 'will' (608).

Graphina does not simply mirror a 'chaste' side of Mariam. Her active choice of chastity is a sign not only of autonomy but of worldly-wisdom: an awareness that few liaisons between noblemen and servants end in marriage. She both asserts and subordinates herself, claiming sexual autonomy but acknowledging male sexual power. This portrait, which is sourceless, provides a reading model for Mariam's story by interrogating the function of women's utterance and establishing female sexual vulnerability and resistance as a dynamic of the play.

This interchange is a key part of Cary's rewriting of her source to focus on the sexual agenda of Mariam's story. Graphina's vulnerability to rape is a function of courtship as opposed to marriage. Nevertheless, the interpolation of her story into Mariam's sets up a parallel between her relationship with Pheroras and Mariam's marriage, which may be enhanced by Mariam's craving for a still lower social position:

> Yet had I rather much a milke-maide bee,
> Then be the Monarke of *Iudeas* Queene.
>
> (59–60)

The portrait of Graphina gives the lie to this fantasy of carefree lower-class existence; not least because Graphina does prove subject to Herod's power, when he forces Pheroras to give her up.[16]

Cary focuses on the sexual conflict between Herod and Mariam by condensing the action, by making Mariam's refusal to sleep with her husband central to the play, and by locating that decision in the context of contemporary marital ideology. When she learns of Herod's imminent return from his visit to Rome, and knowing that he had ordered her death in the event of his own, Mariam articulates her determination to resist him sexually and emotionally:

> I will not to his loue be reconcilde,
> With solemne vowes I haue forsworne his Bed.
> (1135–6)

Herod anticipates a passionate response from Mariam; he apostrophises her:

> Be patient but a little, while mine eyes
> Within your compast limits be contain'd:
> That obiect straight shall your desires suffice,
> From which you were so long a while restrain'd.
> (1290–3)

After this, Mariam's articulation of 'discontent' (1357) and her scepticism about his love for her make clear her adherence to her vow. She upbraids him:

> No, had you wisht the wretched *Mariam* glad,
> Or had your loue to her bene truly tide:
> Nay, had you not desir'd to make her sad,
> My brother nor my Grandsyre had not dide.
> (1376–9)

This combines two moments from Josephus. The charge of not loving her comes from an earlier episode, where it is backed up by her knowledge of Herod's command that she should be killed if he dies.[17] The reference to the murders, however, comes directly from the scene in which Mariamme 'would not lie with him, nor entertaine his courtings with friendly acceptance' (p. 398). Although this is more explicit than in Cary's version, it has less impact because it occurs a year after Herod's return.

By unifying the time-scale and anticipating both Herod's sexual demands and Mariam's resistance, Cary clarifies and intensifies the

sexual nature of the conflict between them.[18] Herod's awareness of
the sexual implications of Mariam's rejection of him immediately
provokes his murderous anger and facilitates his assumption that she
is unfaithful. When he describes her after death as 'the partner of
my now detested bed' (2134), the ambivalence of the wording – the
fact that she rejected him in life as well as abandoning him in death
– underlines the reason for her execution.

Mariam's resistance is both sexual (physical) and verbal (mental).
This equivalence implies a contiguity of mind and body, which becomes a contentious issue in the play. By refusing to sleep with
Herod in punishment for his behaviour, she rejects the conventional
opposition of the two. However, Salome's slander and Herod's
belief in it derive from the contrary position. Herod defines Mariam
as a 'faire fiend' with 'heauy semblance' (1477–8):

> ... Hell it selfe lies hid
> Beneath thy heauenly show.
> (1467–8)

Salome argues that Mariam's body refuses to register its sins: she
'wil neuer blush, / Though foule dishonors do her forehead blot'
(1677–8); and that her eloquence is deceptive:

> She speaks a beautious language, but within
> Her heart is false as powder: and her tongue
> Doth but allure the auditors to sinne,
> And is the instrument to doe you wrong.
> (1701–4)

This is opposed by Mariam's assertion that 'if faire she be, she is as
chaste as faire' (1856), and Herod accepts this position after her
death (2181–8). Yet the act of execution itself, paradoxically, confirms Mariam's assertion. Herod images death as 'losse of breath'
(1482); by destroying her capacity for speech as well as her body,
execution confirms the contiguity of mind and body. The end of
the play effects yet another reversal, encouraging us to read Mariam
as defeating Herod on a spiritual level despite his destruction of
her body.

Details of Mariam's death associate her with Christ.[19] This makes
of her a martyr, so that she, like Cleopatra and Laura, can be associated with the female martyrs in a way that elevates her above the

ambiguities of her life. The association of mind and body employed in this tradition conventionally portrays women as mentally or spiritually transcending the physical suffering of rape; in Mariam's case, it combines with Graphina's perspective to point to another course of action open to Herod. By raping her, it implies, he would defeat a rebellion both physical and mental. If Pheroras, the brother of the king, has the power to make a woman 'yeeld to [his] high will', Herod should be even more capable of such an action. The analogy between regal and husbandly power is, of course, a commonplace.[20] Herod's equation between his political and his verbal power – 'My word though not my sword made *Mariam* bleed' (2131) – alerts us to the missing third term in the equation: they are not, as they might be, matched with sexual power. On the contrary, his execution of Mariam in response to her denial registers his sexual disempowerment.

In symbolic terms, then, the execution might be read as a substitute for rape. Herod's reference to Jove and Leda retrospectively suggests this:

> . . . *Ioue*, if *Ioue* he were, would sure desire,
> To punish him that slew so faire a lasse:
> For *Lædaes* beautie set his heart on fire,
> Yet she not halfe so faire as *Mariam* was.
> (2157–60)

Like the analogies in other plays of the period, which deploy rape stories while rewriting or ignoring the rape, Herod's speech has two effects. Ostensibly, it contrasts the two couples, yet by bringing them together, it makes rape available as an analogy for Herod's action. This analogy, however, is effected primarily in retrospect. The execution itself is neither staged (as with classical drama, it takes place off-stage), nor reported using erotic language (indeed, the Nuntio's account is taken up with his relation of her final speech: the act of execution is announced in a single line (2032)). Where prose fiction frequently eroticises scenes where no rape occurs, as well as those where murder fulfils a narrative demand for rape, *Mariam* actually purges the execution of any such associations. The analogy between the execution and rape is thus posited retrospectively instead of by means of eroticising the violence itself. Cary thus focuses on the sexual conflict in the play without providing titillation with scenes of sexual action or threat.

\*\*\*

The wife hath not power over her own body, but the husband: and likewise also the husband hath not power over his own body, but the wife.

Defraud ye not one the other . . .

(1. Corinthians 7.4–5)

Throughout *Mariam*, images of women's sexual vulnerability clash with images of their sexual power. Mariam's stance of celibacy and her alignment with Graphina in this sort attempt to define her as a paragon of chastity. However, Cary's introduction of a Chorus into the play facilitates the voicing of contemporary marital ideology which contradicts this definition. Such ideology implicitly defines Mariam as *un*chaste, both because of her refusal to satisfy her husband and because of her intrinsic sexual power.

The Choruses echo the ideas on marriage to be found in contemporary conduct literature. The most significant text is Paul's injunction above, which is referred to as 'due benevolence' and forbids either partner to refuse sexual relations if the other demands them.[21] One justification for this rule points to a connection in *Mariam* between Mariam's rejection of Herod and his conviction that she is unfaithful: 'such vnfaithfull desertion is almost neuer separated from adultery'.[22] Although the marriage debt is mutual,[23] the emphasis is on uxorial subordination. According to Whately, 'she must be a monstrous and vnwomanly woman, that being drawne by [her husband's] entreatie will not yeeld' (p. 29). A definition of chastity thus emerges which ensures the sexual compliance of the wife. Marital chastity involves not only fidelity but the fulfilment of sexual duty. Vives states that a wife may not make a vow of chastity since her body 'is in an others power'.[24] The consequences of such a vow are rarely contemplated, and the idea of marital rape barely conceived of.

Strictly speaking, then, Mariam does not merit her claim to chastity. When Herod accuses her of being 'vnchaste' (1705) he is correct in ideological terms, although she has not committed adultery. That she achieves autonomy through sexual abstinence allows her to claim chastity, the cardinal female virtue, for herself; indeed, she convinces many characters of the legitimacy of this claim, eventually including Herod.

The Chorus echoes the marriage tracts:

When to their Husbands they themselues doe bind,
Doe they not wholy giue themselues away?

> Or giue they *but their body* not their mind,
> Reseruing that though best, for others pray?
>                              (1237–40; my emphasis)

More significant than its brief challenging of the wife's right to mental independence is the *un*challenged assumption of this passage:
that with marriage a woman forfeits any right to sexual autonomy.
The connection between resistance and infidelity appears here too,
in relation to the mind: denial of the husband's control leaves a
vacuum for other men.

The Chorus to Act IV, following the confrontation scene and Mariam's farewell, glorifies submission to reinforce the idea that Mariam
is rebelling against a duty. It advocates 'scorni[n]g to reuenge an ini-
urie' (1905), regardless of the oppressor's character. This argument is
located subtly in the sexual context:

> We say our hearts are great and cannot yeeld,
> Because they cannot yeeld it proues them poore.
>                              (1916–17)

The implicit accusation here of refusing to 'yield' is followed by a list
of actions which a 'noble heart' should 'scorne', particularly 'to owe
a dutie ouer-long' (1922–3). The final stanza makes the application
clear:

> Had *Mariam* scorn'd to leaue a due vnpaide,
> Shee would to *Herod* then haue paid her loue.
>                              (1934–5)

The concept of 'due benevolence' thus condemns Mariam. It is not
the first appearance of the idea. Mariam recalls in her opening
speech that her rage against Herod 'kept [her] heart from paying
him his debt' (24); her vow of celibacy adds the sexual implications
to the term.

However, a wider interrogation of the nature of 'debt' in relationships contextualises Mariam's position. Salome proposes to her husband a warped model of emotional debt:

> If once I lou'd you, greater is your debt:
> For certaine tis that you deserued it not.
>                              (479–80)

This flawed argument further loses credibility when she uses it to validate her claim to divorce. A third model of 'debt', this time between friends, receives more serious treatment. Babus's sons tell Constabarus that their 'liues as sau'd by you, to you are due' (636), but he counters that 'With friends there is not such a word as det' (648). His rejection of 'strong necessitie' (1574) in friendships destabilises the Chorus's insistence on Mariam's duty to her husband.

Another context may be available for this debate. *Mariam* stages, though without foregrounding, the conflict between spouses of different faiths and races, Mariam's Judaism versus Herod's 'Mongrell' race, 'party Iew ... party Edomite' (244, 243); biographical criticism of Cary has drawn the parallel between this and her own marital situation.[25] The ideological definition of chastity voiced by the Chorus is fundamentally a Protestant one. The Catholic position, although far from advocating that wives deny their husbands, does praise abstention from marital intercourse in a way that Protestantism does not.[26] Vives goes so far as to praise women who vow chastity without considering their husbands.[27] Mariam's action, then, is partially validated by Catholicism; this intensifies the tension between different positions contextualising her within the play.

The fourth Chorus's list of actions the virtuous woman should reject culminates in 'to scorne a free-borne heart slaue-like to binde' (1927). With an ambivalence characteristic of the play's presentation of Mariam, this leaves unclear whether it is her own heart that a woman should not subdue, or a man's. The surrounding material, however, which advocates humility and bowing even to a foe, suggests the latter. This recalls the injunction against sexual excess within marriage, which causes greater concern among the marriage theorists than the issue of one partner rejecting the other.[28] Behind this lies the fear that female sexuality once unleashed can prove insatiable. Like celibacy, Vives claims that it can cause adultery:

Be not thou *that* desireste to haue a chaste wife ... *the* firste that shall inflame her to letchery, and to thinke euyll.[29]

An 'vnbridled' wife, then, is liable both to commit adultery and to dominate her husband. The third Chorus combines its assertion that husbands own their wives with an attack on marital excess and on Mariam's bid for glory. It argues that 'tis thanke-worthy, if she will not take / All lawfull liberties for honours sake' (1229–30), suggestive of the excess in married ('lawfull') intercourse prohibited by the theorists. Its condemnation of Mariam demonstrates that for a woman to proclaim her virtue or take a stand in its name is a contradiction in terms:

> And euery mind though free from thought of ill,
> That out of glory seekes a worth to show:
> When any's eares but one therewith they fill,
> Doth in a sort her purenes ouerthrow.
>
> (1249–52)

Even the implication of 'but one', that to speak to a husband is safe, is to be proved false.

Herod's anxiety about Mariam's hold over him matches the Chorus's injunction against women's subordination of their husbands. In the confrontation scene he warns her, 'build not on my loue' (1409). As well as warning her not to presume on his affection (a presumption to which she later admits (1799–1802)), this intimates an anxiety about her sexual power – her capacity to 'build' on his lust by tempting him sexually. He confirms this a few lines later:

> Yet let your looke declare a milder thought,
> My heart againe you shall to *Mariam* binde.
>
> (1415–16)

He refers subsequently to his 'bondage' (1766) to Mariam, and claims that she has 'fetter[ed]' his wit and locked up his heart (1489, 1493).

Herod's sense of Mariam's power over him enhances our reading of an anomalous passage in one of his speeches. After accusing Mariam of attempting to murder him he tells her:

> . . . Yet neuer wert thou chast:
> Thou might'st exalt, pull downe, command, forbid,
> And be aboue the wheele of fortune plast.
>
> (1468–70)

The incongruity of female power (whether sexual or political) and chastity accounts for his accusation in the first line: her power over him is a departure from the feminine ideal comparable with being unchaste. If 'neuer' is deleted, Herod's accusation becomes a condition; this too is incongruous, as it loses the equation between such power and the absence of chastity which the play underlines.[30]

Herod's belief in Mariam's adultery, after all, is closely linked with her ability to command, whether it is by smiling on him or by rejecting him.[31] His accusations also register the congruence of sexual and linguistic power in Mariam's rebellion. He images her as a kind of *vagina dentata*: 'shee's vnchaste, / Her mouth will ope to eu'ry strangers eare' (1705–6). This creates her as the sexual aggressor, although represented by the mouth which is both the site of her language and equivalent to the vagina.

Mariam's presentation of herself is open to as wide a range of interpretation as her conduct. Like Sidney's Cleopatra, her renunciations of power display her awareness of it. She boasts, illogically:

> I know I could inchaine [Herod] with a smile:
> And lead him captiue with a gentle word,
> I scorne my looke should euer man beguile,
> Or other speech, then meaning to afford.
> (1166–9)

The subsequent claim, 'O what a shelter is mine innocence' (1174), loses credibility after this certainty of power. Her claims to reject political power display the same duality. She asserts:

> Not to be Emprise of aspiring *Rome*,
> Would *Mariam* like to *Cleopatra* liue.
> (204–5)

This does not imply that she would reject power consistent with purity; yet whether this is possible for a woman is a fraught question, ideologically and in this play. Herod's charge, 'with vsurpers name I *Mariam* staine' (1494), articulates the connection between political and sexual rebellion.

Mariam's political power itself is a strong force in the play. As the descendant of Sara, her right to the throne is stronger than Herod's, the usurper. This infiltrates even her final claim:

> You Princes great in power, and high in birth,
> Be great and high, I enuy not your hap:
> Your birth must be from dust: you power on earth,
> In heau'n shall *Mariam* sit in *Saraes* lap.
> (1845–8)

Mariam's political empowerment through Sara, 'on earth' as well as 'in heau'n', undermines this speech. Sohemus actually reveals that, when believing Herod dead, she claimed power on her son's behalf (1196–9); this retrospective glimpse of her political self-assertion is not in Josephus. After the execution, Herod wonders why the Jews do not rise against him (2115–16). The final Chorus provides a further perspective on this:

> This morning *Herod* held for surely dead,
> And all the *Iewes* on *Mariam* did attend ...
> (2208–9)

Whether the Jews were waiting to see how she would act, or whether they were actually rallying round her, is once again ambiguous.

Alexandra asserts Mariam's potential to have gained political power not through her blood but through her sexual attractions:

> More Kings then one did craue,
> For leaue to set a Crowne vpon her head.
> (221–2) [32]

Moreover, if she had sent her portrait to Anthony,

> His life from *Herod*, *Anthony* had taken:
> He would haue loued thee, and thee alone,
> And left the browne *Egyptian* cleane forsaken.
> (193–5)

Mariam's mother thus suggests that Mariam might have brought about Herod's death, as well as triumphing over Cleopatra. Cary thus brings this suggestion closer to Mariam than in Josephus, where the idea that Anthony might fall in love with Mariamme is Herod's (p. 387).

In fact, Mariam's triumph over Cleopatra was not in winning Anthony from her, but in keeping Herod despite Cleopatra's attempts to seduce him:

> ... her allurements, all her courtly guile,
> Her smiles, her fauours, and her smooth deceit:
> Could not my face from *Herods* minde exile,
> But were with him of lesse then little weight.
> (1815–18)

While Mariam eschews 'guile', her celebration of this superiority undermines her claim to purity. Her enjoyment of her victory over Herod's first wife Doris is also striking. Her boast,

> He not a whit his first borne sonne esteem'd,
> Because as well as his he was not mine:
> My children onely for his owne he deem'd,
> These boyes that did descend from royall line,
> (140–3)

underlines her political position, and contradicts her prior assertion, 'Nor did I glorie in her ouerthrowe' (139).

Doris, like Octavia in *Antonius*, provides a reminder of the ambivalence of Mariam's marital status as a second wife. She claims:

> You in adultry liu'd nine yeare together,
> And heau'n will neuer let adultry in.
> (1851–2)

Mariam claims that 'If faire she be, she is as chaste as faire' (1856) and cites a biblical source to support her position (1861ff.), but when Doris curses her and her sons, begs her, 'let it thee suffice, / That Heau'n doth punishment to me allow' (1880–1). Her apparent concession that she is receiving divine justice may be insincere, to protect her sons; yet even with this motive, insincerity would seem inimical to her claims about her honesty in speech (1169).[33]

Mariam's revolt, then, falls short of adultery, but undermines her claims to chastity and innocence. As the comparison with Cleopatra and with Alexandra's hypotheses demonstrates, her conduct is in many cases a legitimised version of rebellion. Her assumption of political power is validated by her belief in Herod's death, her triumph over Cleopatra by the fact that she is Herod's wife, her victory over Doris by the validity of divorce for men in Jewish law, her renunciation of Herod's bed by its ready alignment with the idea of celibacy rather than adultery. Yet in each case the validation falls short of what is required. The resultant tension, which the presence of Doris and the Chorus heightens, challenges Mariam's rhetoric of chastity and virtue, without detracting from the sympathy in the portrayal.

In underlining the ambivalence of Mariam's conduct and claims, Cary brings her closer to the 'bad' female character, Salome, than the ostensible contrast between them in the play would suggest.[34]

Mariam tells Salome: 'With thy blacke acts ile not pollute my breath' (252). The striking similarities between them, however, not only enhance our sense of Mariam's self-determination but do also threaten to 'pollute' her. It is Salome who proclaims the right of women to divorce, vowing to be the 'custome-breaker' (319), but Mariam's sexual repudiation of Herod is an effective divorce almost as radical and transgressive. Verbal parallels bring out the proximity of their positions; Mariam's 'I haue forsworne his Bed' (1136), for instance, echoes Salome's 'now I must diuorse him from my bed' (327). Despite Salome's protestations, a sexual, non-legal divorce is after all the only kind available to her too, as a woman. She is eventually 'diuorst' (ll. 1339, 2216) only by enraging Constabarus to the point of renouncing her.

Salome's motivation in seeking sexual autonomy – 'varietie' – fulfils the model found in conduct literature and threatens to pollute Mariam by association. The Chorus, like Herod, attribute this motivation to Mariam:

> Still *Mariam* wisht she from her Lord were free,
> For expectation of varietie.
>
> (532–3)

Mariam herself comes perilously close to justifying a second love, in terms which prefigure Salome's charge to Constabarus, 'thy Iealousie procures my hate so deepe' (432):

> . . . *Herods* Iealousie
> Had power euen constancie it selfe to change:
> For hee by barring me from libertie,
> To shunne my ranging, taught me first to range.
>
> (25–8)

Despite her denial that she could love another (29–30), 'range' has connotations which Salome's promiscuity seems to confirm.[35]

Mariam's rhetoric of chastity, then, deliberately masks the transgressive nature of her insistence on autonomy and of her manipulation of sexual resistance in her battle with Herod. That the play's characters eventually declare her unanimously to be virtuous, however, suggests not only that Mariam's definition of herself has prevailed, but that Cary has radically distinguished 'virtue' from 'chastity' and defined it instead as truth to oneself.

## 'LOUE IN CRIMSON CARACTERS': MARIAM AND HEROD

After Mariam's death, Herod laments: 'Were I not made her Lord, I still should bee' (2011). This perception that male power (the analogy between husband and ruler is particularly potent here) can destroy the marriage in which it operates, is central to Cary's complex presentation of marriage. Cary's Mariam differs from Josephus's not only in her radicalism, but also in the depth of emotion she is shown to feel for Herod. In the *Antiquities* she finds her life with him 'very intolerable' (p. 397), while in the *Warres* she hates him (p. 589). Cary's play, by contrast, dramatises the conflict between the imperatives of power and desire.

The play opens with Mariam attempting to rationalise the complexity of her feelings for Herod. Believing him dead, she feels again 'the loue I bare him then, / When virgin freedome left me vnrestraind' (73–4): an association of courtship with sexual freedom which is in direct opposition with Graphina's sense of vulnerability. Herod's tyranny over Mariam is sexual as well as political, whether because of her duty to him or her passion for him.

Herod too is poised between the extremes of love and hatred. He tells Mariam, 'euen for loue of thee / I doe profoundly hate thee' (1464–5). After three acts in which he is portrayed in his absence as a tyrant, the romanticism of his first speeches (1258–62, 1264–99) comes as a shock. Alexandra's demand of her daughter, 'readst thou loue in crimson caracters?' (113), proves apt, for Herod's love is at once genuine and not preclusive of the murder of Mariam's relations or herself. Mariam recognises this love for what it is. She refers to 'his loue for me' (57) without scepticism, and her description of 'him that saues for hate, and kills for loue' (64), if bitter, is accurate. His resolution on executing her epitomises the dual nature of his passion:

> For neither shall my loue prolong thy breath,
> Nor shall thy losse of breath my loue remoue.
>
> (1481–2)

Herod's combination of love and hatred for the wife he eventually murders recalls Othello's relationship with Desdemona. It is credible that Cary might have seen *Othello*, first performed in 1604. The intrinsic similarity of the two plots is heightened by further parallels, and Cary's play has been linked with Shakespeare's in early textual criticism of the latter.[36] Where Othello alludes to the 'base Indian' (or, in the Folio, 'base Iudean') who 'threw a pearl away, / Richer than all his tribe' (V.ii.348–9),[37] Herod laments:

> I had but one inestimable Iewell,
> Yet one I had no monarch had the like,
> And therefore may I curse my selfe as cruell:
> Twas broken by a blowe my selfe did strike.
>                                         (2061–4)

His rationalisation of her murder recalls Othello's 'Yet she must die, else she'll betray more men' (V.i.6):

> Thou shalt not liue faire fiend to cozen more,
> With heauy semblance, as thou cousnedst mee.
>                                         (1477–8)

The anxiety Herod betrays over his wife's sexual power has, too, been attributed to Othello.[38] Where Othello tells Desdemona 'I will kill thee, / And love thee after' (V.ii.18–19), Herod tells Salome:

> . . . Why let my loue be slaine,
> But if we cannot liue without her sight
> Youle finde the meanes to make her breathe againe,
> Or else you will bereaue my comfort quite.
>                                         (1657–60)

After her death he accordingly asks the Nuntio, 'Is there no tricke to make her breathe againe?' (2031). His impulse is comparable to the necrophiliac implications of the Talmudic version of the story, in which Herod preserves Mariamne's body.[39] Cary's intensification to the point of ludicrousness of Herod's wish to recall his wife reveals the desire of these tragic protagonists for absolute power over the love object, and their ultimate impotence.

### 'ONE INESTIMABLE IEWELL': MARIAM AND ISABEL

> Thou gavest me birth, and yet denyest me being; . . .
> . . . Thou to me art like a graceless mother,
> That suckles not, but basely sells her children . . .
> The poorest soul that claims in thee a dwelling

Is far more happy than thy royal issue.
But time will come thou wilt repent this error,
If thou remember this my just prediction;
My offspring will revenge a mother's quarrel,
A mother's quarrel just and fit for vengeance.

(*Edward II*, pp. 184–5)

Isabel's farewell to France illustrates both the predicament of the royal woman and the complexity of Cary's portrayal of Isabel and Isabel's construction of herself. The portrait of Isabel extends the image of queenship provided in *Mariam*, and congruities both of predicament and imagery underline the relationship between the two queens. Though neither is a queen regnant, both have or attain political power: Mariam through her blood, both through their sons and, to different degrees, through their own actions.

Where Mariam is Herod's 'one inestimable Iewell', a corresponding image of Isabel imputes to her greater agency: she is 'a jewel, which not being rightly valued, wrought [Edward's] ruin' (p. 100). Both women's value as 'jewels' is politically charged. The image of Isabel as a 'handmaid', moreover, used twice, extends the implications of *Mariam*'s deployment of Graphina to effect an awareness of uxorial subordination:

> [Isabel], seeing into the quality of the time,
> Where [Spencer] was powerful, and she in name a wife,
> In truth a handmaid . . . .
>
> (p. 130)

She also calls herself her brother's 'poor handmaid' (p. 174).[40] The image locates her in relation to the power-dynamic of marriage indicated in *Mariam*'s use of this metaphor.

Isabel takes Mariam's rebellion to the furthest extreme, fulfilling the potential implied in the ambivalences of the earlier work. She commits adultery, deposes her husband, is involved in his murder and assumes political power. In her farewell to France (above), she hovers between two roles, that of the passive political pawn, sold into marriage to cement male allegiances, and a more active political role, albeit at this point through her son. While the curse is the traditional refuge of the powerless, her portrayal of herself as a victim clashes with her self-determination even up to this point, and with her active role in the rebellion. The implied ambivalence here relates to a wider tension in *Edward II*, manifested both in the author's portrayal of Isabel and in the attempts of other characters to categorise her.

Isabel's portrayal in the emotional and sexual domain is comparably ambivalent. Cary focuses on her political manoeuvres at the expense of her emotional and sexual needs; but she introduces the issue of adultery with an attempt to justify her conduct:

> She saw the king ... revelling in the wanton embraces of his stolen pleasures, without a glance on her deserving beauty. This contempt had begot a like change in her, though in a more modest nature, her youthful affections wanting a fit subject to work on, and being debarred of that warmth that should have still preserved their temper, she had cast her wandering eye upon the gallant Mortimer. (p. 166)

Cary portrays Isabel here as less culpable in adultery than her husband. Yet the image of the queen as a wronged wife with youthful impetuosity sits uneasily with the further depiction of the relationship with Mortimer. The 'silent rhetoric' of their 'sparkling love' is imaged as 'private trading [which] needs few words or brokage' (p. 166). The pragmatism implied by this metaphor is confirmed when

> with a sweet correspondency, and the interchange of many amorous letters, their hearts are brought together, and their several intents perfectly known; hers, to prosecute her journey; his, to purchase his freedom, and to wait upon her. (pp. 166–7)

The incongruity between the 'amorousness' of their letters and the practicality of their 'intents' underlines the political agenda of the liaison. However, the relationship receives no further attention. Without repudiating the association in contemporary thought between sexual and political rebellion (an association available in *Mariam*), Cary thus minimises attention to Isabel's sexual conduct. The connection between political or sexual and verbal licence found in the play also functions differently in *Edward II*.

The dualities indicated here in the presentation of Isabel are, to a great extent, dualities in her presentation of *herself*. Even more self-consciously than Mariam, Isabel fashions herself in ways that will win support from her male auditors or observers. In her few, but crucial speeches, this fashioning clearly involves her eloquence; elsewhere, however, her self-image is controlled as much by visual, as by verbal effects: discursive strategies in a wider sense. This leaves space for Cary to deploy images of language in a strikingly different way from *Mariam*.

*Mariam* and *Edward II* share a prevalence of images of ears, mouths and tongues, which convey the association between language and sexuality. In *Mariam* such images primarily denote female sexual and verbal power; in *Edward II*, by contrast, they are employed with reference to Edward and his minions, rather than to Isabel.[41] The association of language with a corruption at once political and sexual thus centres on the king, despite Isabel's flouting of sexual ideology. The few images of ears and tongues that are used in connection with Isabel, with one exception, seem to lack overtones of corruption.[42]

Isabel's discursive strategies receive a more complex treatment. The assertion that 'women ... make their tongues their weapons' (p. 132) prepares us for something comparable to Mariam's 'vnbridled speech'. Yet, while her eloquence plays a key role in her rebellion against her husband and ruler, she is given only a few speeches: her speeches pleading for help from France and Hainault, the farewell, and a much later speech to Mortimer arguing against the murder of Edward. This last proves ineffectual, with Isabel subsequently conceding to Mortimer; the farewell speech may be a private utterance, or overheard only by her own supporters. It is the pleas, then, that most strikingly stage Isabel's discursive powers.

Isabel's first speech to the French court is the first of three pleas for aid, and the only one which employs direct speech. Here, not only does she call herself her brother the French king's 'poor handmaid' (p. 174), but she manipulates the image of the wronged woman to win sympathy, and utilises the analogy between queen and country to enhance her plea: 'My tears speak those of a distressed kingdom' (p. 173). In so doing, she draws on the erotic fascination available for 'wronged' women:

> My blushing cheek may give a silent knowledge,
> I too much love and honour the cause of my afflictions,
>     to express it.
>
> (p. 173)

That her 'blushing cheek' is at least as important as her words is suggested when, as in her courtship of Mortimer, she employs a 'silent rhetoric' (p. 166):

> Her willing tongue would fain have moved farther;
> But here the fountain of her eyes poured forth their treasure;
> A shower of crystal tears enforced her silence;
> Which kind of rhetoric won a noble pity.
>
> (p. 174)

This first line recalls the 'moving tongues' of *Mariam*, and with it, the play's debate about the power and function of female speech. Yet if Isabel's words are emotive, her 'enforced' silence is equally so.

Isabel's 'wrong', here, is Edward's infidelity to her, which appropriately mirrors his infidelity to his kingdom. 'Wronged' women, however, are more frequently those who have 'fallen', whether or not through their own agency: these alternative definitions coincide for Isabel, because of her adultery with Mortimer. In this scene, Isabel easily imposes the definition of the wronged woman as a wronged wife, over the available definition of her as a 'fallen' woman. Shortly afterwards, however, her self-definition is drastically challenged when Edward persuades the Pope to inform the French of her treason and adultery. The definition of 'wronged' now shifts in Isabel's discourse. In her second appeal to the French, she defines it as 'slandered'. Here too, her visual impact is as important as her words:

> She falls upon her knee imploring pity,
> If not to give her aid, to right her honour,
> Which was eclipsed with so foul a slander.
> A shower of mellow tears, as mild as April's,
> Thrill down her lovely cheeks, made red with anger.
>
> (p. 180; my arrangement)

'Slander' here displaces adultery as the stain on Isabel's 'honour'.

The progressive shift from verbal to visual or sexual appeal culminates in Isabel's manipulation of the brother of the Earl of Hainault: significantly, this is successful where her persuasion of the French was not. Here, where she no longer need address the issue of adultery, she fashions herself as an attractive damsel in distress:

> She makes her winning looks (the handmaids of
> Her hopes) express their best ability,
> More to inflame the heart of her protector.
>
> (p. 190; my arrangement)

This reappearance of the 'handmaid' metaphor furthers Isabel's manipulation of her sexuality. Yet this 'protector' too is motivated partly by 'ambition of glory' (p. 190).

Cary's versions of the 'female complaint' in *Edward II*, then, draw on the same erotic fascination which we know to have fuelled the complaints of the 1590s and beyond; yet they show the woman controlling discourse to eliminate the only too available image of the fallen woman, and replace it with a definition of female 'wrong' which obliterates her sexual stain. The narrator colludes with Isabel, moreover, by marginalising the relationship with Mortimer once it has been established. Further, Isabel's 'complaints' function not to ensure her poetic 'fame' but to facilitate her assumption of political power.

The connection between sexual licence and rebellion for Isabel is thus both available and marginalised. Her deployment of sexuality both confirms the equivalence and is negated by it, as the political agenda in each case proves more compelling and receives more attention. This conflict between sexuality and political expediency mirrors a wider duality in Cary's portrayal of the queen.

Despite the emotional justification suggested by Cary for Isabel's rebellion, her actions are presented largely as the result of reason. The French, however, trivialise her by invoking passion as a feminine motivation which invalidates her arguments. Despite being 'moved' by Isabel, they refuse to help her because

> A woman's passion was too weak a motive
> To levy arms alone on that occasion.
>
> (p. 177)

Isabel's 'passion' here works against her eloquence. Cary earlier presents her caught in a battle between the two, in which reason proves the stronger. When Edward refuses to send her to France,

> Reason at length o'ercame her sex's weakness,
> And bids her rather cure than vent her passion.
>
> (p. 167; my arrangement)

Cary presents Isabel as politically astute and strong-minded. She '[sees] into the quality of the time' (p. 130) and feigns a diplomatic acceptance of Spencer. When they become enemies, he recognises her as 'a woman of a strong brain, and stout stomach, apt on all occasions to trip up his heels, if once she found him reeling' (p. 163).

Her manoeuvring to be sent to France contrasts with Edward's emotional indifference and political incompetence, and she 'courts her adversary with all the shows of perfect reconcilement' (p. 167). Cary departs from the histories and from Marlowe in making Isabel's departure self-motivated. Her departure from France too is a triumph of 'wit', as she deludes both English and French into the belief that she is returning to England when actually escaping to Hainault: 'Thus women's wit sometimes can cozen statesmen' (p. 186).

Isabel's enemies deploy a misogynistic rhetoric simultaneously to categorise her as a transgressive woman and to trivialise the threat she poses. Yet the inconsistency of the stereotypes Spencer deploys betrays an anxiety about Isabel's power. When he advocates sending her to France, he invokes two common ideas about foreign queens, suggesting both that she might be used as a 'pleader' on Edward's behalf and, alternatively, that if allowed to stay in England she might receive French spies (pp. 164–5). His assertion that 'wise men dare not trust in female weakness' (p. 165) is incongruous with the basic premise of his argument, the queen's potential power. He later describes her as 'a chamber-mischief, that was more to be feared at home, than with her brother' (p. 169). This makes of her a shrew; but the trivialising image is itself unstable. Locating this 'mischief' in the 'chamber' implies a sexual threat which is both equivalent to Isabel's political rebellion and actualised in her adultery. The political sense of 'chamber' also undermines Spencer's attempt to domesticate and trivialise Isabel.[43]

## 'A QUEEN, A WOMAN AND A VICTOR': TRIUMPH AND FEMININITY

The narratorial attitude to Isabel undergoes a marked change once she achieves political success. The portrait of Edward's corruption does, of course, imply sympathy with Isabel's cause. Several tropes, however, have simultaneously positive and negative implications for her. Nature is troped as favouring and validating Isabel's actions, aiding her journey to France and her return.[44] When she invades England she is presented as a natural, but violent, purging force: 'a thunder-shower... [which] doth make the cattle run to seek for succour' (p. 193). While aiding Isabel, 'the elements of earth, of air, of water, conspired all at once to make [Edward and Spencer] hopeless' (p. 201).

When Isabel and Mortimer escape, Cary's claim that 'the glorious power of heaven is pleased to punish man for his transgression' (p. 169) strengthens the intimation of divine sanction for Isabel's actions. This may be radical in view of her transgressive behaviour. Yet such a sanction does not necessarily validate Isabel's actions on a personal level; the idea that 'unnatural' women may be sent by God to punish male transgression abounds in misogynistic literature about female rulers.[45] Her relationship to nature is further confused when she is presented as acting against it by resorting to violence, particularly in her treatment of the Spencers. Setting out to capture Spencer and Edward she is associated with a darker side of nature and charged with blood-lust: 'Now is the queen settling her remove for Bristol, where the prey remained her haggard-fancy longed for' (p. 198).

The image of Isabel and Mortimer as 'our pilgrims' (pp. 168 and 186) is similarly ambivalent. While the image is elevating, Isabel's use of the pilgrimage as a cover for her escape may be regarded as a moral crime. The invocation of the concept of 'reformation' offers equally ambivalent implications. A term which can be associated with divine justice, it appears at the deposition parliament as a mere excuse:

> Many ways of reformation for form's sake are discussed, but the intended course was fully before resolved. (pp. 204–5)

Cary subsequently attributes the deposition 'partly [to] his own disorder and improvidence, but principally [to] the treacherous infidelity of his wife, servants and subjects' (p. 206).

Isabel's violence after the invasion prompts unprecedented criticism from the narrator:

> The queen used not to jest where she was angry;
> [Spencer's] father's end assured her inclination
> And bade him rather venture any hazard,
> Than that which must rely on female pity.
> (p. 201; my arrangement)[46]

Spencer's perception is available here behind the portrait of 'female' cruelty, but the author is clearly anxious about her protagonist's lack of mercy. She produces a similar stereotype after the murder of Arundel:

we may not properly expect reason in women's actions; it was enough the incensed queen would have it so, against which was no disputing. (p. 204)

It is at this point of greatest criticism for Isabel, in her treatment of Spencer, that Cary associates her with an equation of language with political and, implicitly, sexual power. Her visits to him appear as an orgy of sight and sound: Isabel's 'eyes with sight, and [tongue] with railing glutted' (p. 202). Yet the narrator's criticism subtly displays its patriarchal bias. When Isabel leads Spencer in progress before his execution, Cary charges her with 'a kind of insulting tyranny, far short of the belief of her former virtue and goodness' (p. 202). She leads Spencer 'not as the ancient Romans did their vanquished prisoners, for ostentation, to increase their triumph; but merely for revenge, despite, and private rancour'. The insinuation that Isabel is more culpable in this act than were her male predecessors reveals itself as gender-specific. The implicit claims that 'ostentation' is an admirable aim, while the others are not, and that the Romans would not have been motivated by 'revenge, despite, and . . . rancour', are clearly dubious; that Isabel's 'rancour' is 'private' is still more loaded. Here, where involved in a particularly public display of power, the woman is accused of acting from private emotions, personal bitterness. The charge illustrates the clash between the private and public spheres attendant on a woman's engagement in public or political action. Paradoxically, her tyranny is at once troped as specifically female and as a contravention of gender decorum.

That the criticism directed at Isabel is self-consciously predicated on gender stereotypes, is suggested by a subsequent passage in which the gender-based criticism comes from an unreliable source:

> To see such a monster so monstrously used,
> No question pleased the giddy multitude,
> Who scarcely know the civil grounds of reason.
> The recollected judgement that beheld it,
> Censured it was at best too great and deep a blemish
> To suit a queen, a woman and a victor.
>                     (pp. 203–4; my arrangement)[47]

Cary's scepticism about the integrity of the 'multitude' here challenges its condemnation.

It is not only the criticism levelled at Isabel by male opponents, then, that proves gender-specific. The same ideology adheres to the narrator's stated attitude to her after the invasion. Once on the path to success, Isabel seems to forfeit the sympathy she had largely received while striving against oppression. That she fulfils the implications of Mariam's rebellion already necessitates a more ambivalent portrayal; but that, unlike Mariam, she becomes a 'victor' effects the alienation of narratorial sympathy. The extent to which criticism of her actions reveals itself as gender-specific, however, points to an alternative position, which the author never explicitly takes up: a position which would celebrate a woman's victory over political and emotional oppression.

### 'QUOTED IN THE MARGINS'

Despite Cary's overt criticism of Isabel, she chooses to give her a more active role in the rebellion than she would have found in her sources. Most of these are unsympathetic to the queen.[48] The only version not to condemn her, Hardyng's *Chronicle*, instead disempowers her, presenting her as a mere figurehead and omitting her relationship with Mortimer. The range of versions suggests that any active political engagement by Isabel necessitates criticism, while only passivity could guarantee praise or even neutrality. Daniel, in fact, presents her as being passively led but still holds her culpable ultimately.[49]

Faced with a choice between the roles of passive 'good' woman or wronged wife, and active, transgressive, sometimes violent political agent – roles which we have seen her negotiating up until the invasion – Cary ultimately chooses the latter. In contrast to most versions she plays down Mortimer's role, barely mentioning him from the escape to France until the final scenes of the work. Isabel thus becomes the prime instigator of the rebellion and deposition, at whatever ideological cost. However, she renegotiates the balance of power between them in connection with the murder of Edward. In exonerating Isabel from the murder, inevitably, she intimates a power-dynamic with Mortimer, which once again denies Isabel agency, although she retains some scepticism about Isabel's innocence:

> The queen, whose heart was yet believed innocent of such foul murder, is, or at least seems, highly discontented; she acknowledges

[Edward's] present sufferings greater than his offences, or might
become the king, her lord and husband; and holds this act of too
too foul injustice, which styles her son a homicide and her a monster. (p. 219)

Her sincerity is borne out by her long speech arguing against the
murder, in which the competition between reason and passion as
motives appears again. The speech displays great political astute-
ness, as well as compassion; it lists concern for her soul and the
cruelty of the act, but argues that the murder would not silence their
enemies. Its conclusion, 'Ne'er can my heart consent to kill my husband' (p. 220), is inadequate as a summary of her argument and, by
implying a purely emotional motivation, facilitates Mortimer's dis-
missive response. Joining previous critics of Isabel, he accuses her of
'female weakness' (p. 221) and ignores her advice. Isabel herself then
capitulates to his categorisation of her, both by stereotyping herself
and by giving up effective power:

> ... I am a woman;
> Fitter to hear and take advice, than give it; ...
> I dare not say I yield, or yet deny it;
> Shame stops the one, the other fear forbiddeth.
> Only I beg I be not made partaker,
> Or privy to the time, the means, the manner.
> With this she weeps, and fain would have recanted,
> But she saw in that course a double danger.
>
> (p. 222)[50]

With this intimation of Mortimer's power over Isabel, Cary exonerates her from the stain of husband-murder. Although she ends the
work by attributing to Isabel the greatest responsibility for Edward's
downfall,[51] she here recreates for her the marginal position of disempowerment, indicating a sorry end beyond the limits of her text:

> The queen, who was guilty but in circumstance, and but an
> accessory to the intention, not the fact, tasted with a bitter time of
> repentance, what it was but to be quoted in the margins of such a
> story. (p. 223)

Cary does not stage the latter stages of Isabel's story.[52] Her reference
to 'repentance' might suggest personal attrition as much as political

come-uppance and punishment. The literary self-consciousness of her image of Isabel's relegation to the 'margins' of the story in which she has portrayed her as central, emphasises instead the complex relationship of women to the process in which Cary has engaged, the writing and rewriting of history.

Like Lumley and Mary Sidney, Cary depicts the cultural conditions shaping women's agency and discourse. By dramatizing her heroines' fashioning of themselves in language, she reflects back both on the issues of linguistic determination which were concerns of Lumley and Sidney, and on the vexed question of the relationship between mind and body which is an even wider preoccupation of the time. In so doing, she explores the complex interconnection between women's sexual agency and their self-definition.

# 8

# 'Liberty to say anything':
# Lady Mary Wroth

## INTRODUCTION

Ther lady euer told her owne story, and beeing, her self.[1]

The themes of female autonomy, self-determination and expression are central to the works of Lady Mary Wroth (c. 1586–1651/53).[2] Her *Urania* and its sequel, 'The secound part of the Countess of Mountgomerys Urania', contain a considerable number of rape narratives, which contrast significantly with the conventional treatment of sexual violence. Her treatment of rape, however, is interesting not only in providing such a comparison, but as an integral part of her portrayal of women's autonomy: sexual, political and linguistic.

The consciousness of the 'lady' Sophia (above), that to control narration – 'her owne story' – is to control or protect one's 'self', is paradigmatic of the treatment of narrative in Wroth's work. The *Urania* is a work of great literary self-consciousness in which many of the 'adventures' are related as 'stories', and its proliferation of female narrators and poets inevitably genders this self-consciousness. We shall see that issues of identity, virtue and agency for women are raised by their control of language in *Urania*, whether spoken or written.

In its multiplicity of plots and characters, Wroth casts and recasts narrative motifs and patterns; a motif that at one point results in attempted rape, for instance, at another produces quite a different scenario. One of the first occurrences of a rape narrative in *Urania*, the attempted rape of Antissia by two men, is a dark inversion of a prominent motif in the work: the triangular love relationship. Wroth's naming of her text and heroine 'Urania' invokes her uncle Philip Sidney's use of this relationship at the beginning of *The New Arcadia*, a work on which *Urania* is partly modelled.[3] Sidney's paradigm makes the two shepherds Strephon and Claius suffer equal passion for an absent love-object, the shepherdess Urania, who never appears in his work. Where this love triangle depends for its immutability on the absence of the love object, Wroth explores the implications both of the woman's presence and of her desire. In one recasting, the woman desires both men in return.[4] Urania herself, however, is spared any imputation of impropriety, since an enchantment achieves her change of lover for her.[5] Parselius's love for another woman, which had necessitated this change, is of course an inversion of the triangle. Another appearance of this version, with two women desiring one man, leads one character, Celina, to 'distraction'. Antissia's attempted rape shows the dangerous potential of the desire of two men for a woman who is present but undesiring.

This technique enables Wroth to explore the implications of any idea in several different ways. It also allows her to suggest darker alternatives to the stories of her two heroines, Pamphilia and Urania. These characters, as is well known, also assume such an oppositional relation to each other. From the contrast between Pamphilia's autonomy of singleness and Urania's subjection to the 'traffic in women', and conversely, between Urania's empowering instability and Pamphilia's subjection to the principle of constancy in love, emerges a debate over the options available to women and their relative merits.[6] The stories and attributes of both characters also find alternative manifestations elsewhere. Antissia in particular, as the other most developed female figure in *Urania*, reflects on them both.[7]

Antissia's story matches the pattern of Urania's. Both are stolen as infants, stolen again from their abductors, and restored as young women. Urania, however, is brought up by loving foster-parents, and if her subsequent instability (she is rescued from an inappropriate love) connects symbolically with her childhood, it also empowers her. In contrast, Antissia recalls that until the age of sixteen she had 'continuall misfortunes' (p. 267). Her instability is connected to her transgressive behaviour, which at its most extreme leads her to a state labelled 'madness'. Wroth allows her portrayal of Antissia to work out some of the darker implications of Pamphilia's situation and character, particularly through the relationship between Pamphilia's love-melancholy and Antissia's insanity. Both states find expression in their poetry.

Rape in *Urania* turns out to be crucially bound up with narration and representation. As Helen Hackett has argued, the work creates 'correspondences between the body, selfhood and narrative', and clearly contains 'a concept of interior selfhood, and of experience as formative of the self'.[8] We shall find that rape both impacts upon women's identity in the work, and may be exploited by them as a narrative tool.

Wroth's gender poses interesting questions regarding her inclusion of rape narratives in her text. As a woman writer of romance, she has several options concerning rape narratives. She could exclude the topic which, however, is one of the genre's stock motifs. That all rape attempts in *Urania* fail may be her answer to this dilemma. She may also describe rape from the female viewpoint and rework some of its conventions, for instance, by establishing a model where the victim is not dependent on a male rescuer. Wroth does this on several occasions, and in these scenes the amount of sexual detail seems to be kept to the minimum, perhaps to avoid titillation. Yet, as Wroth proves, she can also write female sexuality back into the structure of the rape narrative, negating the threat to the woman. I shall discuss this in my final section. Her authoring of rape narratives finds a precedent in the work of a prominent woman writer of the previous century, Marguerite de Navarre, whose *Heptaméron* includes a great many stories of rape, attempted rape and seduction. Not only might Wroth have read this work in French, but a partial English translation had appeared in 1597.[9] The *Heptaméron* is also analogous with *Urania* in its exploration of the implications and effects of narration, particularly in terms of gender.[10]

The relationship between rape and narrative in *Urania* finds a context in the exploration in this work and Wroth's play *Love's Victory* of the ways in which women can express or conceal desire. Pamphilia negotiates the conceptual boundary between public and private, publicising her love by carving poems on trees, but retaining privacy by denying the congruence of writing and desire: 'many Poets write as well by imitation, as by sence of passion' (p. 77). Many other women express their feelings in poetry or relate their stories. Others obey the injunction against female self-expression in the hope of male approval, as Dalina advises in the play (III. 251–6). The drawbacks of this strategy, however, are made clear when a maiden's lover 'not once imagining my end, married another Lady' (p. 245). Alternatively, women may eavesdrop or be eavesdropped upon, whether by accident or design. Amphilanthus eavesdrops on Pamphilia as she expresses her love for him, and this brings them to greater intimacy (ii. f. 50ff.). Orilena unintentionally expresses her love to her disguised beloved, Philarchos, which also leads to their union (pp. 169–72). As an authorial strategy for the expression of female desire, these voyeuristic acts are successful. However, other scenes in *Urania* show voyeurism, whether visual or aural, to contain an implicit sexual threat to women.

The image of female utterance as 'swansong' occurs again in Wroth's work. She describes a widow's lament:

> Like to women spinning, [she] staid but to fasten the thread to begin againe to turne, and twine her sorrowes: but now she had spun them into Rime, like the Swan in a most weeping Verse. (p. 303)

Although the idea of swansong is conventional, this image also emphasises the craft of the woman's utterance, by combining it with the image of spinning: like weaving, a familiar image of female discourse. Occurrences of the image of weaving in *Urania* register the full ambivalence of its associations. A connection can be made between Wroth's evident concern with female narrative and the mythical origin of women's textual production in their resistance to sexual violence. Some examples, however, show a woman controlling language not to lament, but to seduce a man. Of Lycencia we are told, 'the truest worke, or weft of her Loome was ... to winne [Dorileus]' (p. 529). Another woman recalls that she had

> no meanes, saue my owne industrie, and strength of mind busied like a Spider, ... and so did I, out of my wit weaue a web to deceiue all, but mine owne desires. (p. 244)

These images, then, denote female sexual power rather than disempowerment. As we shall see, women narrators in the *Urania* weave stories both to disempower men and to save themselves from disempowerment.

The princess of Argos's version of the text(ile) image, which invokes the legend of Ariadne and Theseus, makes a practical, rather than originary, connection between female language and rape. Having told Lusandrino her story – one which, we shall see, brings arranged marriage into conjuction with rape – she comments: 'how is it possible for you, ore any to enter into our hoped for safety, *without* this thread to guide vs *with*' (i. f. 29). This explicitly valorises the tendency in romance rape narratives to stage female language as a cue for male action. Sophia's strict control over her own story too turns out to relate to rape: she is threatened with rape by her usurping uncle. However, Wroth also makes clear the limitations placed on such language. When Antissia is threatened with rape, the male narrator will not admit that female language may be empowering: 'crying for helpe would not auaile her' (p. 32). When Veralinda is pursued by a bear, it is empowering only as a cue for male action:

> the rest of the women crying, and assisting her onely with their lamentable voyces, the only helpe that sex can yeeld in such a danger, yet now came it wel, for the noise brought *Leonius* to her aide. (p. 365)

I begin by outlining *Urania*'s treatment of rape in relation to romance conventions.

## REDEFINING RAPE

Renaissance romance defines rape as the theft of a woman from a man and as the theft of the woman's chastity. In rape-and-rescue scenarios, the battle over the woman demonstrates male power. In *Urania*'s narratives of attempted rape, Wroth undermines many of the standard assumptions about rape and its narrative function, sometimes by reworking conventional types of narrative, sometimes by creating unconventional ones.[11]

Nowhere in *Urania* is it suggested that it is physically impossible to rape a woman, a belief we know to be common in other romances. In one episode, the aggressor, Lansaritano, chooses to try persuasion rather than rape, but there is no suggestion that rape by force is impossible. On the contrary, he repeatedly asserts his capability of raping Nallinea, justifying himself because she is his 'vassall by birth' (p. 80). This episode exemplifies the function of rape as an expression of power-relations. He explains that 'she whom I might command, I haue bin contented to woe; she, who shuld obay, ignorantly refuseth'; her relatives '[feared] violence would haue been by me *iustly* vs'd vpon her' (p. 80; my emphasis). He has brought her to the court with her beloved to fight a single combat, in which the champion must 'giue her to one of vs and fight with the other'. If Lansaritano wins he will, presumably, rape the woman. Yet the narrative differs from others of its type in that the woman actively desires a man other than her champion. The champion's victory would unite her with her lover; his power over her is thus limited and in accordance with the knightly ethos laid down by the king: 'surely no braue man will giue her from her owne affection'.

Even in Wroth's most conventional rape narrative, she brings out the woman's perspective. The threat of rape is presented as an occasion for a female heroism: 'I fled hither, more spirit then being in mee, then I could euer haue thought I should haue found in my selfe' (p. 518). By contrast, she mocks male heroism. When the Duke of Wertenburg offers to 'loose my life, or saue you', she replies, 'Nay Sir . . . that needeth not', undermining the usual function of rape narratives. That some knights treat threatened rape as a cue to display their valour is also made clear elsewhere. When Melasinda is attacked, Alliamarlus is considered lucky to be the first to find her and rescue her (i. f. 63). More extremely, the 'Knight of the Fair Design' is allowed to fight all the Bulgarian queen's attackers single-handed, as an opportunity for proving himself (ii. f. 29).

Wroth's few invocations of the common idea of the inviolability of virtue contrast with the convention. The narrator comments of Pamphilia when under threat:

> force must not preuaile against such a spirit, if not to bring death for hate, but no affection or submission, threats can worke with her no more, then to command men to giue resistance. (p. 429)

If force '*must* not preuaile', rather than *cannot* or *should* not, the injunction seems to be against the prospective rapist and not against the woman. Wroth seems to be saying that a woman of Pamphilia's spirit cannot be forced into love or submission (although perhaps into death). When Alliamarlus defends Pamphilia against sexual slander, he asserts:

> Pamphilia beesids is soe well knowne in all Vertues, and beauties of minde as itt is impossible to bee thought that either loue, ore force can conquer her, and make her his, whos loue is knowne soe firmly setled, her friends soe infinite. (i. f. 57v)

At first this seems to be a familiar claim: neither love nor force can win a virtuous woman. However, the balance of emphasis between Pamphilia's virtue and her friends' protection also lends itself to a different reading, whereby her virtue (and love for another) keeps her safe from love, and her friends protect her from force.

The idea of unassailable virtue appears again when Candiana dresses as a nymph: 'Chastetie beeing a profession vntouchable, and such as will fright the rudest to violate' (ii. f. 44v). Yet Wroth surprises the reader by revealing an unconventional motivation for this action: like Florimell, she is pursuing her lost lover. Rather than protecting her virginity, then, the role of chaste nymph facilitates her pursuit of desire. Such a reversal of expectation proves common in the *Urania*s.

Where beauty or love are blamed for attempted rape, Wroth gives the argument to men connected to the rapist and further undermines the idea by bringing out the political agenda involved. When Antissia is threatened by two brothers, as one of their knights explains,

> beauty first intic[ed] them, then ambition wrought to compasse a kings daughter to their pleasure; much commending themselues for placing their loues so worthily, yet still forgetting how vnworthie and dishonourable their loue was. (p.32)

Their political agenda is here apparent. Wroth also undermines the role of the rescuer by having the two rapists kill each other long before Amphilanthus arrives to rescue Antissia:

> then grew a strife for the first enioying her, so farre it proceeded, as from words they fell to blowes, and so in short time to this conclusion. (p. 32)

Wroth eliminates the familiar definition of rape as the theft of a woman's chastity in a scene in which Polydorus's wife is 'intreated' by Nicholarus. In this scene she also reworks a familiar scenario from the novella, in which an intruder enters a woman's bedchamber with the intention of enjoying her. In Boccaccio's *Decameron*, the woman typically is delighted by this event; Patricia Francis Cholakian has shown how Marguerite de Navarre rewrites the scenario as rape.[12] Wroth too makes her heroine outraged by the man's intrusion, which she identifies as sexually threatening: 'I wonder...my maids haue thus betrayed me, leauing the Chamber open to my shame' (p. 316). There is an irony in this, however, as the door has actually been left open for the woman's lover, rather than by a bribed maid for an intruder. It is to her lover that she remains 'chaste' rather than her husband: she later refers to having escaped 'breach in faith to her beloued' (p. 320). Since she is an unfaithful wife the threat of rape cannot be a threat to her chastity; she avoids the issue by invoking 'the honour...which borne with me, is my fathers, and my brothers, and my houses' (p. 317): her husband's name is conspicuously absent from this list. Her reaction to seeing Nicholarus when she is expecting her lover highlights this situation: 'her smile was frowning, her ioy displeasure, her rising to embrace him, to turning her face from him, her speech to welcome him, to crying out' (p. 316). In the fourteenth novella of the *Heptaméron*, Marguerite of Navarre had shown a male narrator arguing that a woman's infidelity with a lover validates her rape by another man: an idea challenged by his female listeners.[13] Wroth takes this further by portraying women as capable of making choices based on their desire or lack of desire, and thus defines rape as an attack on sexual autonomy, rather than the theft of chastity.

Polydorus's wife defines Nicholarus's entreaties as a form of assault: 'I neuer was more molested' (p. 317). After this rebuff he draws his sword, either 'to threaten her with harme, if shee consented not, or to make her yeeld, by offering violence on himselfe'. This ironic ambiguity undermines Nicholarus's threat, while underlining its proximity to courtship. When her lover arrives, moreover, he leaves without a fight. His power is again undermined when he goes mad; the woman 'was (no question) sorry in a noble sort, but not in respect, that had he beene other [than mad] she must haue runne a greater danger in hazard of her honor' (p. 320).

Madness here deflates a sexually forceful male character. I turn now to Wroth's more complex portrayal of madness in relation to women.

## MONSTERS AND MADWOMEN: IDENTITY AND INSANITY IN *URANIA*

Through the stories of Antissia and Nereana, as well as a great number of minor characters, Wroth intimates a complex set of connections between rape, identity and female transgression. Insanity proves to be a key motif through which she explores all three. Madness and rape are associated in two Ovidian stories with which Wroth would have been familiar.[14] In his version of Philomela's tale, the women's 'furious' revenge is as horrifying as the rape.[15] Medusa's story strikingly literalises the symbolic equivalence of transgressive 'rage' and monstrosity for women, and the connection of both with rape; it is after rape that she is metamorphosed into the gorgon.[16]

In exploring such connections between monstrosity, madness and 'fury' with her female characters, Wroth, like Cary, destabilises the conventional opposition between transgressive and virtuous women. She shows how sexually transgressive behaviour in women is labelled as 'monstrous', and how actively desiring women can be perceived as 'frenzied', full of 'phantasies' or actually insane, a particular form of monstrosity. Antissia and Nereana are both at different stages criticised as sexually transgressive, threatened with rape and become, or are perceived as, insane. Insanity, moreover, turns out to relate to women's linguistic autonomy. Like the writers with whom the last chapters were concerned, Wroth's explorations of female expression and autonomy within her text reflect her own position as a writing woman.

One of the lengthiest accounts of attempted rape in *Urania* suggests a relationship between trauma and the transformation or destabilisation of the 'self'. Leatissia tells Pamphilia how she was metamorphosed into a water nymph to protect her from rape and murder at the hands of the man who had just attempted to rape and then murdered his own daughter. This is the only occasion in the work where a victim of attempted rape dies; her defender, Leatissia's lover, is also killed, and the horror is compounded because the original attempt at rape is incestuous.

The father, Demonarius, as his name suggests, is a type of the habitual rapist traditionally found in romance: 'rauishing, if to death, was little, or nott att all thought to bee a fault' (ii. f. 32v). He 'fell in liking (for it were sinn for mee to giue soe sacred a name as Loue to such a detestable beast)' with his daughter, Lydia. When she and her mother flee he catches them, and orders his wife 'to hold [Lydia], while hee tooke his full pleasure of her'. In the ensuing fight both Lydia and her brother (Leatissia's lover) are killed. Wroth thus conveys the horror of rape without staging it, and without undermining its force with a happy ending.

Demonarius's desire to rape is then directed towards Leatissia. Pursued by him, she dives into a fountain and Diana transforms her into a water nymph, saving her from the rape. This story of attempted rape prevented by metamorphosis differs from its closest Ovidian prototypes, the stories of Arethusa and Daphne. Arethusa and Daphne are still desirable and vulnerable after their metamorphoses, suggesting that metamorphosis provides a substitute for rape. Alpheus, being a water-god, attempts to 'mingle with' Arethusa in her new form as a spring, from which she is only saved by the ground splitting beneath her; Apollo is successful in embracing Daphne 'even now in this new form'.[17] By contrast, Leatissia is absolutely protected from Demonarius, vanishing from his sight. Nor is she made inanimate, becoming instead a *'liuing* sepucher [*sic*]' representing 'chaste suffering misfortune' (f. 33; my emphasis). Her description, moreover, gives equal weight to her bereavement as the cause of her suffering.

Leatissia's metamorphosis thus enacts literally a transformation of 'self' that seems often to occur to women in the *Urania*. This is frequently the effect of frustrated desire but, as here, it may result from threatened rape. The sexual attack on the Queen of Bulgaria, for example, leaves her 'soe strangly undrest, and tattered in her habitts, her heare soe ruffeld', but after rescue she 'quickly came better to her self' (ii. f. 29v). The idea that an attack may disturb a woman's sense of 'self', as we shall see, occurs most strikingly in the story of Nereana.

Threatened with rape, Lydia is 'distracted and wilde *with* ouerswaying sorrow' (ii. f. 32v). Such 'distraction' also frequently results from both love and grief in *Urania*. Although the portraits of Nereana and Antissia are its only sustained and detailed investigations of the idea of insanity, many other stories establish a connection between women's mental instability and their experience of cruelty or frustrated love. The wronged wife of Allimarlus is full of 'rage':

> Then did she as one distracted, fall from one passion into another, leauing complaining, and chafing, and from crying fell to singing, and twenty of those passions had she. (p. 466)

Celina's reaction to love trauma is extreme. She lies on the ground 'carelesse of order, or modesty, allmost distracted' (p. 546). Her disordered discourse reflects her mental instability:

> some lines she put together, but so few, as could make no kind of verse, not hauing proportion, or number: these indeed, said she, are fit for my making, vnmeasurable thoughts leaue me, as hope & help abandons me. (p. 547)

'Distraction' has been identified as one of the most extreme terms for insanity in this period – and one that is associated with raving, or idle or incomprehensible talk. Edward Jorden's *The Suffocation of the Mother* (1603) states that mad people will 'laugh, crye, prattle, threaten, chide, or sing'.[18] In *The Anatomy of Melancholy* (1620), Robert Burton further associates madness with 'want of governement', and images the descent into madness as a metamorphosis: 'we metamorphize our selves, and degenerate into beasts'.[19] Burton's characterisation of madness as 'raving... full of anger and clamor, horrible lookes, actions, gestures' (i. 132) will prove pertinent to several of Wroth's characters.

Jorden defines depravity as the possession of a distorted perception and as being 'furious' or 'distracted through loue, feare, griefe, ioye, anger, hatred &c' (f. 13v). Madness is connected to the imagination, 'whereby sometimes they will waxe furious and raging depriued of their right iudgement' (f. 13v). Burton makes this connection, but adds other causes including sorrow, fear, shame, desire of revenge, anger, envy, hatred, pride, too much studying, imprisonment and poverty (i. 250–355). He also claims that diet affects melancholy, particularly the quantity of food consumed (i. 220 ff.) and therefore recommends dieting as a cure. The other most recommended cure is marriage. Although Burton emphasises this as a cure for love-melancholy (iii. 242), he also believes that coition in itself will cure the malady (i. 416), as the sub-plot of Shakespeare's *Two Noble Kinsmen* illustrates.

The perception of madness in these quasi-medical texts is closely connected to deviation from behavioural norms, particularly for women. This is strikingly illustrated by Tomaso Garzoni's *Hospital of Incurable Fooles* (1600). The section treating female inmates is taken up almost entirely by anecdotal descriptions of the women's pranks, rather than with any account of how or why they became mad.[20] Women are believed to be particularly prone to madness; Jorden states: 'the passiue condition of womankind is subiect vnto more diseases and of other sortes and natures then men are' (f. 1), particularly 'suffocation of the mother' ('hysteria'), which he describes as 'monstrous and terrible to beholde' (f. 2).[21] A mad woman, moreover, is characterised as driven by an unruly body and sexual appetite. As Katharine Hodgkin puts it, mental instability in a woman would be 'located in her restless and greedy body rather than her restless and creative mind'.[22]

The idea of female madness as transgression reflects the social attitude evidenced in an advice book by 'M.R.', *The Mothers counsell* (1630).[23] 'M.R.' defines 'madnesse' as being 'Out of Compasse in Temperance', and characterises it as unruliness or evilness. A mad woman is 'like a rough stirring Horse' (p. 15) who needs sharp restraint; she suffers from 'excesse of passions' (p. 19); she is cunning in her speech and vicious (p. 17). In fact, her definition of a mad woman is identical to that of an 'ill' or 'odious' woman in several points; both are a danger to the commonwealth (pp. 17, 30). 'M.R.' categorises as mad any woman who is 'proud and vnruly' (p. 17), indiscreet, passionate or sensual. Her definition of pride also embraces presumption in intelligence:

It is a great madnesse in any woman to amuse vpon those things which are farre beyond her vnderstanding. (p. 18)

Phyllis Chesler has found that 'what we consider "madness" [may be] . . . the total or partial rejection of one's sex-role stereotype'.[24] This insight will prove pertinent to Wroth's portrayal of Antissia and Nereana.

The connections implied in medical texts and conduct literature between madness, monstrosity and (sexual) transgression are given substance in the two parts of the *Urania*. Wroth's frequent use of the words 'fury' and 'frenzy', denoting both anger and madness, reinforces such a connection.[25] We have seen how love trauma in the published text can lead to 'distraction', and how in the sequel this state may be produced by pride and imagination. I turn now to female characters whose sexual behaviour renders them monstrous, and to Wroth's version of a female monster whose sexuality renders her more nearly human.

Sexually assertive women in *Urania* are frequently labelled monsters. Leonius is captured by a woman who is described as 'an inchantress, a deuile, and a harlott' and a 'monster' (i. ff. 58, 58v). She is 'free of all things as com*m*une, euen to her owne person' and 'the greatest libertine the world had of female flesh' (f. 58v). There are many such sexually rapacious women in the work, and their licentiousness is often associated with language.[26] This woman is 'as full of faulshood as of vaine and endles expressions, beeing for her euer acting fashion, more like a play boy dressed gawdely vp to show a fond louing woemans part, then a great Lady'. Sexual voracity is here equated with linguistic plurality, with 'busied braines' (f. 59v), and with acting.[27]

Wroth indicates, however, the agenda behind the categorisation of 'worthless' or transgressive women as monstrous, and shows how their behaviour evokes complex feelings of disgust and scorn in the men who fear their voracious sexuality. When Leonius is taken

prisoner by another woman, who 'hated all worth' (p. 404), it tran-
spires that her hatred of him is due to his father's cruelty to her mother.
Another woman pursues the lover who abandoned her and has him
tortured. The justification of this vengeful woman counterbalances
the contention that 'women inraged they say are Deuils' (p. 477).

The implications of male hostility to female sexual assertiveness
are displayed most strikingly when a knight, Clavorindo, encounters and kills a monster with a woman's face. The tale is told from a
male perspective, by Clavorindo himself. Although female monsters
are mentioned elsewhere in the work, and although she also has
biblical precedents,[28] this creature specifically recalls three from
Spenser's *Faerie Queene*. Error is half woman, half serpent (I.i.14); the
Echidna has a maiden's face and 'former parts' and a dragon's
'hinder parts' (VI.vi.10); the Echidna's daughter is a 'huge great
Beast' who 'of a Mayd . . . had the outward face, / To hide the hor-
rour, which did lurke behinde' (V.xi.23). Arthur's destruction of her
– 'Vnder her wombe his fatall sword he thrust' (V.xi.31) – we have
seen to have symbolic resonance as rape.[29] Wroth's recreation of
Spenser's female monsters interrogates patriarchal attitudes towards
transgressive women. By making her monster more explicitly sexually assertive and seductive, she brings out the male sexual aggression which is the subtext of such battles.

Throughout the scene, a striking ambivalence in the knight's
attitude to the creature conveys male hostility to female power.
While fighting her as a monster, he simultaneously refers to her as
though she were a woman, and invokes the rules of courtly conduct
which he is drastically transgressing. With a comical literalism he
records: 'I grew soe unciuill to the face of womankinde, though to
that sex I ame a faithfull seruant, as I strake her ouer the head,
cleauing itt in tow' (i. f. 22). Many more similar monsters appear,
and he claims that 'fury made me now forgett all cerimony', as
though he had used great 'ceremony' originally.

Where the Echidna and her daughter have the faces of 'maidens',
Wroth's monster makes no claim to virginity. Other uses of the
word 'monster' for women have prepared us for the characterisation
of this creature as sexually voracious and aggressive. Clavorindo
first calls her face 'som what tolerable', but he soon describes it as 'as
flattering a face, and countenance as the most dissembling creature
of woemen kinde could haue'. Her approach to him is recounted in
such language as to suggest a sexual advance; she is at her most
'beastly' to the knight when at her most 'womanly':

this thing monstrous, and fauning, came towards mee, wagling her head, like a light wanton, licking her lips for treacherous kysses and bowing, as idolators doe to images, courting as farr, as beast-lines can doe and performed by a beastly creature.

This recalls in minute detail three women in the published volume who are sexually assertive and threatening. Lycencia is 'false beyond expression, and what not, that might make a woman change nature with a beast' (p. 516). She 'shak[es] her head like a bowgh in a storme of wind, or nodding like and [sic] old wife sleeping in an afternoone, licking her lips, and glaring like a Cat in the darke' (p. 517). The monster's 'wagling' head also appears in the description of a woman who seduces and imprisons men:

Vnsteady she was in her fashion, her head set vpon so slight a necke, as it turn'd like a weather-cocke to any vaine conceit that blew her braines about. (p. 346)

When the Queen of Bulgaria attempts seduction,

she onely lickt her lipps, that when they returned to sight, they might looke like cherries after raine, red and plumpe, and totterd her head. (p. 461)

These descriptions establish a type on which Wroth draws in the portrait of the monster.

Clavorindo's foe, then, is literally rendered monstrous by her sexual assertiveness, which is indistinguishable (by the knight) from violence, for her lips are as ready to eat him as they are for kisses. His violence towards her thus expresses the hostility of men towards female voracity; it is legitimised by her monstrosity even while we are reminded of her womanliness. His first blow responds specific-ally to signs of disdain: 'I saluted her frownes *which* grew high vpon me *with* a sound blowe ouer her hating, and to mee hatefull eyes' (f. 22). This is an ironic touch to what is supposed to be a portrait of sexual assertion, for the monster's frowns recall those of the Petrarchan mistress upon the lover whose vows she will not hear. Clavorindo is literally striking a blow here for the spurned lover. The monster's 'fury' links her with the idea of insanity found in the med-ical texts and with the passionate and transgressive women found in both parts of *Urania*. Yet Wroth ironises this monstrous characteristic when she attributes it to Clavorindo, whose 'fury' makes him 'forgett all cerimony'.

Clavorindo's analysis of the creature's language is significant as a comment on female educational and linguistic capability. Roaring is 'the only language I heard her use'. He announces:

> vnhumane creatures may bee taught to speake some thing, to purceaue some thing and soe to express that, butt neuer can be brought to true knowledg, noe less, to ciuilitie, butt as beasts will keepe their owne natures, *fury* being their best guide. (f. 22; my emphasis)

Spenser's Echidna's daughter has been read as alluding to the Sphinx, an intelligent female monster who challenges male intelligence.[30] It is ironic, then, that Wroth's version is derided by her male observer as incapable of 'true knowledg'. This irony, I shall argue later, contributes to Wroth's use of this episode to undercut her male critics.

Nereana's and Antissia's stories pursue in greater depth these connections between identity and sexual/emotional trauma. Antissia's story both parallels and inverts Nereana's. Their implicit models of cause and effect conflict not only with each other but within each story.

The outline of Nereana's story suggests a model of cause and effect by which a transgressive woman is punished by hardship for her pride and self-assertion. Yet this is complicated by her relationship to insanity and by the connection implied between sexual threat and identity or mental stability. Nereana's identity is central to her portrayal throughout *Urania*. During the course of the romance she takes on (or is forced into) the roles of queen, knight-errant, lover, madwoman and goddess. She is 'Knightlike' when she pursues her straying lover, Steriamus (p. 163). She is later attacked, in a scene which contains at least six references to 'self', beginning with reflexives but becoming increasingly significant. Nereana 'for that time laid aside State, and to recreate her selfe after her owne liking, went into the Wood' (p. 164). She loses her way 'and at last quite lost her selfe' (p. 165), an enactment of her 'emotional confusion and lack of self-direction'.[31] Attempting to cast off, temporarily, the encumbrances of her position as queen, she is soon to find that she has lost the power incumbent on that position. She is now a blank page or void;

rather than 're-creating' her self, she is re-created by the madman Allanus, first as his mistress Liana and then as the goddess of the woods.

In this scene a veiled threat of rape is followed by an unusual substitute for it. Allanus mistakes Nereana for his disdainful mistress
and tries to implore or force her to 'embrace mee with thy pardoned
loue' (p. 165). He then decides that she is the goddess of the woods
and worships her instead. This worship has many of the hallmarks
of a rape narrative:

> whether she would or noe, [he] would worship her, and that he
> might be sure of her stay, hee tide her to a tree; then to haue her in
> her owne shape out of those vestures...hee vndress'd her, pull-
> ing her haire downe to the full length; cloathes hee left her
> none... (p. 166)

In his search for 'her owne shape' he creates a new one for her. This
scene comically undermines the aggressor's power; it culminates:
'then setting her at liberty he kneeled downe and admired her'. Yet
this conjunction of sexual and physical aggression with worship or
admiration conveys the closeness of the two. Nereana's reaction prepares us to identify his transformation of her as a violation: 'Villaine
said she, touch me not, nor dishonor not my habits with thy rude
handling them' (p. 166). Elizabeth Harvey has shown that images of
the 'good' woman at this time do not differentiate 'between bodies
[and] their coverings'; Nereana clearly sees Allanus's assault on her
clothes as a sexual affront.[32] It is not simply a slur on her honour and
a signal of the possibility of actual rape, but is itself an attack on her
self-definition, which is fulfilled when he transforms her into the
goddess of the woods.

In a striking inversion of the Narcissus myth, Nereana is saved
from suicide by horror at her own new image. Running away,
'almost hating her selfe in this estate', she prepares to throw herself
into a spring:

> But the picture of her owne selfe did so amaze her, as she would
> not goe so neere vnto her metamorphos'd figure.

The same disjunction of self appears later when she tries to hide 'euen
as it were from her owne selfe' (p. 168). Three uses of the word
'metamorphosis' make more explicit the tangential connection
between her identity crisis and attempted rape. As well as the

narrator's use of it (above), Allanus uses it of her; she is then 'amazed with what hee said, neuer hauing heard of any such thing as a *Metamorphosis*'. These references locate Nereana in relation to the Ovidian idea of metamorphosis, as associated with the threat of rape. Nereana's metamorphosis, though not as literal as Leatissia's, frees her from being raped, providing another channel for Allanus's desire to 'worship' her. However, it also destabilises her perceived identity, with drastic effects.

Nereana's new appearance earns her the label of madness from Philarchos, who rejects her plea for help. Her speech also leads to this diagnosis, showing her 'as vaine, as her apparell was phantast-icall' (p. 167). His contention that 'a woman and being madde, had liberty to say anything' both licenses and disempowers female utter-ance. That Nereana is only mad according to the definition of female madness as transgression makes more striking his trivialisation of female speech.

Wroth's attitude to Nereana is hard to gauge. When she dismisses Allanus we are told she does so out of pride (p. 168). Hardship sub-sequently 'wrought kindnesse in her, who else despised, and con-temned all'. Yet earlier attitudes to Nereana's amazonian behaviour have been ambiguous. The king of Morea's wonder at her 'such con-stant fury' (p. 163), although recalling the frenzies of 'monstrous' women, might be commendation or criticism. Pamphilia calls her pursuit of Steriamus 'great pitie' but praises her for it, perhaps iron-ically (p. 163). It is not possible to read Nereana's story straightfor-wardly as 'pride comes before a fall', which would implicitly posit sexual or identity trauma as a just punishment for female transgres-sion. If there is a latent awareness of this ideology in the scene, it is not one that the author necessarily endorses.

Wroth maintains this ambivalent attitude to Nereana through the rest of her story. Her isolation in the cave seems to teach her self-control; although her spirit is 'none of those the exactliest ruld', she becomes 'a Lady that must tell her selfe to be one' (p. 277). As a measure of her reform, she now criticises her own 'want of judg-ment' (p. 278) in pursuing Steriamus. When she is rescued, however, she resumes her original state:

> like a garden, neuer so delicate when well kept vnder, will with-out keeping grow ruinous: So ouer-running-weedy pride, in an ambitious creature proues troublesome to gouerne, and rude to looke on. (p. 279)

Pride – thinking Perissus loves her – leads to her categorisation again as mad. Echoing contemporary views on diet in relation to madness, Perissus decides that 'with good feeding [she is] growne into her fury againe, and fullnesse had renewed her madnesse' (p. 290). Nereana's period of want is here read as a cure for her madness. It is repeated when her subjects, out of fear of her 'tempest of rage' and her 'iust anger' (p. 290), depose her and lock her in a tower. Here she is 'fed neately, and poorely to keepe downe her fancy' (p. 291). Ambiguously, Wroth calls the imprisonment 'punishment justly allotted for such excessiue ouer-weening', but also condemns it. Her people's eagerness to categorise her as insane underlines the misunderstanding and marginalisation of unconventional women:

> [she was] told still shee was mad, and threatned to bee vsed accordingly, if shee raued, accused of fury, and that made the cause to satisfie the people, who ignorant enough, had sufficient cause to belieue it, seeing her pasions, which though naturall to her, yet appeared to their capacities meere lunatick actions. (p. 291)

Although she subjects Nereana's pride to comedy, Wroth's treatment of her marginalisation as a madwoman shows her 'madness' to exist largely in the perception of individual men and society.[33] This stage of Nereana's story recalls that of Lady Arbella Stuart, another royal woman punished for sexually and politically transgressive behaviour by being locked in a/the Tower and reported 'distracted'. Stuart died in the Tower in 1615, where she was imprisoned for marrying against James I's wishes. Wroth had danced with Arbella Stuart in Jonson's *Masque of Beauty* in 1608, and would have been aware of the circumstances of her incarceration and death.[34] Unlike Arbella, however, Nereana is eventually restored to rule (p. 421).

By the beginning of the *Urania* sequel, Antissia, we are told, has 'growne now to be accounted farr wurse then euer Nereana was for frenzies' (i. f. 11v). Like Nereana, but more extremely, Antissia's rapid alternations between sexual victimisation and sexual self-assertion constitute a form of instability which may contribute to this madness.

Antissia is abducted as a baby and before being restored is, as we know, attacked by two brothers who attempt to rape her. She then has a brief love affair with Amphilanthus, and is distressed and 'distracted' by his desertion of her. Her suffering in love leads in her perception to a fragmentation of self; when they go fishing she 'thought her selfe each fish, & *Amphilanthus* still the nette that caught her, in all shapes, or fashions she could be framed in' (p. 270). She mistakenly thinks he is meeting Pamphilia in secret (in fact it is Pamphilia's brother Rosindy) and enters the state of 'fury' associated with madness and transgression, 'vowing to reuenge, and no more complaine' (p. 91). Her rejection of the more conventional role for wronged women, 'complaining', in favour of 'rage' and 'revenge', precipitates her categorisation as mad. We are soon told that 'madnes grew so vpon this, as she burst out into strange passions' (p. 92). Discovering her mistake, she becomes 'a meere *Chaos*' (p. 95) and apologises, 'I . . . haue mistaken my selfe, or indeed my better selfe'.

The constructed opposition between Antissia and Pamphilia as bad and good readers, Antissia frequently deluded, Pamphilia ever wise, is a source of much comedy at Antissia's expense. It is, however, misleading. Antissia is actually a good reader; she correctly identifies Pamphilia's poems as hers and the emotion in them as genuine rather than imitated. Although much is made of her misreading of Rosindy as Amphilanthus, she is correct in realising that Amphilanthus is fickle. Her vituperative attack on him (p. 93), although addressed to the wrong man, is entirely justified by his subsequent conduct. Moreover, Wroth demands sympathy for her when she is deserted, looking forward too to Pamphilia's abandonment by the same man: 'this was the reward for her affection, and which most poore louing women purchase' (p. 273).

In her 'furie' (p. 310), Antissia arranges Amphilanthus's murder. When it fails she 'came to her good nature againe' (p. 311), and believes she is one of 'the worst weeds' in her country, 'which ought to be destroyed, least they infect the earth' (p. 312). Recalling the image of Nereana as an 'ouer-running-weedy' garden, the author compares her to 'a Nettle [which], hardly scaping the weeders hand, but growing on, turnes to seede, and from thence springs hundreds as stinging' (p. 313). Antissia's story exemplifies Burton's model for jealousy leading to madness (iii. 304). Yet Amphilanthus's hypocrisy in blaming her for 'causeles fury' (p. 339) increases our sympathy.

Antissia is then married to Dolorindus, 'she discreetly louing him, but he doting of her' (p. 341). Her 'discretion' seems ironic in this context, and the match is clearly an attempt to control her; medical texts, as we know, recommend it as a 'cure' for madness. However, like many cures in *Urania*, Antissia's marriage neither tames her nor, it seems, helps her to forget Amphilanthus, for she later addresses Rosindy as 'Amphilanthus owne image' (i. f. 11v) and has to be 'cured' a second time, by Melissea.

These signs of Antissia's mental instability prepare us for the portrait of her insanity in the *Urania* sequel. The sequel shifts the emphasis from love trauma to pride and imagination in its portrayal of female insanity. One woman is 'deform[ed] . . . nott onely in her person, butt in her minde farr higher flying' (ii. f. 59v). Another is 'a phantasticke younge creature', whose 'wandering thoughts' lead her to write verses 'to choke vp the other phantasies, and giue mee a little scope of expression' (f. 59v).

The equivalence of insanity and monstrosity appears in a male onlooker's description of Antissia as having a 'brutish demeaner' (i. f. 13). Here her madness is characterised in terms of anger: 'raging, rauing, extrauagent discoursiue language' (f. 13). It is also bound up with her intelligence and use of language, and with her poetry in particular. In the published volume her stories had been labelled as 'friuolous discourse' (p. 270). The sequel pushes this idea to its furthest extreme, fulfilling the association between the female imagination and insanity.

Antissia's madness, a male narrator tells us, was brought on by studying: 'beeing a dangerous thing att any time for a weake woeman to studdy' (i. f. 13).[35] Not long after this we are to be told that a monster is incapable of education beyond a certain point (i. f. 22); here, conversely, a woman becomes 'monstrous' through attempting to study. The fragmentation which characterised Antissia in the published volume now intensifies. Her nephew describes her

neither waulking, running, nott standing still, yett partly exercising all, she neither sange, nor spake, nor cried, nor laughed but a strange mixture of all thes together, soe discomposed as if pieces of all throwne into a hatt, and shooke together to bee drawne out, like valentines to be worne by seuerall persons. (f. 11)[36]

Her madness, at least in Antissius's eyes, is also signalled by her state of dress. He calls her 'neither drest nor vndrest' and describes her outlandish garments in a blason of female insanity. Her language he finds equally hard to classify, for she speaks 'something, butt whether prose, ore Verce I can nott tell' (f. 11v). She is credited with 'frekes, and follys' and is notorious for her 'phantisies'.

Melissea diagnoses Antissia as having 'high wrought' brains and 'high expressions' unusual for a woman (f. 16). She magically 'cures' her, which produces a crisis of identity similar to Nereana's after her 'metamorphosis':

> now her ancient woemanish thoughts came about her ... in an extreame passion shee ran to her bed, and couered her dispised self soe close, as she had neere stifled her self, being soe consious to her self, as she was afraid, and asham'd, her owne self should see her, thus she lay wishing from her soule she might dy as vnknowne, as she was then to her owne knowledg. (f. 16v)

Nereana could not bear to see the creature into which Allanus had forcibly metamorphosed her; Antissia cannot bear to see the outlandishly dressed woman she has created as herself.

If Antissia's sexual self-assertion previously led her to insanity, her return to 'woemanish thoughts' seems to make her vulnerable to rape: almost immediately, she is threatened with rape by a giant. Wroth explicitly contrasts her two selves:

> poore Antissia grew fearfull seeing his lookes filled *with* ardour, quaked when hee spake in the gentlest way to her, when hee frownd, euen terror shooke her, if hee touched soe little as her hand, she sounded [swooned], Oh change of dispositions, late frantick, fearles, now trembling reddy to dy *with* feare, beefor dreadles, now knowing, gasping for quiett breathe. (i. f. 16v)

Antissia's transformation from fearlessness to terror thus appears as the acquiring of knowledge, implying that fear is the natural condition of sane women.

The pattern of victimisation here is in marked contrast to Nereana's story. If Antissia's first experience of attempted rape partly resulted from and partly contributed to her instability, this second experience suggests that sexual vulnerability and disempowerment are conditions of conventional femininity, from which her madness was an escape. Wroth laments the predicament of women threatened with rape: 'how miserable are all woemen in this kinde'.

Antissia is rescued, but she is later captured yet again, by the giant Tomardo. Like Nereana, she is imprisoned:

my self often nay allmost euery day whiped, and dietted for feare
of beeing fatt *with* water, and crusts of bread, naked, and alone.
(ii. f. 16v)

Although she is not explicitly accused of madness, the forcible dieting is a familiar 'cure', and her enforced nakedness also makes her
seem sexually vulnerable. If Antissia is being 'treated' for madness at
this point, however, we must see her as the victim either of such a
misunderstanding as Nereana experiences, or of a policy of 'preven-
tion rather than cure'. Such treatment would prevent her from
regaining her old state of madness, a condition in which she would,
according to the logic of her story, be less sexually vulnerable and
more difficult to handle.

The role of male perception in classifying madness is made clear
in Antissia's story. It is easy to posit a contrast between her sanity in
the published volume and insanity in the sequel, to see her as 'going
mad' at some point between the two.[37] Yet characters in the text do
not draw this line; for them any alteration in her mental stability is
merely a difference in degree. Rosindy actually sees Antissia's madness in the sequel as less serious than the earlier madness which led
to her misplaced 'fury' against him. Recalling that state of 'almost
madness', he suggests:

many of thes fitts, might haue led her to an vncurable distraction,
*which* I fearr still hath left reliques beehind itt, . . . for I beeleeue
she cannott cure the smutts, though a little she may haue slaked
the flames. (i. f. 11)

Antissia eventually narrates her story for herself and blames her 'fol-
lyes' and 'younge pride' (ii. f. 16) for her later sufferings. However,
the idea that her suffering has been a punishment for folly is belied
by the fact that, as she recalls, her fortunes were 'neuer fixt butt
mouing'.

Wroth does not explicitly reject the idea that female folly is a cause
of later suffering, including attempted rape, but her portrayal of
Antissia's life suggests other models, some contradictory. Antissia's
story implies that sexual vulnerability can be the result of instability
(the attempted rape by the two brothers in part a function of her
being a perpetual victim of abduction as a young girl); it also implies
that sexual victimisation can result in mental instability (this attack
contributing to her subsequent madness). At the same time, sexual

self-assertion (her love for Amphilanthus) is also credited both as producing and constituting madness; yet we can also read this as another form of sexual trauma, since her 'fury' is a result of his desertion. The idea that mental instability is a protection against rape provides a further model: or conversely, that vulnerability to rape is a condition of passive, conventional femininity (the attack immediately after her 'cure').

Antissia's story, then, is both similar to and also an inversion of Nereana's. The hardship endured by Nereana is her time in the cave, a result of being labelled insane; Antissia's hardship is insanity itself. Yet these periods of trouble have opposite effects on the two women. Nereana's 'breaks' her, curing her madness; while oppressed she voices conventional ideas about women and transgression, but resumes her old 'self' once restored to her former power. Antissia's hardship is liberating, giving her a new linguistic freedom and, perhaps, freeing her from the condition of vulnerability to rape which characterises her when 'sane'. Her 'cure' comes later – but when it does, she too then voices the conventional ideas that seem to be related to this vulnerability. The models of cause and effect concerning sexual trauma, conduct and insanity, then, are not only in conflict within Antissia's story, but also conflict with that implied by Nereana's experience.

If Wroth does not come down categorically in favour of one model of female behaviour and experience above the others, this is a strength of her portrayal of Antissia and Nereana. After all, to promote the idea that sexual vulnerability is the plight of passive and conventional women would be a negative model, while the transgression–punishment scenario is equally problematic. Wroth not only avoids an ideological impasse, then, but creates more complex portraits of the characters and opens up significant questions about women's sexual transgression, vulnerability and self-determination.

Wroth's portrayal of 'madness' in *Urania* is radical in several respects. It is rare to find a woman writer dealing with the topic at all; Juliana Schiesari points out that Hildegard of Bingen is the only *pre*-modern woman to have done so, and the only early theorist to have considered the issue of gender.[38] Wroth underlines the connection of madness to transgression for women and emphasises the role of (male) perception in diagnosing it. She implicitly refutes the conventional wisdom that marriage cures the malady, by showing it to have no effect (unless a negative one) on Antissia's sanity. Moreover, she is radical in challenging the opposition between admirable (Aristotelian) melancholy, associated with men, and degrading (Galenic) melancholy or madness, often associated with women.[39] She casts a woman, Pamphilia, in the elevating role of melancholic traditionally reserved for men, but explores ideas about women's transgressive madness through the figure of Antissia and others. However, the opposition between Antissia and Pamphilia turns out to be collapsible; their shared experiences destabilise it. Pamphilia might be 'diagnosed' as a 'love-melancholic' (her love of solitude and darkness are common symptoms),[40] but erotomania has played a role in Antissia's state too. Moreover, if Antissia's mental state at least partly results from Amphilanthus's treatment of her, this brings her closer to Pamphilia. Although Pamphilia is praised for her constancy, Wroth makes it clear that the melancholy that goes with it is problematic. Conversely, while Antissia is ridiculed by many for her ignominious conduct, Wroth shows that to some extent madness liberates her.

These contrasts and connections find a manifestation in the portrayal of Antissia and Pamphilia as alternative models of the woman writer.[41] Pamphilia's emotional control relates to her production of sonnets, which are widely respected. Antissia shows the potential for grief to become uncontrollable; her poetry reflects her fragmentation and transgression and is therefore despised. Nereana's experience establishes that 'a woman and being madde, had liberty to say anything' (p. 167); Antissia's use of language is a major signifier of her madness.

Not only is Antissia associated with 'friuolous discourse' (p. 270, i. f. 11v), but Antissius (her nephew) calls her poetry 'olde sickly stuff, as if poetry were fallen into a consumption' (i. f. 11v). Her insanity, then, is measured by the poor *quality* of her poetry. As the chief signifier of her madness in the sequel, Antissia's 'poetticall furies' (ii. f. 16) are almost unprecedented.[42] It is, of course, a standard dramatic convention that women who go mad sing bawdy songs, but where they would usually sing existing songs, Antissia has composed her own.

Wroth has established an association between female insanity and the breakdown of language in her portrait of Celina in the published volume. Antissia's language is close to this model; her 'mad' poems are free and (at first hearing) obscure, and much of her spoken language fluctuates between verse and prose. This formal instability may relate to conventions in representing madwomen on stage.[43] Wroth is not, here, writing a verse drama, so she does not have the same opportunity to use or reject such conventions. However, her emphasis on Antissia slipping between the two modes may have a more radical effect. Her linguistic instability renders her almost incomprehensible to her male listeners, Rosindy being disturbed by his inability to categorise her language, just as Burton is bewildered at the speech of madwomen (i. 45). Antissia's radical instability reaffirms that unconstrained female discourse may be incomprehensible to a male audience; her language, then, mirrors her mental instability or fluidity which is a source of her power. Unlike Celina, however, Antissia does produce some complete poems.

Antissia's performance of one poem is as unusual as its content; she is 'stiring vp and downe like a new broke colte, in a haulter' (i. f. 16). This recalls Jorden's account of madmen who 'cannot abstaine from motions and gestures' (ff. 14v–15). The image suggests the wild passion of one whose subordination is not fully achieved, and the image is appropriate for the process of training a woman to behave according to social ideology. Wroth thus intimates that the behaviour of this unconventional woman has been caused by her society, and that her 'madness' represents the last vestiges of her struggle against it. (We recall that 'M.R.' is to describe a madwoman as a 'rough, stirring horse' in need of restraint.) As such, the image might describe the 'cure' which Antissia is about to be given by Melissea, rather than her present state. Another explanation, however, might be that Antissia is now married; marriage may be the 'haulter' attempting to break her in to society. As such, however, it is clearly unsuccessful.

Antissia actually gains a new source of power through insanity. Her 'mad' poems voice sexual power and enjoyment in a way that shocks her audience. In 'Come lusty gamesters of the sea' she celebrates a sexuality that women are supposed to suppress, extolling Venus and rejecting Diana. Not only does Antissia equate love with 'Varietie', she also seems to be rejoicing in a specifically female sexual pleasure:

> Venus, my deere sea borne Queene,
> Gives mee pleasures still unseene...
> (i. f. 15v)[44]

The idea of unseen female pleasure is clearly sexual. Antissia's poetic enjoyment of this pleasure is readily associable with the French feminist idea of 'jouissance': boundless sexual/textual pleasure.[45] Not surprisingly, Antissia's audience are unable to cope with her poetic sensuality or 'poeticall furies', and consider this a 'tedious ditty'; Melissea is to pronounce her 'high expressions' unladylike. Dolorindus chides her:

> I see you will...straine your expressions to immodesties in your vaine phantesies did euer a chaste lady make such a songe, or chaste eares indure the hearing itt, fy fy Antissia, if you will write, write sence, and modestie, not this stuff, that maides will blush to heere. (f. 16)

This rebuke strikingly recalls the 'advice' given to Wroth by Lord Denny after the publication of the first part of *Urania*. Outraged by the veiled portrayal of his own family crisis in *Urania*'s pages, Denny attacked Wroth as a 'hermaphrodite'. Condemning *Urania* for its 'lascivious tales and amorous toyes', that is, for its staging of female desire, he tells her to 'followe the rare, and pious example of your vertuous and learned Aunt, who translated so many godly books'.[46] This scandal brought about Wroth's undertaking to recall all copies of the work, although it is not certain that this was carried out. It has been suggested that she might have stopped writing the sequel after this attack by Denny. Yet although it may well be feasible that Wroth did not intend to publish the sequel after all this trouble, there is no evidence that it actually discouraged her from continuing with it in manuscript.[47] On the contrary, I would argue that Wroth's portrayal of Antissia in the sequel and her version of Spenser's Echidna could both function as answers to Denny's attack.

The portrait of the woman/monster may be connected to Denny's poem 'To Pamphilia from the father-in-law of Seralius', in which he calls her a 'Hermophradite in show, in deed a monster'.[48] In his poem Wroth-as-monster is, like Clavorindo's foe, 'wrathfull' (l. 3). Moreover, she is accused of insanity ('thy witt runns madd' (l. 12)), her text is compared to 'a drunken beast' (l. 18), and Denny's image of her indiscriminate literary malice is strongly connotative of sexual promiscuity:

> Yet common oysters such as thine gape wide
> And take in pearles or worse at every tide.
>
> (ll. 9–10)

If the monster who is capable of some self-expression but not 'true knowledg' is an ironic response to Denny's characterisation of Wroth as monstrous for writing a romance, she may have enjoyed intimating its sexual power, while conveying in the scene the hostility of men towards female sexual and literary self-assertion.

The implications of unconventionality in writing, however, are developed with Antissia. Antissia's poetry is frequently called 'fustian' (f. 15v) and 'olde, sickly stuff' (f. 11v), which might connect her to her author, since Wroth's chosen genres, the romance and the sonnet sequence, were associated with the generation before her own. We have seen that Dolorindus's advice that Antissia should write 'sence, and modestie' explicitly recalls Denny's 'advice' to Wroth. Moreover, Antissius's description of Antissia also recalls Denny's imaging of Wroth as a 'Hermophradite': she has a 'brutish demeaner fittinger for a man in woemans clothes acting' (i. f. 13). Wroth's portrayal of Antissia in the sequel, then, along with that of the woman-monster, strongly suggests that they function in part as a response to Denny's vilification of her as scandalous, monstrous and insane.

## 'THE DISCOURSE OF THRALLDOME': COURTSHIP, RAPE AND POLITICS

> I ame in double danger, either to haue my country quite ruind, and I taken by force, to bee forced to yeeld to that brutish beast the Souldan of Percia ... ore to yeeld to bee his wife *which* is wurse then millions of death to mee to think on.
>
> (i. f. 57)

Pamphilia's plea for help articulates the symbolic equivalence between the queen's body and her country which the Sultan's threatened invasion and rape would literalise. As in Elizabeth I's Tilbury speech, Pamphilia's constancy becomes representative of the security of her country and both here come under attack. The same equivalence, though implicit in every attack on the queen, is exemplified by the King of Celicia's attack after her refusal of marriage:

> with an inuincible Army, [he] was come neare the confines of her Country, by force to win, what he could not by loue, or faire meanes gaine. (p. 429)

That country and queen share a name heightens their symbolic congruence. The king's attempt to invade the country Pamphilia – his approach to its 'confines' – prefigures the rape of its queen he hopes to achieve.

In underlining the equivalence of invasion and rape, Wroth inevitably recalls Elizabeth I's troping of her virginity as ensuring national security. This is not the only moment at which Pamphilia may be identified with Elizabeth. As well as her status as queen regnant, the politicisation of her adherence to chastity or constancy marks her as a recollection of Elizabeth. At one point she appears in costume reminiscent of Elizabethan iconography, and like Elizabeth she argues that she is married to her country in justification for refusing a suitor (p. 218).[49] Although Pamphilia's emotional life is the focus of much of her story, Wroth increasingly conveys its political significance. I turn now to the political significance of rape in Wroth's works, and the way in which the rhetoric of courtship masks its threat.

Elizabeth's political rhetoric finds reflections in contemporary literature. In Lyly's *Euphues and his England* (1580), for example, Hackett has suggested that national 'self-determination' is figured as 'the impregnability of the Queen's body to either inner turmoils of love or outer assaults by suitors'.[50] In the *Old Arcadia*, moreover, Musidorus's plan to seize the Arcadian throne after marrying Pamela links rape with invasion. The monarch's impregnability, then, involves deflecting not only rape impulses, but also marriage proposals. Wroth's own relatives, including Philip Sidney, had been involved in the debate over Elizabeth's proposed French marriage. Around forty years later, Wroth's interest in the queen's body becomes part of her wider investigation of the connections between rape, invasion and rebellion, and the rhetoric of courtship.[51]

Pamphilia's appeals for help, unlike the inarticulate cries of many distressed damsels in romance, take the form of letters, written discourse. This is a fitting means of resistance for Wroth's so literary heroine; her response to sexual and political threat, like her response to love and grief, is not only articulate but written. This connection is underlined by an episode which links the queen's body to her discourse, when a messenger delivering Pamphilia's letters to her subjects is waylaid:

> [he] maliciously, and bacely vsed the letters beefor hee rent them, saying hee would haue dun*n* as much by her, if she had nott the

better liked him, as hee had dun*n* by her papers had she fallen as luckily into his hands, for of any thing, hee loued to haue a faire, great Queene vnder his vassallage. (ii. f. 39)

This makes explicit the congruence between a woman's body and her writing which is implicit in contemporary injunctions against women's literary production: thus seeming to prefigure the topos in later seventeenth-century epistolary fiction whereby '"breaking open" the woman's letter is an act of "mind-rape"'.[52] Like the invasions, this is a political assault (the destruction of letters from a queen) which figures itself as equivalent to a sexual one.

This attack has further political significance, undertaken as revenge for Pamphilia's refusal to marry the King of Lydia (who also attacks her friends in revenge). The king's brothers reject the rape-as-revenge topos, and expose its rhetoric as flawed:

if a man refused will thinke to right his loss w*hich* is non since non can lose that they neuer had, hee must reuenge him self vpon him self for his fond hopes, and not on thos are fitter to bee honored then contended w*ith*. (ii. f. 19v)

One of the king's cousins, however, has Pamphilia abducted by a rabble: 'to teach her she might haue maried my Cousine' (ii. f. 45v). That a woman's rejection of a suitor might justify his raping her implies that courtship and rape might be two sides of the same coin.

Wroth's treatment of the male rhetoric of worship, in which the woman is troped as all-powerful, the wooer as her 'vassal', suggests that the possibility of violence underlies all courtship. This 'discourse of thralldome', as one woman in the sequel calls it, receives extensive interrogation in *Urania*. When the woman is the more powerful, Wroth brings out the paradox inherent in the language of courtship. A queen literalises the trope when she takes prisoner a knight, who tells her, 'I am in your royall hands a Vassall at command' (p. 257). Wroth also describes Venus as '[Adonis's] suppliant, hee her God, and she the great Queene of loue yett his vassall' (ii. f. 9). Where the wooer is male, his 'vassalage' is rhetorical because of his physical power to overcome the woman; here, with a female lover, it is rhetorical because of her power as a deity. Wroth underlines this power structure by comparing the youth to Ganymede, exemplar of male sexual vulnerability.

Women frequently mock men's rhetoric in *Urania*. When Steriamus describes himself as a dead man, Pamphilia replies, 'I neuer heard till now ... that dead men walked and spake' (p. 56). Her assessment of the Sultan's letter to her, more seriously, points out the masquerading of threatened rape as courtship:

> a loue letter itt should haue bin*n*: and was in a strange kind, for if denyde *with* such brutish threatning fitter for turcks to deale *with* then tender Christian Ladys. (ii. f. 18)

The conjunction of male sexual aggression and the male rhetoric of love is exemplified in the scene between Nicholarus and Polydorus's wife. The narrator's claim not to know whether his sword is drawn 'to threaten her with harme, if shee consented not, or to make her yeeld, by offering violence on himselfe' (p. 317) shows the closeness of the rhetoric of courtship to sexual aggression. Moreover, the woman's reaction – 'shee was distemperd with the manner' – underlines the danger. Nereana's encounter with Allanus displays the same reversibility or disappointment of expectation, but inverted: it is after demanding love, tying her up and stripping her that Allanus 'admired her' (p. 166).

Several episodes in the sequel make explicit the function of such rhetoric in masking actual male power. When Licandro liberates a castle from bondage and falls in love with one of the prisoners, the Tartarian princess, his language of bondage and thraldom contrasts pointedly with her powerlessness. The blason which first describes her conventionally equates beauty with power, crediting her with eyebrows 'as if bent to destroy all harts that yeelded nott subiection to the powrfull boss of their comaunds' (i. f. 24v); as for Licandro, 'meere siuility taught him obedience to such a spirite'. His friend Olymandro, however, underlines the real balance of power between them, when he reminds him that she 'is now in your dispose' (f. 25).

The princess's repeated pleas for freedom display an acute awareness of her compromised position. She requests to be 'vntoucht, and safe', and 'quiett and free to my self' (ff. 25–25v), clearly aware of the possibility of sexual danger. Licandro's response confirms the sexual agenda: 'non shall euer say, that by my meanes, especially vnder my commaunde the least shadow of insiuility, much les force shall euer bee vsed' (f. 25); this does not reassure her. Articulating the position of other rescued women in romances, she tells him that if he has freed her 'a great obligation I must owe vnto you'. Cutting through his rhetoric, she emphasises the real meaning of thraldom: 'I ame nott used to the discourse of thralldome farder then my owne misirie hath brought mee, to bee a prisoner' (f. 25).

Such a power-dynamic is a feature of courtship whether or not the lady is royal. When it involves a queen and a foreign ruler, as we have seen, 'the discourse of thralldome' conceals the threat not only of rape, but of invasion. The analogy between ruler/ruled and lady/ vassal, however, is destabilised more thoroughly when a subject (a political vassal) attempts to rape his queen. The intersection of rape with rebellion most strikingly reverses the power-relationship between women and men in a situation of courtship or 'admiration'.

In the published *Urania* a high proportion of the sexual attacks are on queens or princesses and some, as we have seen, acknowledge the relationship between political and sexual power. Rebellion in this text, however, is linked with sexual profligacy, rather than with rape. The Romanian rebellion results directly from the queen's adultery (pp. 60ff); later, a one-man rebellion is associated with inconstancy in love, as the rebel's jilted lover dies for his sake (p. 379). The rebellion in Hungary (pp. 63ff.) has a sexual agenda that brings it close to some of the rape scenarios in the sequel, as the rebel demands to marry the queen; however, although Melasinda eventually agrees, she enjoys her lover in secret. This twist in the story makes the woman the victor.

The sequel dramatises at least ten rebellions, and rebellion comes to be associated here neither with female licentiousness nor with male inconstancy, but with rape.[53] Wroth thus develops the connection between the two implied in Sidney's *Old Arcadia*. Here, Musidorus's attempted rape of Pamela can be associated with the attempted rebellion which takes place at the same time. Wroth's royalist attitude to rebellion, though tempered with a strong sense of the contrast between good rulers and bad, facilitates such an association.[54]

The intersection of narratives of rebellion with rape narratives literalises the connection between the instability of the political relations between ruler and ruled and that of the balance of sexual power between a lady and her 'vassal' or admirer. Such intersections occur several times in the *Urania* sequel. When Ollorandus's widow makes a vow of chastity and retreats into a monastery, her rapacious suitors, forbidden by law to disturb her, try to start a rebellion as the only way of bringing her out (ii. f. 56v). The Sultan of Persia threatens his niece Sophia, the rightful heir, seeking to marry her 'by force if I consented nott' to cement his authority: 'soe liking mee as hee calls itt, but my right better' (i. f. 61). Melasinda's capture by rebels who attempt to rape her emphasises the inversion of the power structure involved in both rebellion and rape: 'she now beesought, who lately commaunded, yett had nott preuaild, for the Arch traiter was hee who then had taken her, and had her in his wicked power' (i. f. 63). However, she is assertive of her right to revenge, unlike several merciful women in *Palmerin*, and adamant that her assailant should not be spared.

Wroth extends her portrayal of the sexual-political dynamic of rebellion by bringing it into play with forced marriage, a theme which also coincides with stories of invasion. It is not surprising that most attempted rapes of queens in *Urania* and its sequel are attempts to force marriage, since this is clearly the most effective way of seizing political power. Wroth also demonstates the proximity between forced marriage (forced by the 'suitor') and arranged marriage (forced by the parents).

Arranged marriage provides the main plot in *Love's Victory*. Like Pamphilia in the *Urania* sequel, Musella has agreed to marry a man she does not love, the boorish Rustic, and having changed her mind, she is forced by her mother to honour her promise. A series of comments emphasises that this marriage, although not involving physical compulsion, would constitute a sexual violation. Dalina's warning that

> ... att night,
> I'le undertake much mirth will not apeere
> In faire Musella, she'll showe *heavy* cheere ...
> (V. 133–5; my emphasis)

is followed by Silvesta's lament for

> Musella to bee forc'de and made to ty
> Her faith to one she hates, and still did fly.
> (174–5)

The scene is illuminated by its counterpart in the *Urania* sequel, which also features a character nicknamed 'Rustick'. Using the characteristics of rape narratives, this scene constructs an indifference to female sexual volition as boorishness. The shepherds explain that 'soe right a Rustick hee is, as for to haue his mistress loue him whether she will, ore nott' (ii. f. 7). Wroth's treatment of the traditional theme of forced marriage thus underlines its sexual significance.

In the *Urania* sequel, the rebellion in Argos further suggests an equation between parental coercion and rape, mediated by rebellion. Lupus, the commander of the rebel army, proposes marriage to the princess as a condition of her father being 'king during his lyfe by title'; her husband would subsequently 'commaund all by commaunding mee' (i. f. 29v). The episode is not constructed as a rape narrative; indeed, the princess acknowledges that Lupus 'vseth Ladys, and woemen siuilly'. It shows more strongly for this how the sexual autonomy of royal women is bound up with political life. Her mother the queen's story of forced marriage underlines this equivalence between 'force' by a stranger and 'force' by parental or political pressure. Her father's insistence is coupled with a degree of forcefulness in the suitor which, expressed as it is in terms familiar from rape narratives, suggests that he might have attempted to rape her or force her into marriage: 'noething butt his hauing mee could satisfy him' (i. f. 32v).

In a work so crucially concerned with male–female power-relations as the *Urania* sequel, its backdrop of political rebellion is particularly connotative. The high incidence of rebellion establishes a strong sense of the power-polarity between ruler and subject, but at the same time destabilises that relationship, conveying its instability and reversibility. The familiar equivalence of ruler/subject with husband/wife and especially with lady/'vassal' becomes resonant here; if the world of the *Urania* sequel is one in which the polarity of ruler and ruled is ever vulnerable to inversion, it is also one in which we are made aware of the reversibility of the power-relations invoked during courtship. The term 'traitor', generally used in the published *Urania* as a term of moral opprobrium, particularly for men who attempt rape, acquires added force in the sequel when rapists are also political traitors. The contiguity of the political and the sexual for women and for queens in particular gives this effect added weight.

Pamphilia's awareness of the power-dynamic behind courtship appears as one factor behind her rejection of so many proposals. When Rodomandro, king of Tartaria, proposes, she answers:

> you who are soe fitt to commaund, why should you stile your self a seruant, noe my lord you are borne to rule, and god forbid I should assume any such power ouer you. (ii. f. 21v)

Yet she is clearly aware of the limitations of her 'power' as a wife, and accuses him of seeking power over love and, implicitly, over her:

Your greatest presumption ... is to my sight the greatest, since ... your ambition is to conquer loue, since if I com*m*aund in soueraine power, you must needs if you win*n* mee bee master of him, soe I take this as your desire to haue sole power ouer loue to make mee your instrument for itt.

Pamphilia's 'soueraine power' is not only over love but over her country and subjects. This power will be affected as much as her personal autonomy by her marriage to a foreign king.

In persuading her to marry him, Rodomandro utilises Pamphilia's sexual vulnerability, perhaps the cumulative effect of the many attacks in the work. He offers to 'serue you as a guard' (f. 21v), and although he identifies serpents and beasts as the threat, earlier events have made it clear that she is most at risk of abduction and rape. Leandrus makes this suggestion when he offers to guard her from 'traitors' who might 'assaile' her. Pamphilia then claims that her 'greatnesse, and these walls' (p. 178) are warrants for her safety. If the numerous attempted abductions and attacks to which she is subjected give the lie to this sense of security, it may be that her words are as much a warning to Leandrus not to 'assaile' her with unwanted marriage proposals. To him she is adamant that she does not wish for 'ones power I could not loue' (p. 178): his power over her, as well as in her defence. Her marriage to Rodomandro achieves revenge on Amphilanthus for marrying someone else, but is also an abandonment of this principle.

Wroth undermines the power of the male protector or rescuer yet again when Rodomandro marries Pamphilia, for at this point he too seems to become vulnerable to attack. One aggressor swears he will kill Rodomandro 'for mariing Pamphilia w*ith* out his leaue' (ii. f. 44). Shortly after this she and her 'new husband' (ii. f. 45v) are attacked by the King of Lydia's cousin, seeking revenge yet again. A husband is not necessarily a protection against attack, despite the manipulation of female sexual vulnerability in the male rhetoric of courtship.

## 'SO PRETTILY IN SUCH DANGER':
## RAPE NARRATED, RAPE TRANSFORMED

Wroth's demonstration of the reversibility of the power-relations posited by the rhetoric of courtship, is analogous with the structural principle governing many of the *Urania*'s key episodes. The literary playfulness which produces the inversion and reinversion of patterns in the work frequently involves the manipulation of expectation to create a sense of infinite reversibility. We have seen this at work in the fortunes of Antissia and Nereana, and it produces, for example, Nereana's 'worship' by the man who seemed intent on assaulting her, and Melasinda's triumph over her rebel-husband by enjoying her lover. This technique of manipulating expectations so as to frustrate or shock them intersects with Wroth's specific frustration of the expectations surrounding rape, when she transforms rape narratives by interpolating into them active female desire.[55]

We have already seen how Wroth presents rape narratives and the implications of sexual trauma from a distinctively female viewpoint. She also deploys rape as a stock motif of romance, a narrative device with its concomitant ideological and structural implications. Several women narrators within the two *Urania*s manipulate the conventions of the rape narrative to empower themselves; Wroth as the *Urania*'s narrator takes such manipulation further. In extending the *Urania*'s literary playfulness to this area, she suggestively empowers many of her female characters. In so doing, she demonstrates the power of narration.

Central to Wroth's manipulation of expectation is her portrayal of voyeurism and deployment of its paradigmatic literary manifestation, the blason. Recent work on the blason has established that it renders its (female) subject sexually vulnerable.[56] Wroth both endorses and complicates this sexual association, blasoning male and female subjects alike. Her treatment of voyeurism more generally both demonstrates its danger for women and suggests means for female empowerment. Her playfulness with literary expectation, as we know, involves an invocation and recasting of patterns and ideas from Sidney's *Arcadia*. She recasts the erotic triangle from the beginning of the *New Arcadia* in different ways to show its implications when the woman is present rather than absent. One version inverts it by having the woman, beloved by two male friends, love them both in return, thus presenting a problem not encountered by Strephon and Claius. This situation is the result of a deliberate act of voyeurism, set up by the prior lover to titillate his friend:

> I intreated to see her legge, she refused not, he being just before vs saw it too, then did his loue increase, while I ignorantly and

foolishly stroue to make him see excellencies to robb my selfe of them. (p. 384)

When she had added an undesiring woman (Antissia), the impasse had been resolved by attempted rape and murder. Here, it is resolved by the men's homosocial union. Interestingly, it is the second case which involves voyeurism. Other episodes, however, invoke both possibilities – rape and reciprocated desire – in quick succession.

The setting in which Amphilanthus finds a nymph bathing is a conventional one for a rape narrative: 'besides a priuate and vnfre-quented place, each Angle and wanton winding embanked with trees' (p. 555). The nymph 'vndressed her, and pulled off her fine aparell, as her vpper garments and ruffe, her necke then remaining bare'; to emphasise her innocence we learn that 'merrily did she this, singing a dainty song concerning chastity'. Amphilanthus's response comically underlines his arousal:

tender he was least the Brooke with his cold . . . armes might make her start and so molest her with such vnpleasing imbracements, therefore to preserue her from such hazard, and her honor from the danger, her naked simplicity might bring her to, in any hands but his, he spake to her. (p. 555)

Her fear heightens his pleasure: 'feare, trembling and all possessing her, yet so prettily in such danger she looked' (pp. 555–6). The pos-sibility of rape, inherent in the combination of female fear and male arousal, becomes explicit at the end of the scene, when Amphilan-thus leaves 'in place of taking, or thinking, of taking these, asking fauour, or vsing power' (p. 556). Yet the possibility of reversal is intim-ated here at the very last stage by a suggestion of the nymph's own desires: as he leaves, she sighs.

The encounter between Parselius and Dalinea shows the reversib-ility of the scenario of potential rape. He is led to his first meeting with her through a 'braue roome richly hang'd with hangings of needle-worke, . . . the Story being of *Paris* his Loue, and rape of *Helen*' (p. 102). This reference, with its in-built ambiguity as to the woman's desire, tantalizingly points to both rape and mutual desire as possible outcomes. The story proceeds, however, as one of court-ship, with Dalinea reciprocating Parselius's passion:

loue creeping into the heart of Dalinea, as subtilly as if he meant
to surprise, and not by open force take her. (p. 103)

The available substitution of 'Parselius' for 'love' here has alarming
implications, and the idea of force is again introduced at the end of
the sentence. These dark implications are retrospectively confirmed
later, when Parselius leaves Dalinea, pregnant and with no proof of
their marriage, to return to Urania.

In the course of restaging this fluid boundary between rape and
courtship, Wroth also rewrites some of the manoeuvrings of Sidney's
Pyrocles. In Leonius's pursuit of Veralinda she separates out the elements of Pyrocles's courtship of Philoclea. Leonius saves Veralinda
from a wild beast in his own shape as a man; he then dresses as a
nymph, rather than an Amazon, bringing their wooing a stage closer
to homoeroticism. The rescue specifically echoes Sidney and, moreover, reinstates and intensifies the 'private' version of the *Old Arcadia*.
Leonius is first aroused, like Pyrocles, by a visual feast which manifests itself to the reader as a blason, and which characterises its object
as innocently disordered: 'her haire carelesly throwne vp, neither tiyde,
nor vntyde, but cast into a delightfull neglectiuenes' (p. 362). The threatening potential of the blason is confirmed by the equation of knightly
with erotic adventure. Leonius is told that it is not 'for a man of your
profession to feare, especially Beauties' (p. 363), and follows Veralinda
'knowing that a man who ment to followe aduentures must not feare
any thing: especially a woman, and so sweete an one' (p. 362).

After these generic markers follows the rescue. Where Sidney's
revision had eliminated the equation of rescuer with wild animal,
Wroth reinscribes it by making Leonius's voyeurism coincide with
the beast's chase rather than following its death:

> as shee ran, her dainty leggs were seene, discouering such excel-
> lency in shape, and swiftnes, as that had bin enough alone to con-
> quer; she passed by him, hee standing still to encounter her
> enemy, yet did his eyes cast amorous wishes after her, his spirit
> raised in hope to meete the Beast, who gaped, as wanting breath
> to hold the ioy hee had in expectations, to deuoure that sweete
> portion of excellent daintinesse. (p. 365)[57]

Like the 'Old' Pyrocles, Leonius is the beast's competitor, the latter
clauses applicable to either. It is again the woman's desire which
transforms this threat of violence into reciprocated passion – a passion

subsequently free of the ambiguity of Pyrocles's union with Philoclea in the *Old Arcadia*.

These transformations contrast sharply with those found elsewhere in literature of the period. As a narrative device, we have seen that rape lends itself to transformation. In drama in particular, the bed-trick can transform consensual sex into rape, and vice versa. Despite its prominence in Sidney's *Arcadia* too, Wroth never uses the bed-trick. As with the bed-trick, however, the implication of rape remains submerged in her 'transformed' narratives. Her introduction of female desire into threatening scenarios also contrasts with the tendency of male writers to attribute desire to women being raped or threatened with rape. This, as we know, sets the urge to portray women as promiscuous against the urge to stage rape, or the rhetoric of all-powerful female virtue against male sexual power. Although Wroth's two strategies – one conveying female suffering from rape, the other asserting female desire – also coexist, the tension between them is not analogous to that in drama or the epyllia, but is suggestively empowering for the female characters.

As substitutes for rape scenarios, Wroth's transformed rape structures, with the woman's desire effecting a shift into the courtship mode, are clearly distinguishable from the phenomenon of 'substitute rape' we have observed in romance. Here, sexual subtexts and titillation are introduced into narratives in which the plot mentions no sexual action, through superfluous nakedness or sexual language. Wroth's submergence of rape in the episodes above seems to have a different function. Moreover, when women are subjected to violence in *Urania*, it often lacks such an erotic component. The torture of Ramiletta lacks sexual overtones (p. 106ff.), as does that of Liana – by an aunt rather than a male relative (p. 208); and in the notorious story of Sirelius, the father-in-law's violence is not expressed in sexual language (pp. 438–40). Conversely, a woman who is killed for her promiscuity actually appears as the sexual aggressor at the moment of her destruction:

> he threw her downe [from the rock], but as she fell louing all mankind, she held him so fast as he went vnwillingly with her, breaking their necks. (pp. 530–1)

Wroth does manipulate expectation with erotic charge, however, in the description of Limena's torture by her husband. As in other romances, he ties her to a tree by her hair:

> Then pulled hee off a mantle which she wore, leauing her from
> the girdle vpwards al naked, her soft daintie white hands hee fas-
> tened behind her. (p. 68)

The progression of adjectives seems deliberately tantalising, anticipating 'breasts' rather than 'hands'. Yet if Limena's torture is sexu-
alised here, she is not necessarily disempowered by it. Hackett
points out that Wroth deploys the imagery associated with Christian martyrdom in describing Limena's torture, in order to validate
Limena's (unconsummated) love for a man other than her husband, and suggests that her wounds may symbolise 'the combined
emotional, psychological and physical scarring of marital rape'.[58]
Using Traub's discussion of the shifting of gender identification in
readers or viewers of erotic scenes, she argues that a female reader
or writer 'might take both sadistic and masochistic pleasure' in this
moment.[59] The sexualisation of Limena's torture, moreover, also
empowers her more explicitly. The voyeurism in which Parselius is
implicated leads to her freedom when he kills her husband. She
herself then manipulates erotic display when telling him and Perissus
her story:

> he opened my breast, and gaue me many wounds, the markes
> you may here yet discerne, (letting the Mantle fall againe a little
> lower, to shew the cruell remembrance of his crueltie) which
> although they were whole, yet made they newe hurts in the louing
> heart of Perissus. (p. 71)

Limena's erotic verbal and physical self-exposure confirms her lover's
attachment, just as her husband's and the narrator's exposure of her
had prompted her rescue and her union with Perissus. It thus provides a figure for the exploitation by the narrator of such sado-
masochistic eroticism. Such self-exposure matches that of several other
women in *Urania*, both 'innocent' and 'worthless'.

Several women in *Urania* use narrative and self-display to empower
themselves, two constructing rape narratives to trap men. Their
exploitation of the stock motifs of the narrative which usually
records and perpetuates women's subordination may mirror the
*Urania*'s. It is a false rape narrative which lures Amphilanthus away
from the vision of Pamphilia's torment in the Hell of Deep Deceit,
and its extravagance underlines its fictitiousness:

when [Lucenia] would haue throwne her selfe into the Sea, . . . the rude wretch tyed her by the hayre, to his leg, and so road away with her, *Musalina* from the wood againe claiming ayd, with her hayre rudely cast about her, and lowdest cryes. (p. 554)

The widow of Terichillus too creates a false rape narrative in order to take revenge on Amphilanthus for killing her husband. He and Ollorandus encounter her 'running, her haire loose, couering her face, her cries loud and fearefull, her cloathes halfe on, and halfe off, a strange disorder in her words, she spake as if danger pursued, and helpe requisitly demanded' (p. 237). She thus strictly observes the decorum of rape narratives, precisely by counterfeiting '*dis*order'. She then delivers a narrative in which her suitor 'vowed to haue me by force, since no other meanes would preuaile'; her misery, she claims 'hath quite destracted me'. When Amphilanthus fulfils his knightly role, he is attacked by her men. A second woman plays the same trick on Ollorandus, 'with as fearefull cries, & shriks pass[ing] by' (p. 238). Appropriately to this scene of illusion, the rape narrative is visually inverted here, for we first see her pursued by Ollorandus, rather than by the posited rapist.

Both knights are disempowered by the women's narrative control; Ollorandus is almost literally 'held with discourse' by the maid. The scene exhibits an appropriate self-consciousness about narration. After all the enemy knights are dead and the widow has killed herself, 'then did [Amphilanthus and Ollorandus] striue to bring some of them that lay on the ground to life, if but to tell the plot, but in vaine for they were all dead' (p. 239). The men who have been characters in the women's narratives as well as in the *Urania* narrator's, thus register their total confusion as to the 'plot'. Aptly, it is the second woman/narrator who finally explains it to them.

All these women thus empower themselves more powerfully than the few women in other romances who 'cry rape'.[60] When Lycencia attempts to seduce Dorileus, however, she deploys a strategy comparable to Acrasia's in *The Faerie Queene*. She combines her story with careful self-display, prefacing it with 'some business of his intreaty, and her modest-like bashfulnes' (p. 517). The story is one calculated to arouse her male audience, complaining of her husband's impotence: 'I feare he had only the face of *Venus*, but not the affections': As if this were not enough to convey her sexual appetite, she explains that she has come in search of a water that will ease grief, perhaps an aphrodisiac. In this search, she claims:

I met some few dayes, since an unruly consort, who mooued with
my beauty, as they pleased to call this poore part of mee, would
needs haue that, and all.

Lycencia arouses her male audience not only by inspiring pity, but
by portraying herself as sexual prey. Her strategy seems a more literal version of Acrasia's construction of herself in the Bower of Bliss;
both characters deploy the erotic charge that usually victimises
women in order to pursue their own desires.[61] Like the Spenserian
version, this episode underlines the power of rape narratives to titillate the male reader, and the power such self-representation confers
on the female narrator.

Olixia, another lustful woman, also manipulates self-display. Her
'care . . . to be neglectiue in her apparrell' (p. 256) recalls the 'delightfull neglectiueness' of Veralinda's dress. The contrast between Olixia's
sexual tyranny and Veralinda's innocence might imply an opposition here between 'art' and 'nature'. Yet the echo also points to a
congruity between them. Olixia's (like Lycencia's) deliberate staging
of her own dishabille to attract men, like other women's staging of
rape narratives to lure men into their traps, becomes a figure for the
narratorial staging of such voyeuristic moments which empower
Veralinda and Limena, by the text's woman author. Such acts thus
figure the *Urania*'s wider manipulation of literary and erotic expectations to overturn convention.

While self-display and narration thus prove to be closely connected to
women's pursuit of their desire, Wroth does not forget the danger
incumbent on such strategies. An encounter between Philarchos and
an unnamed maiden in the sequel stages eavesdropping as a form of
aural voyeurism which creates a situation of sexual threat, thus
pointing back to the debates in the published text over whether and
how a woman should express desire, and counterbalancing Wroth's
portrayal of women being empowered by voyeurism. In its reversals
of expectation, it invokes and undermines an important function of
rape narratives, and suggests the effect of gender on narration.

The episode is another version of the scenario featuring an intrusion into a woman's bedchamber, which we have seen Wroth
rewrite in the scene between Nicholarus and Polydorus's wife.
Where Nicholarus was quickly expelled and comically deflated,
Philarchos presents a greater threat to the woman. This time, the intruder himself is the narrator. Philarchos relates how he accidentally

entered the maiden's bedroom at night by a secret door and overheard her lamenting her love for him. Her lament is predicated on
his unavailability: he is married, so she is 'neuer to injoye' (i. f. 45v);
this facilitates her image of herself as Venus to his Adonis. Like Strephon and Claius, she has not anticipated the love-object's presence.
When he sits on her bed and kisses her hand, she reacts in fear:

> [she was] infinitely amased to see her self thus surprised, att such
> a time of night, and in such a place, her chamber, all alone in bed,
> and wholy at my mercy . . . and therfor to trust to my fauour, ore
> lose that she soe deerely, and [better] esteemed than her lyfe, her
> honor. (i. f. 46)

The word 'surprised' here provides a generic marker derived from
the military language associated with rape.

Philarchos clearly enjoys his narrative, as he enjoyed his power
over the woman. Like Amphilanthus with the bathing nymph, his
erotic satisfaction is proportionate to her fear and reluctance:

> I tooke many most sweet, and pleasing kisses from her, *which* she
> loath to lett mee haue, made them farr the sweeter, striuing soe
> pretily, as the more pleasingly to make mee take more that she
> might haue more cause to refuse. (f. 46v)

Philarchos – a 'good' knight and Pamphilia's brother – boasts about
refraining from raping the maiden in such a way as to make clear
that he was quite capable of it:

> Truly if [her] words, and *with* thes words such floods of teares
> had nott com, I knowe not how farr my libertie on such delicate
> opportunities might haue shaped.

Begging for mercy, the woman assures him that she had no idea of
his presence when she declared her love; if she had, he ought 'to
haue hated mee for such impudent im*m*odestie'.

The strategy by which the union of lovers is facilitated by one
eavesdropping on the other is evidently highly problematic when it
is the female who displays herself. This story is a negative version of
Orilena's, who married Philarchos in the published *Urania* after
using the same strategy. That it is Philarchos who is the eavesdropper
in both cases underlines the reversibility of the scenario. The

maiden's sexual peril in this scene is based on Philarchos's inability to right any sexual 'wrong' by marrying her. Yet it also suggests more generally the danger of self-display for women. Her narrative – which she presumed private, but which generically anticipates an eavesdropper (if only the reader) – has been 'a snare to beetray my honor in and by soe shamefull a way, as of all the most shamely'. By giving Philarchos knowledge of her love, it has made her 'prostrate my self to your powr'. Where women 'surprised' in bed typically prove compliant with the intruder, Wroth twists this scenario in two directions. Not only does she emphasise the danger of rape, like Marguerite de Navarre, but she also rewrites the idea of the desiring victim. This woman had indeed been desiring (the absent) Philarchos, but is no less frightened by his actual presence.

Philarchos claims, like many male writers, that the woman's 'no' means 'yes'. He concludes: 'itt may bee I had better pleased the sweet sad soule *with* kind and louing imbracings then as I did' (f. 46v). Wroth thus shows him projecting his desire onto his potential victim, and separates it from the issue of the woman's own desire and expression.[62]

Rather than raping the maiden, Philarchos demands her 'story'. This is the only story in *Urania* which is given reluctantly, and it literalises the rhetoric of many people in the *Urania* sequel who 'obey' what they call a 'command' to tell their stories. Despite the woman's control of narrative, then, her story also functions as a sign of her disempowerment; her description of herself here as his 'vassal' (f. 46v) is not merely rhetorical. Her narrative, like her kisses, is more delightful to him because delivered in fear: Philarchos 'being on the bed then holding her by the trembling hand, her voice then weake *with* feare of . . . danger'. The equation of sexual with narrative pleasure suggests that Wroth here finds another substitute for rape.

The woman's story is titillating not just because it is delivered in fear, but because it is a story of her unconventional pursuit of desire. She had disguised herself as a princess to dance with Philarchos at court: 'brought on the stage like a player acting an other part nott conserning my self butt in phantastick conseit, fouled by mine owne phansie' (f. 47). Both acting and fantasies are, as we know, associated with assertive female sexuality. Unlike Lycencia, however, she is ashamed of her 'presumptious part'.

Philarchos takes her story as an opportunity to turn the tables on her by moralising about her immorality and advising her to follow a chaste life:

what is ore should be more deere to a Lady, and a faire one, than her honor, heere you lose itt in choise, and aduenture itt to all ... [W]ash away the shamely desire in the teares of true repentance. (f. 47v)

The high moral tone of his sentiments is ironically undermined by their context. Yet it finds a precedent in prose fiction, in the novellas which advocate female chastity as the conclusion to stories of rape or attempted rape. By echoing this literary model, Wroth creates Philarchos as a culpable, exploitative narrator. The novellas had exploited the rape narrative to frighten a posited female reader into maintaining her chastity. Wroth's scene casts its two characters in a variety of roles. Philarchos is both the figure of sexual threat, and the moralising narrator; the maiden is both the near victim of the story and the female reader/auditor. Where the novellas encourage the woman reader to identify with the threatened heroine of the story, here the identification is literal. Conversely, Philarchos's combination of roles identifies the male narrator (both creating the story of sexual threat and moralising) with the rapist figure.

However, the tale-within-the-tale, narrated unwillingly by the 'heroine', does provide an application for Philarchos's moral. The moral thus appears not as an inept conclusion which responds to the woman's story while ignoring the present situation (his consideration of raping her), but as a deliberate act of narrative control. By imposing the moral, Philarchos-as-narrator *writes* the woman's transgression as responsible for her present compromised position and danger. He is as manipulative a narrator as the women elsewhere in the work who empower themselves through narrative. Wroth thus wittily reworks conventional rape narratives, and emphasises narrative power.

Perhaps fittingly, Philarchos's female audience, Pamphilia and Veralinda, seem taken in by his construction of the tale. When he has finished, they thank him for the story and for 'sweete expressions in itt' (f. 48v), perhaps explicitly referring to its 'moral'. Yet there is one indication that they do not share his titillation at the woman's sexual peril. Veralinda interrupts the story when he boasts of his sexual power, to comment that 'a dreadfull man itt seem'd you appear'd to her' (f. 46), to which Philarchos gives the rather lame excuse, that it was 'butt for fear she should bee too willing to mee'.

Wroth's rape narratives are most often told by the narrator of *Urania*. The women's accounts then function as tales-within-tales in these narratives, such as Melasinda's relation of her attempted rape. The effect of gender on narrative is further suggested, however, by episodes narrated wholly by either a male or female character. Antissia's first attack, as we know, has a male narrator; this distances the reader from her experience and distress. Conversely, the most detailed account of attempted rape has a female narrator, Leatissia; her tale, moreover, is told exclusively to a woman auditor, Pamphilia. Finally, Philarchos's narrative shows a male narrator writing female fear as titillating and female desire as culpable. It also reiterates the problematic nature of female self-expression. Wroth thus shows the perilous side of a narrative strategy which has elsewhere empowered her female characters.

Mary Wroth's treatment of rape, then, proves significantly different from that of other romance writers. Recognising the potential of rape both as an expression of the power-relations between men and women and as a narrative structure, she uses it as a key part of her exploration of wider themes. Attempted rape thus functions as an intrinsic part of her exploration of female identity and mental stability, while the fact that the possibility of sexual violence lies behind courtship is an important element in her portrayal of sexual politics. She is perhaps most innovative, however, in her displacement and mockery of the rape narrative's conventional functions (such as exemplifying male power), and in her creation of new functions for it, by using its structure to play with the idea of female desire and narrative control.

# Conclusion

You shall finde [knights] as ready to defend you, as your enemy
dare presume to molest you.

(Palmerin, i. f. 81)

Nay Sir (said shee) that needeth not.

(Urania, p. 518)

The contrast between the presentation of rape found in *Palmerin* (a
1596 translation of the early sixteenth-century original) and Wroth's
playful exploitation and transformation of its conventions in *Urania*
in 1621, is illustrative both of the development of a theme over time
and of the impact of gender-difference. If this study has shown that
the functions of rape both vary from genre to genre and develop
through the period, it has also revealed the *un*changing centrality of
rape to the portrayal of gender-relations.[1]

Both gender-difference and cultural difference have been themes
implicit in this study. I have sought to combine an arguably 'modern'
perspective on sexual violence with an investigation of the specific
meanings and functions of rape in the early modern period. I have
thus highlighted the ways in which ideological circumscriptions on
women, as manifested in literature, so often centre on and are tested
by the depiction of violence against them. I have also sought to add
an understanding of the depiction of rape in literature to the wider
picture of rape in the period: a picture which is made up of the existing
historical and sociological studies, and will I hope continue to expand.
While literary depictions of rape may not produce 'evidence' of its
historical 'reality', they have clearly been connected to the legal
attitude to 'rape' and 'ravishment', and to the semantic complexity
of these terms.

We have found that a tension characterises most portrayals of
rape in early modern literature, so that overt condemnation of rape
is repeatedly challenged by various strategies which normalise,
inscribe and even validate it. This strikingly parallels Bashar's finding that the legal attitude to rape was at odds with the actual low
reportage and low conviction rate. In fact, this historical anomaly
seems to be analogous with literary representations in several
respects. The dual position of women as both male property and the
(potentially more active) keepers or destroyers of male honour, is

one ideological clash that resonates in literature. The conflicting functions of rape scenarios as defining female virtue or as titillating a male readership, provide another analogy. And just as, when rape was regarded as a crime against (and thus actively *involving*) the woman, conviction seems to have become even less likely, so the significance accorded to the mental state of the raped woman often problematises literary portrayals.

Where in the modern legal system male and female voices generally compete to define a sexual act either as consensual or as rape, early modern literature does not usually stage such 'courtroom' situations.[2] The competition to define rape is largely manifested here in tensions within the texts, rather than in specific conflicts between male and female characters or 'viewpoints', although such conflicts do occur. The engagement of women writers with the subject of rape, however, clearly provides another version of this conflict of representations.

Caroline Lucas's contention that a woman writer will treat rape differently from a male writer has been borne out by *Urania*. However, her suggestion that a woman writer might 'view [rape] in a personal, more direct way, rather than from the standpoint of a detached (male) observer' needs qualification.[3] For one thing, not all representations of rape by male writers can be characterised as 'detached'. This hardly seems to acknowledge erotic or political agendas or other narrative or ideological purposes. Moreover, Wroth clearly shares with other writers an awareness of the literary or narrative potential of the rape scenario (just as polemical writers draw on it as a topos which can counter misogynist charges of female wantonness). Where 'difference' comes in, then, is in her exploitation of this narrative situation to convey, in many cases, a 'female' perspective.

Without setting out to seek 'gender-difference', this study has nevertheless found significant differences in the way one woman writer treats rape, and in the ways women writers engage with issues of female sexual and linguistic autonomy. In so doing, it has also revealed the complex engagement of these writers with their literary and ideological contexts.

The depiction of sexual violence is paradigmatic of attitudes towards women represented in early modern literature. As a means of either proving or affecting a woman's sexual status, we have seen that rape (or its threat) is closely involved in the polarity between chaste and unchaste women which is prominent in early modern thought. It also exposes the problematic relationship between mind and body and the anxiety about female knowability which is prevalent in this period. These issues have proved central to the works of Mary Sidney, Cary and Wroth, who reflect on them using rape or female sexual shame in different ways as a narrative or figurative tool, or as a generic context.

The question of titillation is worth reflecting on here for the contrast provided by juxtaposing male- and female-authored texts. We have seen that the portrayal of rape is frequently titillating, and that in male-authored narratives the eroticisation of violence against women sometimes serves no other purpose. Of course, like any other effect of representation on a posited 'reader', titillation does not necessarily relate to authorial intention. Nevertheless, it is interesting that in the case of two women writers a contrast in this function is available. While it is possible to see Mariam's execution as an alternative to rape, Cary makes this suggestion without recourse to an eroticisation of the violence against her. In *Urania*, titillation is certainly a dynamic in many episodes, but itself comes under scrutiny as Wroth plays with the idea of female self-display and voyeurism (visual, aural and narratorial).

I should like now to revisit a critical work that has had a significant place in the feminist project to uncover female roles in the production of literary and visual art: Nancy Vickers' article 'The Mistress in the Masterpiece'. Vickers 'reads' together Benvenuto Cellini's bronze relief, 'The Nymph of Fontainebleau', and his account of its production, to 'locate the position of ... a specifically female body, within it'.[4] I wish to reread in particular Cellini's written description of his treatment of his model for the Nymph, Caterina.

Having caught Caterina being unfaithful to him, Cellini marries her off to her lover but continues to 'use' her artistically and sexually. In her account of Cellini's treatment of his model/mistress, Vickers argues persuasively that 'Caterina's flesh is positioned to serve ... both sexual and artistic needs; she provides not only bodily but also visual pleasure ... through the "delightful" spectacle of beauty under pressure'.[5] She also points out that Cellini's sexual 'use' of Caterina is explicitly presented as his revenge on her husband, so that her body is caught in a battle between male sexual rivals.[6] However, while arguing that male art is heavily reliant upon female subjection (whereby the manipulation of the image of woman *in* the relief is parallel to the exploitation of the artist's model), she does not draw attention to the way in which Cellini's account represents his sexual relationship with Caterina in a way that approximates to rape.

Since the sexual act is used and represented as revenge, it already functions as an appropriation of the female body analogous to rape. Cellini represents it as follows:

> I made her pose in the nude ... and then I had my revenge by using her sexually. ... I also made her pose in great discomfort for hours at a stretch. Her discomfort annoyed her as much as it pleased me ('me dilettava'), since she was very beautifully made. ... [She 'insults' him and he beats her up.] When I had given her a good pummelling, she swore she would never return; so for the first time I realized what a mistake I had made. ... I saw her all torn, bruised, and swollen, and I realized that even if she did come back it would be necessary to have her treated for two weeks before I could use her.[7]

The issue here is not whether or not the phrase 'using her sexually' masks a rape. Rather, it is the closeness in Cellini's *representation* between the sexual act (which presents the woman as a passive object), physical violence and artistic manipulation which I wish to highlight. The 'discomfort' of the woman's posing is clearly close, in this representation, to her experience of his physical violence. It is also readily alignable with her experience of the sexual act. Analogously with many of the writers we have looked at, Cellini both inscribes and eradicates rape in his representation. He writes out the issue of her volition in his sexual appropriation, while taking pleasure in describing her lack of volition in his physical brutalisation of her; the description of her 'torn, bruised, and swollen' is too close to those of the sexual act and of her beauty in posing to be devoid of erotic signification. He then represents himself and Caterina as replaying a cycle of sex, violence and art, as she returns to him, to '[enjoy] sexual pleasure', be beaten and model for him: 'My figure came out beautifully'.[8]

In re-reading this depiction, I seek to add a violence which is specifically *sexual* to the interconnection Vickers notes between female beauty and representation here. Vickers' article returns the 'mistress' to the 'masterpiece' and forms part of a wider project of establishing the 'Poetics of Gender'[9] in a way that facilitates the reading of women's texts as well as of women's depiction in male art. I have sought to add, further, an understanding of the ways in which represented gender-relations in the early modern period have exploited the subject of rape, and to use this as a way into the issues of sexual and discursive autonomy which figure so largely in so many women's texts of the period.

As well as enhancing our understanding of the representation of gender-relations in early modern literature (and the gendering of that representation), this study has attempted, conversely, to add early modern literary representations of rape to the widening picture of the portrayal of rape across literature. This picture is itself part of the process of understanding rape as a social and cultural phenomenon. In what ways, then, do early modern literary representations of rape extend our understanding of its cultural functioning, or bear out existing theories and findings? They clearly bear out the feminist contention that rape is 'more a political than a sexual act', that is, motivated foremost by the desire for power, rather than by desire *per se*.[10] The prevalence of rape in early modern literature suggests its importance for the represented power-dynamic between men and women, while its various functions show rape being exploited as both a narrative and an ideological tool. We have, moreover, examined the ways in which narratorial condemnation of rape tends to be counterbalanced by its inscription. The tendency for rape to be troped as 'something else', too, is widespread. In these ways, rape's portrayal in this period confirms more general findings.[11]

The idea that rape is often portrayed as seduction, however, proves particularly complex in this period. Because 'rape' at this point is no longer defined straightforwardly as a property crime, a concern with the mind of the raped woman competes with a tendency to define her as unchaste regardless of her volition. The idea of pollution mediates this opposition, but does not resolve it. However, the ideological imperatives that shape female conduct crucially affect the presentation of her volition, too. Seduction and rape, then, are blurred not only by the projection of male desire onto its victim (although we have seen this at work in poetry in particular), but also by the conflation of coercion *and* temptation as threatening female virtue, which writes out female desire. Conversely, we have seen female-voiced polemical writers in particular writing seduction *as* violation. In these cases, an apparent vagueness of the boundary between rape and seduction functions as part of the polemicists' conflation and equation of verbal persuasion and sexual violence as

equally coercive and damaging, rather than (for example) the epyllion writers' eradication of female volition in their representations of
the sexual act.

The relationship between female desire, resistance and virtue is
thus problematic. One woman writer, Lanyer, chooses to endorse
the contention that resistance through lack of desire does not qualify
as virtuous conduct.[12] More radically, Cary shows Mariam manipulating sexual resistance to ensure an autonomy which is emotional,
discursive and (potentially) political as well as sexual, while Wroth
explicitly challenges the idea that a woman's sexual resistance must
be based on her concern for chastity rather than on her sexual
choice.

It is worth, finally, reflecting on continuities as well as differences
between our own time and the period of this study. The presentation of rape in modern law as a matter of competing representations
would seem to render self-evident the relevance of studying earlier
representations of rape today. Until 1994, in a case of sexual assault
or rape with no corroborative evidence, the judge was required to
advise the jury that it would be dangerous for them to convict solely
on the evidence of the complainant.[13] This legal formula seems to
have descended from Sir Matthew Hale's contention in 1678 that
rape 'is an accusation easily to be made and hard to be proved, and
harder to be defended by the party accused, tho never so innocent'.[14]

I have not sought 'psychological' reasons for female reactions to
violence, beyond the parameters set up by the texts. I noted at the
outset that self-destructive responses to rape, such as self-mutilation
and suicide, relate in early modern texts to ideological tropes (such
as the power of beauty) and economic realities (the status of women
as male property). It is nevertheless thought-provoking to consider
the congruence between these motifs of early modern literature and
the self-mutilation and suicide attempts which may result from rape
today. This might lead us to ponder the impact on modern women
of the cultural heritage concerning rape.

Such questions cannot be answered here. Instead I should like to
bring the insights of this study to bear on a modern film representation of rape, *The Accused* (1988), for the light it sheds on rape as a narrative device and on the uneasy relationship between rape and the
female voice. In this film, which purports to expose the 'reality' of
modern rape law, the rape of the heroine, Sarah Tobias, is carefully

manipulated to produce the optimum dramatic and cinematic effect. To achieve this, it must be moved from its chronological place at the beginning of the story and staged virtually at the end of the film, providing its climax. This graphic depiction of gang rape has received much criticism for being voyeuristic: and perhaps the depiction of rape can never escape such charges. The positioning of the scene as the film's climax, however, makes such an effect more likely; that the rape is preceded by an erotic dance by the heroine, however intrinsic to the plot, also heightens the sense of the viewer's voyeurism.

There are clear continuities here in the narrative functions of rape in art, whether literary or cinematic. The issue of voice is prominent too. The function of the trial in *The Accused*, after all, is to give Sarah a voice; after the rape charges against her attackers have been reduced to lesser, non-sexual charges before trial, the trial of the men who incited the rape is supposed to allow her to tell her story. This she does, but it is not this narration of rape by its female victim that accompanies the portrayal of the scene in flashback. Instead, it is the testimony of a male witness, Kenneth Joyce, that has this role, reflecting the fact that his story carries greater weight than hers in the trial. In fact, the camera 'eye' shifts during the flashback rape scene from representing Kenneth's view, to Sarah's, and to the rapists' and other witnesses'. By destabilising the link between Kenneth's voice and the enacted rape, this might seem to challenge his prerogative in taking over the narratorial role at this point.

The gendering of voice in relation to rape, then, continues to be problematic in modern depictions. While the trial's verdict vindicates Sarah, the film privileges the graphic representation of rape over her narration of it, and severs the one from the other, even if somewhat uneasily.

Absolute certainty about sexual violence against women is in *The Accused*, as in the trial it depicts, provided by male corroboration. This perhaps reflects a sense of the 'unknowability' of women and their sexual history which is now familiar to us from the early modern period. Yet if female knowability or its impossibility is a theme of early modern texts (and it is this idea Wroth plays with when she teasingly inscribes female desire), female *knowledge* is, conversely, a theme of the women's texts we have considered here. Where Lumley's Iphigenia early in the period is striking in her 'wit' but is denied knowledge of the male bargain that will cost her her life, Wroth's Nereana, in 1621, is baffled by allusions to 'metamorphosis' because 'her wit [lies] another way' (p. 168): and this metamorphosis both reflects and impacts upon her knowledge and definition of herself. And in 1616, Leigh's conduct book posits book-learning as a sign of the chaste woman and as a means of guarding her ears from male erotic persuasions or coercions.

The conditions by which female utterance is licensed and/or circumscribed have been a central theme of this book; the women writers considered in it stage, negotiate and experiment with these conditions within their texts. The mythical origin of women's discourse in resistance to male violence finds a reflection here. Many of the texts considered have resisted or 'rewritten' male-authored discourse. This is manifested as much in the challenging of the precepts of marriage literature, or contemporary views on female insanity, as in the specific relationships between original and translated texts, between Josephus and Cary, or Philip Sidney and Wroth. If in rewriting their sources they follow Philomela and Arachne, whose discourses responded to and challenged male sexual violence, this is to restore something of the 'fury' of these figures, so often written as victims. It also suggests a conception of women's utterance, despite its limiting conditions, as empowering. Female 'unbridled speech' may be as dangerous to the speaker as to the auditor, but this too confirms its power.

# Notes

## INTRODUCTION

1.  John Daye, 'The P[rinter] to the Reader' in Thomas Norton and Thomas Sackville, *The Tragidie of Ferrex and Porrex* [*Gorboduc*] (revised edition; 1570), sig. Aii.
2.  See Wendy Wall, *The Imprint of Gender: Authorship and Publication in the English Renaissance* (Ithaca and London: Cornell University Press, 1993), chapter 3.
3.  See Susan Brownmiller, *Against Our Will: Men, Women and Rape* (NY: Simon and Schuster, 1975); Peggy Reeves Sanday, 'Rape and the Silencing of the Feminine' in Sylvana Tomaselli and Roy Porter, eds *Rape: An Historical and Cultural Enquiry* (Oxford: Basil Blackwell, 1986; rpr. 1989); Ross Harrison, 'Rape – a Case Study in Political Philosophy', ibid., pp. 41–56. Anne Edwards summarises feminist views on rape in 'Male Violence in Feminist Theory: an Analysis of the Changing Conceptions of Sex/Gender Violence and Male Dominance' in *Women, Violence and Social Control*, ed. Jalna Hammer and Mary Maynard (Basingstoke: Macmillan, 1987), pp. 13–29.
4.  Christine Froula argues that this inscription of misogynistic violence in literature puts women readers into the position of 'abused daughter[s]'. 'The Daughter's Seduction: Sexual Violence and Literary History', *Signs* xi (1986), 621–44 (633). For discussions of the visual arts, see, for example, Ian Donaldson, *The Rapes of Lucretia: a Myth and its Transformations* (Oxford: Clarendon Press, 1982); Norman Bryson, 'Two Narratives of Rape in the Visual Arts: Lucretia and the Sabine Women' in Tomaselli and Porter, pp. 152–73. For an analysis of the place of rape in feminist criticism see William Beatty Warner, 'Reading Rape: Marxist-Feminist Figurations of the Literal', *Diacritics* xiii (1983), 12–32.
5.  See Lynn A. Higgins and Brenda Silver, eds *Rape and Representation* (NY: Columbia University Press, 1991); Ellen Rooney, 'Criticism and the Subject of Sexual Violence', *MLN* xcviii (1983), 1269–77; Tomaselli and Porter.
6.  For medieval French literature, see Patricia Francis Cholakian, *Rape and Writing in the* Heptaméron *of Marguerite de Navarre* (Carbondale and Edwardsville: Southern Illinois University Press, 1991); Kathryn Gravdal, *Ravishing Maidens: Writing Rape in Medieval French Literature and Law* (Philadelphia: University of Pennsylvania Press, 1991). See also Donaldson; Kathleen Wall, *The Callisto Myth: Initiation and Rape in Literature* (Kingston and Montreal: McGill-Queen's University Press, 1988). Rape may, of course, be discussed in connection with individual writers. For rape in Jacobean drama, see Suzanne Gossett, '"Best Men are Molded out of Faults": Marrying the Rapist in Jacobean Drama', *ELR* xiv (1984), 305–27; Leonard Tennenhouse, 'The Theater of Punishment: Jacobean Tragedy and the Politics of Misogyny' in *Power*

*on Display: The Politics of Shakespeare's Genres* (NY and London: Methuen, 1986), pp. 102–46.

7. These terminal dates allow inclusion both of the earliest woman's text considered here (Jane Lumley's *Iphigeneia*) and of works by two others, Elizabeth Cary and Mary Wroth, which were not published during their lifetimes but were written in the 1620s.

8. Diane Purkiss emphasises the class backgrounds of these writers as decisive factors in their writing. See her edition of *Three Tragedies by Renaissance Women: The Tragedie of Iphigeneia in a version by Jane, Lady Lumley, The Tragedie of Antonie translated by Mary, Countess of Pembroke, The Tragedie of Mariam by Elizabeth Cary* (Harmondsworth: Penguin, 1998), Introduction.

9. William Shakespeare, *The Rape of Lucrece* (1594), l. 822 in *The Poems*, ed. F.T. Prince (London and NY: Methuen, 1960; rpr. 1985).

10. For the Senecan controversy 'The Man Who Raped Two Women', see Eugene M. Waith, *The Pattern of Tragicomedy in Beaumont and Fletcher* (New Haven: Yale University Press, 1952), p. 89.

11. See, for example, Elaine V. Beilin, *Redeeming Eve: Women Writers of the English Renaissance* (Princeton, NJ and Oxford: Princeton University Press, 1987); Clare Brant and Diane Purkiss, eds *Women, Texts & Histories 1575–1760* (London and NY: Routledge, 1992); Margaret Patterson Hannay, ed. *Silent But for the Word: Tudor Women as Patrons, Translators, and Writers of Religious Works* (Kent, Ohio: Kent State University Press, 1985); Tina Krontiris, *Oppositional Voices: Women as Writers and Translators of Literature in the English Renaissance* (London and NY: Routledge, 1992). For women's reading, see Suzanne Hull, *Chaste, Silent, & Obedient: English Books for Women 1475–1640* (San Marino: Huntington Library, 1982).

12. For the problematic implications of biographical readings of women's texts, see Danielle E. Clarke, 'Translation, Interpretation and Gender: Women's Writing c. 1595–1644' (D. Phil. thesis, Oxford, 1994), p. iv.

13. For a summary of the controversy, see Katharine Eisaman Maus, *Inwardness and Theater in the English Renaissance* (Chicago and London: University of Chicago Press, 1995), pp. 2–3.

14. Ibid., p. 28.

15. I am indebted to Elizabeth D. Harvey's *Ventriloquized Voices: Feminist Theory and English Renaissance Texts* (London and NY: Routledge, 1992) for my understanding of this phenomenon.

16. The swan was traditionally mute till just before death, when it sang for the first and last time. In Orlando Gibbons' popular madrigal, 'The siluer Swanne', the dying swan is female. *First Set of Madrigals and Mottets* (1612), sig. A3.

17. I do not reiterate ideas about women and authorship which are now familiar from the body of criticism indicated above, except as the issue of authorship relates to originary myths of rape.

18. For discussions of the assimilation of these women's texts into the canon, and its implications, see Purkiss, *Three Tragedies*, Introduction, pp. xi–xiii, and Jonathan Goldberg, *Desiring Women Writing: English*

*Renaissance Examples* (Stanford: Stanford University Press, 1997), pp. 3–15. For introductions to the lives and works of Jane Lumley and Mary Sidney, see, respectively, Lorraine Helms, 'Iphigenia in Durham' in *Seneca by Candlelight & Other Stories of Renaissance Drama* (Philadelphia: University of Pennsylvania Press, 1997), pp. 48–71; Margaret Patterson Hannay, *Philip's Phoenix: Mary Sidney, Countess of Pembroke* (Oxford: Oxford University Press, 1990). Mary Ellen Lamb's *Gender and Authorship in the Sidney Circle* (Wisconsin: University of Wisconsin Press, 1990) covers both Mary Sidney and Mary Wroth. For a useful summary of material on Elizabeth Cary and Wroth, see Barbara Kiefer Lewalski, *Writing Women in Jacobean England* (Cambridge, Mass. and London: Harvard University Press, 1993).

19. See, for example, Harvey; Rosemary Kegl, *The Rhetoric of Concealment: Figuring Gender and Class in Renaissance Literature* (Ithaca and London: Cornell University Press, 1994); Linda Woodbridge, *Women and the English Renaissance: Literature and the Nature of Womankind, 1540–1620* (Urbana and Chicago: University of Illinois Press, 1984). I am of course indebted to this body of criticism.

20. See, for example, Beilin, Krontiris, Lewalski. For exceptions to this rule, see Lorna Hutson, *The Usurer's Daughter: Male Friendship and Fictions of Women in Sixteenth-Century England* (London and NY: Routledge, 1994); Wendy Wall. Lamb's book reverses the usual trend by devoting all but one chapter to the writings of the female members of the Sidney circle.

21. Feminist readings of women's writing have often sought the 'feminine difference'. Margaret J.M. Ezell charts the ways in which different generations of critics have read women's works, in *Writing Women's Literary History* (Baltimore and London: Johns Hopkins University Press, 1993).

## CHAPTER 1

1. William Painter, *The Palace of Pleasure* [volume i] (1566), i. f. 6.
2. See Kathleen Wall, p. 173.
3. Higgins and Silver, pp. 2–4.
4. For the purposes of this study, I shall be looking at rapes of women rather than men.
5. Lee Ellis, *Theories of Rape: Inquiries into the Causes of Sexual Aggression* (NY and London: Hemisphere, 1989), pp. 1–2.
6. Tomaselli, 'Introduction' in Tomaselli and Porter, pp. 10–11.
7. See, for example, E. Sue Blume, *Secret Survivors: Uncovering Incest and Its Aftereffects in Women* (NY and Chicester: John Wiley & Sons, 1990), pp. 90–3, 184–91.
8. See Nazife Bashar, 'Rape in England between 1550 and 1700' in *The Sexual Dynamics of History: Men's Power, Women's Resistance* (London: Feminist History Collective, 1983), pp. 28–42 (33–4). This leads Miranda

Chaytor to define her project, despite its focus on legal records, as looking not at history but representation. 'Husband(ry): Narratives of Rape in the Seventeenth Century', *Gender & History* vii (1995), 378–407 (382).

9. Susanne Kappeler, *The Pornography of Representation* (Cambridge: Policy Press, 1986), p. 2.

10. Amy Richlin, 'Reading Ovid's Rapes' in (ed.) *Pornography and Representation in Greece and Rome* (Oxford and NY: Oxford University Press, 1992), pp. 158–78.

11. See *OED*, 'rape' ($v.^2$).

12. See *OED*, $v.^2$, 2: 'To carry off (a person, *esp.* a woman) by force', and 3: 'To ravish, commit rape on (a woman)'.

13. Porter, 'Rape – Does it have a Historical Meaning?' in Tomaselli and Porter, p. 217.

14. See *OED*, 'ravish' (1), (2.a): 'To carry away (a woman) by force. (Sometimes implying subsequent violation)', (2b): 'To commit rape upon (a woman), to violate'; 'deflower' (1): 'To deprive (a woman) of her virginity; to violate, ravish'. An early image of 'deflowering', Ovid's story of Proserpina, asociates it with rape rather than simply initiation. See Ovid, *Metamorphoses*, ed. Frank Justus Mller (Loeb Classical Library, London: William Heinemann Ltd and Cambridge, Mass.: Harvard University Press, 1944), v. ll. 398–401.

15. Elspeth Graham, 'Women's Writing and the Self' in *Women and Literature in Britain 1500–1700*, ed. Helen Wilcox (Cambridge: Cambridge University Press, 1996), pp. 209–33 (215).

16. Corinne J. Saunders, 'Secular Law: Rape and *Raptus*' in 'Against Her Will: The Writing of Rape in Medieval England', Chapter 2 (forthcoming). I am grateful to the author for allowing me to read this in manuscript.

17. Ibid. Early modernists have tended to assume that the definition of 'rape' as sexual violation originated in the late sixteenth century, rather than, to some extent, re-emerging.

18. Bashar, p. 41. This article also summarises the scant existing historical studies of rape in the early modern period.

19. John Bullokar, *The English Expositor* (1616), sig. M8.

20. *The Lawes Resolvtions of Womens Rights: Or, The Lawes Provision for Woemen* (1632), edited by 'T.E.': probably Thomas Edgar. See note in *STC*.

21. Bashar, pp. 33, 40.

22. Ibid., p. 41.

23. *OED*, 'ravish' (3c). See also 'ravishment' (3), 'ravishing' (3). The earliest usages recorded are from the fourteenth century, *c.* 1477 and *c.* 1430, respectively.

24. Gravdal, p. 5. Gravdal is describing the French words 'ravir', 'ravissement' and 'ravissant', but the English is directly equivalent.

25. Ibid. The word 'ravish' now connotes romantic seduction rather than rape.

26. Rooney, p. 1275.

27. Shakespeare, *Lucrece*, ll. 1791–1806.

28. Frances Ferguson, 'Rape and the Rise of the Novel', *Representations* xx (1987), 88–112 (99).

29. Thomas Laqueur traces this argument back to second-century Rome. *Making Sex: Body and Gender from the Greeks to Freud* (Cambridge, Mass. and London: Harvard University Press, 1990), p. 161.

30. *Lawes Resolution*, pp. 396, 400. See also Bashar, p. 36.

31. The realisation that orgasm may coexist with trauma and resistance during rape is relatively new even today. See Blume, pp. 110, 221. Shakespeare's *Lucrece* is discussed in Chapter 3, pp. 65–8.

32. J. Healey, trans. St Augustine, *Of the Citie of God* (1610), p. 31.

33. Vives' note in Healey, p. 27.

34. See Donaldson, pp. 21–39. For an account of the role of the threat of rape in the medieval 'saint's life', see Saunders, 'Against Her Will', chapter 4.

35. Helen Hackett, *Virgin Mother, Maiden Queen: Elizabeth I and the Cult of the Virgin Mary* (Basingstoke: Macmillan, 1995), p. 178.

36. Louis Adrian Montrose, 'The Elizabethan Subject and the Spenserian Text' in Patricia Parker and David Quint, eds *Literary Theory / Renaissance Texts* (Baltimore: Johns Hopkins University Press, 1986), pp. 303–40 (314–6). Hackett argues that Elizabeth's virginity was celebrated as 'an emblem of the defiant impregnability of the body politic' (1995, p. 118). For a discussion of the simultaneous penetrability and intactness of the female body, see Maus, pp. 193ff. For a detailed investigation of the ways in which rape figures in representations of Elizabeth, see Susan Frye, *Elizabeth I: The Competition for Representation* (Oxford and NY: Oxford University Press, 1993), for example, pp. 72–86, 135–9.

37. Ovid, *Fasti*, ed. and trans. J.G. Frazer (Loeb Classical Library, London: William Heinemann Ltd, 1989), ll. 810.

38. William Vaughan, *The Golden-Grove* (1608), i. sig. E7–E7v.

39. Patricia Francis Cholakian discusses the debating of this problem in Marguerite de Navarre's *Heptaméron* (pp. 63–4).

40. Rooney, p. 1272.

41. Kappeler, pp. 157–8.

42. For this formal controversy over the nature of women see Woodbridge.

43. For the vexed relationship between persuasion and coercion, see Maus, pp. 81ff. See also John Forrester, 'Rape, Seduction and Psychoanalysis' in Tomaselli and Porter, pp. 57–83.

44. Gossett sums up the evidence that it was wise for a rape victim to marry her rapist (pp. 310–12). Frances Ferguson discusses the implications of marriage for perceptions of rape (p. 90).

45. See Stephanie H. Jed, *Chaste Thinking: The Rape of Lucretia and the Birth of Humanism* (Bloomington, Indianapolis: Indiana University Press, 1989), p. 3, paraphrasing Aristotle, *The Politics*, trans. B. Jowett (Oxford, 1885), 1311a, 1314b. See also Donaldson, pp. 7ff.

46. Niccolò Machiavelli, *The Discourses*, ed. Bernard Crick (Harmondsworth: Penguin, 1970), iii, chapter 26, p. 477.

47. The conflicting schools of thought are summarised helpfully in Ellis.

48. Teresa de Lauretis, 'The Violence of Rhetoric: Considerations on Representation and Gender' in *Technologies of Gender: Essays on Theory,*

*Film, and Fiction* (Bloomington: University of Indiana Press, 1989), pp. 31–50 (36–7).

49. Monique Plaza, 'Our Costs and Their Benefits', trans. Wendy Harrison, *m/f*, iv (1980), 28–39 (31).

50. Jonathan Crewe, *Trials of Authorship: Anterior Forms and Poetic Reconstruction from Wyatt to Shakespeare* (Berkeley: University of California Press, 1990), p. 141.

51. Thomas Nashe, *The Unfortunate Traveller* in *An Anthology of Elizabethan Prose Fiction*, ed. Paul Salzman (Oxford: Oxford University Press, 1987), p. 281. See Constance C. Relihan, *Fashioning Authority: The Development of Elizabethan Novelistic Discourse* (Kent, Ohio and London: Kent State University Press, 1994), pp. 69–70.

52. See Laura Mulvey, 'Visual Pleasure and Narrative Cinema', *Screen* xvi (1975), 6–18; E. Ann Kaplan, 'Is the Gaze Male?' in Ann Snitow, Christine Stansell and Sharon Thompson, eds *Desire: The Politics of Sexuality* (London: Virago, 1984), pp. 321–38; Nancy J. Vickers, '"The blazon of sweet beauty's best": Shakespeare's *Lucrece'* in Patricia Parker and Geoffrey Hartman, eds *Shakespeare and the Question of Theory* (NY and London: Routledge, 1985), pp. 95–115; Parker, *Literary Fat Ladies: Rhetoric, Gender, Property* (London: Methuen, 1987), pp. 126–54.

53. Gravdal, p. 17, drawing on Norman Holland, *The Dynamics of Literary Response* (Oxford: Oxford University Press, 1968).

54. Caroline Lucas, *Writing for Women: the Example of Woman as Reader in Elizabethan Romance* (Milton Keynes: Open University Press, 1989), p. 56.

55. Valerie Traub, *Desire and Anxiety: Circulations of Sexuality in Shakespearean Drama* (London and NY: Routledge, 1992), p. 100.

## CHAPTER 2

1. See also Bandello, *Certain Tragical Discourses Written Out of French and Latin by Geoffrey Fenton* (1567), ed. Hugh Harris as *Bandello: Tragical Tales* (London: Routledge, 1925); and George Pettie, *A petite Pallace of Pettie his pleasure* (1567), ed. I. Gollanz (London: Chatto & Windus, 1908), which includes Philomela's story.

2. The earliest extant edition of *Amadis* (in Spanish) is from 1508, with all 12 of its books available by 1546. The first cycle of *Palmerin* began to appear in Spanish in 1511 and continued throughout the century. See John J. O'Connor, *Amadis de Gaule And Its Influence on Elizabethan Literature* (New Brunswick, NJ: Rutgers University Press, 1970). The first book of Ortuñez's *Mirror of Knighthood* appears in 1578 in Margaret Tyler's English translation. The 1580s see further volumes of that cycle translated, the first volume of *Palmerin d'Oliua, Palmendos*, and the first English translation (bar extracts) of *Amadis* (book i, licensed 1589). The remaining decade of the reign sees several volumes each of *Amadis, Primaleon, Palmerin of England* and the *Mirror*, as well as a translation of Ariosto's *Orlando Furioso.*

3.  See Lucas, pp. 8–18.
4.  See Hutson, p. 89.
5.  Gravdal, pp. 43–4.
6.  The chivalric romances treated in this chapter are: *The Ancient, Famous And Honourable History of Amadis de Gaule*, part i, trans. Anthony Munday (1589; rpr. 1613); Ludovico Ariosto, *Orlando Furioso. Translated into English Heroicall Verse by Sir John Harington* (1591), ed. Robert McNulty (Oxford: Clarendon Press, 1972); Diego Ortuñez de Calahorra, *The First Part of the Mirrour of Princely Deeds and Knighthood*, trans. Margaret Tyler (1578; rpr. 1599), *The Second Part of the Mirror of Knighthood* (1583, rpr. 1598), *The Third Part*... (books i (1598), ii (1598), iii (1599), iv (1601)) [I shall refer to these as *Mirror*, i, ii, and iii(1), (2), (3) and (4), respectively]; Anthony Munday, trans. *The History of Palmendos* (1589), *The History of Palmerin*, i and ii (1596; rpr. 1616), *The Third and last part of Palmerin* (1602), *The Historie of Primaleon of Greece* (i, 1595, ii, 1596; rpr. i, ii and iii, 1619), *The History of Palladine of England* (1588; rpr. 1700); Bartholomew Yong, trans. *Diana of George of Montemayor* (1598).
7.  See *Orlando*, VIII. 52ff., XVII. 42; *Palmerin*, i. ff. 125ff., 168v, 169v–170; ii. f. 62; *Mirror*, i. f. 70ff.
8.  See *Orlando*, XVI. 30, XL. 32–4; *Primaleon*, ii. f. 15; *Mirror*, ii. f. 26v.
9.  Corinne Saunders finds the forest to be a 'conventional landscape' for rape. *The Forest of Medieval Romance: Avernus, Broceliande, Arden* (Cambridge: Cambridge University Press, 1993), p. 160.
10. In Thomas Lodge's *The Life and Death of William Longbeard* (1593) a woman offers herself to an earl to save herself from rape by soldiers. *The Complete Works* (NY: Russell and Russell Inc., 1963), ii. 61.
11. *Palmerin*, ii. ff. 15 ff.
12. See Chapter 1, n. 44.
13. Painter, *The Second Tome of the Palace of Pleasure* (1567), f. 169.
14. Actual rapes occur in Bandello's 'Modern Lucretia' (*Certain Tragical Discourses*); George Gascoigne, *The Adventures of Master F.J.*; Thomas Lodge, *Euphues Shadow, William Longbeard*, and *Robert Duke of Normandy*; John Lyly, *Love's Metamorphosis*; Nashe, *The Unfortunate Traveller*, Painter, 'Lucrece' and 'Alexander de Medices'; Pettie, 'Tereus and Progne' (*A petite Pallace*). Attempts occur in Bandello's 'Villainous Abbot'; Greene, *Myrrour of Modestie, Penelopes Web, Philomela, Farewell to Folly*; Lodge, *A Margarite of America, William Longbeard, Robert of Normandy*, Lyly, *Love's Metamorphosis*; Painter, 'Apius and Virginia'; Pettie, 'Icilius and Virginia'; Barnabe Riche, *Farewell to Military Profession* and *Don Simonides*.
15. Garter, *Susanna*, ll. 805–6.
16. Lodge, *A Margarite of America* (1593) in *Works*, iii. 30.
17. Lodge, *Euphues Shadow* (1592) in *Works*, ii. 32–3.
18. Lodge, *The Famous, true and historicall life of Robert second Duke of Normandy* (1591) in *Works*, ii. 24.
19. See *Mirror*, ii. f. 26v.
20. See Jonson's notes for the *Hymenaei. Ben Jonson: The Complete Masques*, ed. Stephen Orgel (New Haven: Yale University Press, 1975), p. 81.

21. Such enchantments, Mary Patchell records, are an old motif in romance. *The Palmerin Romances in Elizabethan Prose Fiction* (NY: Columbia University Press, 1947), p. 41.

22. See George Gascoigne, *The Adventures of Master F.J.* (1573) in Salzman (1987); Barnabe Riche, *Riche his Farewell to Militarie profession* (1581), ed. Donald Beecher (Binghampton, NY: Medieval and Renaissance Texts and Studies, 1992), *The straunge and wonderful aduentures of* Don Simonides, *a gentleman Spaniard*, i (1581), ii (1584), ed. Norbert Kind (D. Phil. thesis, University of Cologne, 1989).

23. Greene, *Philomela: The Lady Fitzwaters Nightingale* (1592) in *The Life and Complete Works of Robert Greene*, ed. Alexander B. Grosart (Huth Library, 1881–6), xi. 179.

24. Lucas, p. 56.

25. Greene, *The Myrrour of Modestie* (1584) in *Works*, iii. 17–18.

26. Philip Sidney, *The Countess of Pembroke's Arcadia (The Old Arcadia)*, ed. Jean Robertson (Oxford: Clarendon Press, 1973), p. 406.

27. Elizabeth Dipple blames Mary Sidney for the alteration in 'The Captivity Episode and the *New Arcadia*', *Journal of English and Germanic Philology* lxx (1971), 418–31 (419). See also William A. Ringler, Jr (ed.) *The Poems of Sir Philip Sidney* (Oxford: Clarendon Press, 1962), p. 375.

28. See Ringler, pp. 372–9; Robertson, p. lxii, n. 2; Peter Lindenbaum, *Changing Landscapes: Anti-Pastoral Sentiment in the English Renaissance* (Athens and London: University of Georgia Press, 1986), pp. 55–6.

29. Catherine Bates argues that courtship in the *Arcadia* is characterised by doubleness or ambivalence. *The Rhetoric of Courtship in Elizabethan Language and Literature* (Cambridge: Cambridge University Press, 1992), pp. 110–35 (115). See also Richard McCoy, *Sir Philip Sidney: Rebellion in Arcadia* (New Brunswick, NJ: Rutgers University Press, 1979), p. 40; Lindenbaum, p. 52.

30. See Bates, p. 117; Robert E. Stillman, *Sidney's Poetic Justice: The Old Arcadia, Its Eclogues, and Renaissance Pastoral Traditions* (Lewisburg, London and Toronto: Bucknell University Press, 1986), p. 135.

31. For other such figures in Spenser and Wroth, see Chapters 3, p. 87 and 8, pp. 194–7.

32. Bates, p. 118.

33. See Walter Davis, 'Narrative Methods in the *Old Arcadia*' in Dennis Kay, ed. *Sir Philip Sidney: An Anthology of Modern Criticism* (Oxford: Clarendon Press, 1987), pp. 103–23 (113–15).

34. See p. 240, n. 52.

35. See Blair Worden, *The Sound of Virtue: Philip Sidney's* Arcadia *and Elizabethan Politics* (New Haven: Yale University Press, 1996), pp. 61–3, 300–1.

36. *The Countess of Pembroke's Arcadia (The New Arcadia)*, ed. Victor Skretkowicz (Oxford: Clarendon Press, 1987), p. 17. Quotations from the revised work will be from this text, unless otherwise stated.

37. *Astrophil and Stella* in *Sir Philip Sidney: Selected Poems*, ed. Katherine Duncan-Jones (Oxford: Clarendon Press, 1973).

38. Cecropia's logic is based on the current belief that conception required both the man and the woman to achieve orgasm. See p. 16.
39. Lamb, p. 101.
40. Maurice Evans, ed. *The Countess of Pembroke's Arcadia* (Harmondsworth: Penguin, 1977), p. 681.
41. Bates argues that the revised sex scenes clash with the depiction of love elsewhere in the revised *Arcadia* (pp. 125ff.).

CHAPTER 3

1. Philip Sidney, 'Astrophil and Stella', Second Song, ll. 1–4.
2. Ann Rosalind Jones and Peter Stallybrass discuss the 'strategies of manipulation' employed by lover and courtier alike, in 'The Politics of *Astrophil and Stella*', SEL xxiv (1984), 53–68 (54). For a further exploration of the congruence of courtship and courtiership, see Bates.
3. *Aurora* (1604), Sonnet 84, ll. 7–8, in *The Poetical Works of Sir William Alexander Earl of Stirling*, ed. L.E. Kastner and H.B. Charlton (Edinburgh and London: William Blackwood & Sons Ltd, 1929), ii.
4. Sir Robert Ayton, 'What others doth discourage', ll. 4, 31–2, in *The New Oxford Book of Seventeenth-Century Verse*, ed. Alastair Fowler (Oxford: Oxford University Press, 1991; rpr. 1992), pp. 77–8.
5. Barnabe Barnes, *Parthenophil and Parthenophe: A Critical Edition*, ed. Victor A. Doyno (Carbondale and Edwardsville: Southern Illinois University Press, 1971), p. 39.
6. See Clark Hulse, *Metamorphic Verse: The Elizabethan Minor Epic* (Princeton, NJ: Princeton University Press, 1981), pp. 17–20.
7. Gervase Markham, *The Famous Whore, or Noble Curtizan: Conteining the lamentable complaint of Paulina, the famous Roman Curtizan* (1609), ed. Frederick Ouvry (London, 1868).
8. See my discussion of 'shame' versus 'guilt' cultures, p. 17.
9. John Kerrigan lists these in his introduction to (ed.) *Motives of Woe: Shakespeare and 'Female Complaint': A Critical Anthology* (Oxford: Clarendon Press, 1991), pp. 14–23.
10. 'Lady forsaken' from *The Paradyse of Daynty Deuises* (1576); see Kerrigan, p. 19 (n.).
11. *Thomas Howell's Poems (1567–81)*, ed. Alexander B. Grosart (Manchester: Occasional Issues of Unique or Very Rare Books, 1879), pp. 224–6.
12. In Kerrigan, p. 127. I cite this, and all other poems in Kerrigan's anthology, by line-number.
13. Ruth Hughey, ed. *The Arundel Harington Manuscript of Tudor Poetry* (Columbus, Ohio: Ohio State University Press, 1960), pp. 113–15 (I shall cite by line number).
14. See Thomas Churchyard, 'Shores Wife' in *Mirror for Magistrates* (1563 edition) in Kerrigan, pp. 111–24; Anthony Chute, *Beawtie dishonoured, written under the title of Shores wife* (1593); Samuel Daniel, *The Complaint of Rosamond*, appended to *Delia* (1592), in Kerrigan, pp. 164–90; Michael Drayton, 'The Epistle of Rosamond to King Henrie the Second'

and 'The Epistle of Shores Wife to King Edward the Fourth' in *Englands Heroicall Epistles* (1597), reproduced in Kerrigan, pp. 192–205; John Higgins, 'Elstride' in *The Mirror for Magistrates* (1574) in *Parts Added to The Mirror for Magistrates by John Higgins and Thomas Blenerhasset*, ed. Lily B. Campbell (Cambridge: Cambridge University Press, 1946); Thomas Lodge, *The Complaint of Elstred*, appended to *Phillis* (1593) in *Works*, ii. 59–84.

15. Götz Schmitz lists many of these in *The Fall of Women in Early English Narrative Verse* (Cambridge: Cambridge University Press, 1990).

16. Thomas Blenerhasset, 'The Lyfe of Lady Ebbe' (1578) in Campbell; Drayton, *Matilda* (1594) in *The Works of Michael Drayton*, ed. J. William Hebel (Oxford: Basil Blackwell, 1961), i; William Barkstead, *That which seems best is worst. Juvenals tenth satyre: with Virginias death* (1617).

17. See sigs Gv, G3; and 'The complaint of her waiting women against the wooers' (sig. E2ff.). Peter Colse, *Penelopes Complaint: or, A Mirrour for wanton Minions* (1596).

18. See Robert Roche, *Eustathia or the Constancie of Susanna* (1599), sig. F5v; Robert Aylett, *Susanna: or, the Arraignment of the Two Uniust Elders* (1622), p. 9.

19. Thomas Middleton, *The Ghost of Lucrece*, ed. Joseph Quincy Adams (NY and London: Charles Scribner's Sons, 1937).

20. See Heather Dubrow, *Captive Victors: Shakespeare's Narrative Poems and Sonnets* (Ithaca and London: Cornell University Press, 1987), p. 143.

21. Richard Barnfield, *The Complaint of Chastitie. Briefely touching the cause of the death of Matilda Fitzwater* in *Poems*, ed. Edward Arber (Westminster: Archibald Constable & Co., 1896), pp. 35–7 (36).

22. See Kerrigan, p. 27.

23. See p. 18.

24. Carolyn D. Williams, '"Silence, like a Lucrece knife": Shakespeare and the Meanings of Rape', *Yearbook of English Studies* xxiii (1993), 93–110 (96–7).

25. Sasha Roberts discusses the editorial apparatus and marginalia of editions of the poem to emphasise the 'disjunction between dominant and dissident readings' of Lucrece's innocence. Shasha Roberts, 'Editing Sexuality, Narrative and Authorship: The Altered Texts of Shakespeare's *Lucrece*' in Cedric C. Brown and Arthur F. Marotti, eds *Texts and Cultural Change in Early Modern England* (Early Modern Literature in History. Basingstoke: Macmillan, 1997), pp. 124–52 (129). She also shows how later editions more explicitly define the poem's central act as a rape.

26. See Schmitz, p. 63.

27. See, for example, Thomas Procter, *The Triumph of Trueth* (1585) with its inset 'Helens Complaint' (sigs Evv–Evi).

28. See Schmitz, pp. 63–4.

29. See M.A. Shaaber, ed. *'The First Rape of Faire Hellen* by John Trussell', *Shakespeare Quarterly* viii (1957), 407–48.

30. Schmitz, p. 66.

31. *Hero and Leander* in Elizabeth Story Donno, ed. *Elizabethan Minor Epics* (London: Routledge & Kegan Paul, 1963) (I cite by line number). The

earliest extant edition of the poem is 1598, but it was entered in the Stationer's Register in 1593.

32.  John Weaver, *Faunus and Melliflora* (1600) in Donno.
33.  Francis Beaumont, *Salmacis and Hermaphroditus* (1602) in Donno.
34.  Thomas Peend, trans. Ovid, *The Pleasant Fable of Hermaphroditus and Salmacis* (1565), sig. A7v.
35.  Thomas Lodge, *Scillas Metamorphosis* (1589), stanza 86 and Thomas Edwards, *Cephalus and Procris* (1595), ll. 529–30, both in Donno.
36.  In Donno.
37.  In John Marston, *Poems*, ed. Arnold Davenport (Liverpool: Liverpool University Press, 1979), quoting from Ovid, *Ars Amatoria*, trans. in William Keach, *Elizabethan Erotic Narratives: Irony and Pathos in the Ovidian Poetry of Shakespeare, Marlowe, and Their Contemporaries* (New Jersey: Rutgers University Press, 1977), p. 153.
38.  Edmund Spenser, *The Faerie Queene*, ed. A.C. Hamilton (London and NY: Longman, 1979).
39.  See III.iv.41, which I shall discuss later.
40.  Susanne Lindgren Wofford, *The Choice of Achilles: The Ideology of Figure in the Epic* (Stanford, Calif.: Stanford University Press, 1992), pp. 365–6.
41.  See Montrose (1986); Thomas H. Cain, *Praise in The Faerie Queene* (Lincoln and London: University of Nebraska Press, 1978).
42.  See Frye, chapter 3; Wofford, p. 325.
43.  See Harry Berger, Jr., '"Kidnapped Romance": Discourse in *The Faerie Queene*' in G. Logan and G. Teskey, eds *Unfolded Tales: Essays on Renaissance Romance* (Ithaca: Cornell University Press, 1989), pp. 208–56 (244).
44.  Maureen Quilligan, *The Language of Allegory: Defining the Genre* (Ithaca: Cornell University Press, 1979), p. 30.
45.  Stevie Davies, *The Feminine Reclaimed: The Idea of Woman in Spenser, Shakespeare and Milton* (Lexington: University Press of Kentucky, 1986), p. 72.
46.  Wofford, p. 14.
47.  Sheila T. Cavanagh, *Wanton Eyes & Chaste Desires: Female Sexuality in The Faerie Queene* (Bloomington and Indianapolis: Indiana University Press, 1994), p. 7.
48.  Wofford discusses the congruence and disjunction between rapture and rape, pp. 353–71.
49.  The Argument to IV.x hints at the nature of the appropriation by calling it a 'conquest'.
50.  Davies, p. 83; Cavanagh, p. 3.
51.  Hackett (1995), p. 141.
52.  For the function of landscape as origin in Spenser, see David Quint, *Origin & Originality in Renaissance Literature: Versions of the Source* (New Haven and London: Yale University Press, 1983), pp. 149–66.
53.  This may be due to allegory's dependence on female bodies. Where male sexual power is represented by a single figure, it is in the allegorical figure of Lust (which clouds the issue) or (again, ambiguously) in Busyrane.

54. Judith Dundas traces the images of both the spider and the bee for poetic creativity in *The Faerie Queene*. *The Spider and the Bee: The Artistry of Spenser's Faerie Queene* (Urbana and Chicago: University of Illinois Press, 1985), p. 8. For weaving as an image of specifically female language, see pp. 122–3.
55. See Ovid, *Metamorphoses*, x. ll. 76ff.
56. For the connection between vision, voyeurism and desire, see Theresa M. Krier, *Gazing on Secret Sights: Spenser, Classical Imitation, and the Decorums of Vision* (Ithaca and London: Cornell University Press, 1990).
57. The same phenomenon appears in Jacobean drama; see Chapter 4, pp. 96–7.
58. Frye, p. 130. On the other hand, Berger calls the masque a 'symbolic murder'. 'Busirane and the War Between the Sexes: An Interpretation of *The Faerie Queene* III.xi–xii', *ELR* i (1971), 99–121 (106).
59. For Busyrane as representing Love or Eros, see James Nohrnberg, *The Analogy of The Faerie Queene* (Princeton, NJ: Princeton University Press, 1976), pp. 472, 480–3.
60. See Davies (pp. 96–7) and Cavanagh (pp. 5–6), who locates the scene in the context of violent pornography.
61. Spenser, *Prothalamion* in *The Minor Poems*, ii, ed. Charles Grosvenor Osgood and Henry Gibbons Lotspeich, in *The Works of Edmund Spenser: A Variorum Edition*, ed. Edwin Greenlaw et al. (Baltimore: Johns Hopkins University Press, 1947).
62. Spenser, *Epithalamion* in *Minor Poems*, ii. I am grateful to Dennis Kay for supplying me with these details and connections.
63. See, for instance, Jonathan Goldberg, *Endlesse Worke: Spenser and the Structures of Discourse* (Baltimore and London: Johns Hopkins University Press, 1981), p. 147; Berger (1971), pp. 111, 116; Krier, p. 191.
64. Bates, pp. 138–51.
65. Wofford, p. 363.
66. See Berger (1989), p. 222.
67. Myrrha tricked her father, Cinyras, into sleeping with her, whereupon he pursued her to kill her. See Ovid, *Metamorphoses*, x. ll. 311–518.
68. See Nohrnberg, pp. 446–7.
69. Wofford, p. 315.
70. Wofford, p. 471, n. 24.
71. Cavanagh, p. 162.
72. Ibid., p. 68.
73. Ibid., p. 70.
74. Ibid., p. 119.
75. Susan Griffin, *Pornography and Silence: Culture's Revenge Against Nature* (London: The Women's Press, 1981), p. 144.
76. And, as Nohrnberg argues, the destruction of the golden calf (p. 224).
77. Ibid., p. 707, n. 116. Dennis Kay notes that bare feet are attributes of humiliated or degraded women, in 'Wyatt and Chaucer: *They Fle From Me* Revisited', *Huntington Library Quarterly* xlvii (1984), 211–25 (214). Marina Warner has suggested that they function traditionally as a fetishistic substitute for female genitals. *From the Beast to the Blonde: On Fairy Tales and Their Tellers* (London: Chatto & Windus, 1994), pp. 113, 128.

78. That allegorical figures (representing abstract qualities) are usually female derives, of course, from the feminine gender of Latin abstract nouns; yet this does not obviate the question of violence.
79. See Wofford, p. 14.

CHAPTER 4

Where dates of plays are given they refer to the likely first performance(s) rather than first publication, taken from E.K. Chambers, *The Elizabethan Stage* (Oxford: Clarendon Press, 1923) and Gerald Eades Bentley, *The Jacobean and Caroline Stage* (Oxford: Clarendon Press, 1941; rpr. 1949).

1. Shakespeare, *King John*, ed. E.A.J. Honigmann (London: Methuen, 1954), I.i.254.
2. See Marilyn L. Johnson, *Images of Women in the Works of Thomas Heywood* (Salzburg: Salzburg Studies in English Literature, 1974), pp. 61ff.
3. Thomas Heywood, *The First and Second Parts of King Edward the fourth* (c. 1599) in *The Dramatic Works*, ed. R.H. Shepherd (London: John Pearson, 1874) i, p. 16.
4. Loughrey and Taylor refer to Bianca's 'seduction'. *Thomas Middleton: Five Plays*, ed. Bryan Loughrey and Neil Taylor (Harmondsworth: Penguin, 1988), p. xix. Margot Heinemann admits that Bianca 'has at first little choice', but presents her as succumbing to worldly temptation. *Puritanism and Theatre: Thomas Middleton and Opposition Drama under the Early Stuarts* (Cambridge: Cambridge University Press, 1980), pp. 183–4. Suzanne Gossett, however, defines the act as rape (p. 319), as does Kathleen McLuskie in *Renaissance Dramatists* (NY and London: Harvester Wheatsheaf, 1989), p. 20.
5. Thomas Middleton, *Women Beware Women*, II.ii. 352–3, in *Five Plays*.
6. In the first edition of the play, the stage direction is simply 'Exit above'. Middleton, *Two New Playes: More Dissemblers Besides Women; Women Beware Women* (1657), p. 130.
7. Even Barbara Joan Baines, who is sympathetic to Bianca, says that she both resists and surrenders. *The Lust Motif in the Plays of Thomas Middleton* (Salzburg: Salzburg Studies in English Literature, 1973), pp. 132–3.
8. Leonard Tennenhouse, 'Violence Done to Women on the Renaissance Stage' in *The Violence of Representation: Literature and the History of Violence*, ed. Nancy Armstrong and Leonard Tennenhouse (NY: Routledge, 1989), pp. 77–97 (77).
9. See Doris Adler, *Philip Massinger* (Boston: Twayne Publishers, 1987); McLuskie; Gordon McMullan, *The Politics of Unease in the Plays of John Fletcher* (Amherst: University of Massachussetts Press, 1994); Nancy Cotton Pearse, *John Fletcher's Chastity Plays: Mirrors of Modesty* (Lewisburg: Bushnell University Press, 1973); Robert Y. Turner, 'Responses to Tyranny in John Fletcher's Plays' in J. Leeds Barroll, ed. *Medieval*

and *Renaissance Drama in England: an Annual Gathering of Research, Criticism and Reviews* (NY: AMS Press, 1989), iv. 123–41.

10.  This is equally true of plays with a clear allegorical or satirical import, such as Middleton's *A Game at Chess* (1624), which uses the attempted rape of the White Queen's Pawn by the Black Bishop's Pawn as part of its anti-Catholic and anti-Spanish satire.

11.  William Rowley, *All's Lost by Lust*, ed. Charles Wharton Stork (Philadelphia: Publications of the University of Pennsylvania, 1910).

12.  See Ann Lancashire, 'Introduction' in (ed.) *The Second Maiden's Tragedy* (Manchester: Manchester University Press and Baltimore: Johns Hopkins University Press, 1978), pp. 39, 40–1.

13.  Jean E. Howard, *The Stage and Social Struggle in Early Modern England* (London and NY: Routledge, 1994), p. 7.

14.  For the clash between rape stories and the idea of Christian martyrdom, see Simon Shepherd, *Amazons and Warrior Women: Varieties of Feminism in Seventeenth-Century Drama* (Brighton: Harvester Press, 1981), chapter 13.

15.  See Susan Zimmerman, ed. *Erotic Politics: Desire on the Renaissance Stage* (NY and London: Routledge, 1992).

16.  See both attempts in Beaumont and Fetcher's *The Faithful Shepherdess*, and in *Love's Cure*, and Massinger, *The Bashful Lover*. George Peele's *The Love of King David and Fair Bethsabe. With the Tragedie of Absalon* (1599) is an exception, as Thamar is raped by her brother, Amnon.

17.  See Middleton, *Revenger's Tragedy*, 'Beaumont and Fletcher', *Bonduca*.

18.  *The Humorous Lieutenant, A Tragi-Comedy*, in *The Dramatic Works in the Beaumont and Fletcher Canon*, v, ed. Fredson Bowers (Cambridge: Cambridge University Press, 1982).

19.  *Amends for Ladies*, IV.ii.40–4, in *The Plays of Nathan Field*, ed. William Perry (Austin: Texas University Press, 1950).

20.  *The Woman's Prize, or The Tamer Tam'd* in *Beaumont and Fletcher Canon*, iv (1979), III.iii.7–9.

21.  Thomas Heywood, *The Rape of Lucrece* (1603–8) in *Works*, v, p. 194.

22.  *The Maid in the Mill* in *Beaumont and Fletcher Canon*, ix (1994), III.iii.113–16.

23.  John Marston, *The Wonder of Women, or The Tragedie of Sophonisba* in *Three Jacobean Witchcraft Plays*, ed. Peter Corbin and Douglas Sedge (Manchester: Manchester University Press, 1986), III.i.28–39.

24.  Ben Jonson, *Volpone*, ed. Alvin B. Kernan (New Haven and London: Yale University Press, 1962), III.vii.222.

25.  Cyril Tourneur, *The Atheist's Tragedy* in *Webster and Tourneur*, ed. John Addington Symonds (London: Ernest Benn Ltd, 1948), IV.iii., p. 313.

26.  *Cymbeline*, ed. J.M. Nosworthy (London and NY: Methuen, 1955), IV.iii.13–14. Iachimo's threat to Imogen, though not that of rape, is a violation. See pp. 121–2.

27.  John Fletcher, *The Tragedy of Valentinian*, in *Canon*, iv (1979), I.i.92–4.

28.  *The Queen of Corinth*, in *Beaumont and Fletcher Canon*, viii (1991), IV.iii.83.

29.  *Bonduca*, ibid., iv, IV.iv.117–19.

30.  Anon., *The Reign of King Edward III*, ed. John S. Farmer (Tudor Facsimile Texts, 1910), sig. E.

31.  *A Wife for a Month; A Tragi-Comedy, Beaumont and Fletcher Canon,* vi (1985), IV.iii.43–4.

32.  See Rebecca W. Bushnell, *Tragedies of Tyrants: Political Thought and Theater in the English Renaissance* (Ithaca and London: Cornell University Press, 1990), p. 68.

33.  Fletcher's *The Faithful Shepherdess* provides the rare example of an unchaste woman, Amaryllis, being threatened with rape, which converts her from her former habits. *Beaumont and Fletcher Canon,* iii (1976), V.iii.79–107.

34.  *The Woman-Hater,* ibid., i (1966).

35.  John Milton, *A Masque presented at Ludlow Castle [Comus]* (1634).

36.  Massinger, *The Bashful Lover* in *The Plays and Poems of Philip Massinger,* ed. Philip Edwards and Colin Gibson (Oxford: Clarendon Press, 1976), iv, III.ii.25–6.

37.  Thomas Dekker, *Match Me in London* in *The Dramatic Works,* ed. Fredson Bowers (Cambridge: Cambridge University Press, 1958), III.iii.48–9.

38.  George Whetstone, *The Right Excellent and famous Historye of Promos and Cassandra* (1578), ed. John S. Farmer (Tudor Facsimile Texts, 1910), sig. C.

39.  *The Little French Lawyer* in *Beaumont and Fletcher Canon,* ix, IV.vii.42–5.

40.  Massinger, *The Bondman* (1623) in *Plays,* i, V.ii.84.

41.  Thomas Middleton, *Hengist, King of Kent; Or The Mayor of Queenborough,* ed. R.C. Bald (NY and London: Charles Scribner's Sons, 1938). Raped women commit suicide in *Valentinian, Lucrece, The Revenger's Tragedy* and Massinger's *The Unnatural Combat.* They are killed by their fathers in *Titus Andronicus* and *Alphonsus,* and coincidentally in *Bonduca* and *All's Lost.* In *Promos and Cassandra, The Queen of Corinth* and Middleton's *The Spanish Gypsy,* they marry their rapists. Sophonisba, Virginia and the 'Lady' of *The Second Maiden's Tragedy* kill themselves or are killed to avoid rape.

42.  Massinger, *The Unnatural Combat* (1621–5) in *Plays,* ii, V.ii.186–7.

43.  Gossett, p. 305.

44.  Ibid., p. 306.

45.  Ibid., p. 327.

46.  Ibid., p. 322; Middleton, *The Spanish Gypsy* in *The Best Plays of the Old Dramatists. Thomas Middleton,* ed. Havelock Ellis (London: Vizetelly & Co., 1887), i, p. 374.

47.  See Gossett, p. 324.

48.  McLuskie, p. 154.

49.  Susan Zimmerman, Introduction, p. 8. The erotics of cross-dressing were first discussed in Lisa Jardine, *Still Harping on Daughters: Women and Drama in the Age of Shakespeare* (Brighton: Harvester and Toronto: Barnes and Noble, 1983).

50.  Peter Stallybrass, 'Transvestism and the "body beneath": Speculating on the boy actor' in Zimmerman, pp. 64–83 (64).

51.  *Titus Andronicus,* ed. J.C. Maxwell (London and NY: Routledge, 1989).

52.  See Douglas E. Green, 'Interpreting "her martyr'd signs": Gender and Tragedy in *Titus Andronicus'*, *Shakespeare Quarterly* xl (1989), 317–26 (325); Mary Laughlin Fawcettt, 'Arms/Words/Tears: Language and the

Body in *Titus Andronicus'*, *ELH* 1 (1983), 261–77. Heather James argues persuasively that Shakespeare uses the abuse of Lavinia 'to scrutinize the art of petrarchan representation itself', in *Shakespeare's Troy: Drama, Politics, and the Translation of Empire* (Cambridge: Cambridge University Press, 1997), pp. 42–84 (47).

53. For a threat of literal branding, see *Woman-Hater*, IV.i.166; for a purely metaphorical example, see *Edward IV*, p. 165.

54. *The Maids Tragedy* in *Beaumont and Fletcher Canon*, ii, IV.i.98–109.

55. See Julia Briggs, 'Shakespeare's Bed-Tricks', *Essays in Criticism* xliv (1994), 293–314. G.K. Hunter puts the traditional view in his edition of *All's Well that Ends Well* (London and NY: Routledge, 1959, rpr. 1989), pp. xliv–v. For a discussion of 'the substitutability of one body for another' in Shakespeare, see Maus, pp. 171ff.

56. See *The Two Gentlemen of Verona*, ed. Clifford Leech (London: Methuen, 1969), pp. xxxvi–vii. See also Hutson's discussion of the original story, pp. 57–61.

57. *Alphonsus Emperor of Germany*, ed. Herbert F. Schwarz (NY and London: G.P. Putnam's Sons, 1913). The play was not published until 1654, but dates from 1594. See Briggs, p. 294.

58. Whetstone, sigs Eiv, Fivv, Hii.

59. The play is based on the Senecan controversy 'The Man Who Raped Two Women'. See Waith, p. 89.

60. The complex issue of betrothals and their status is summarised in J.W. Lever, ed. *Measure for Measure* (London and NY: Routledge, 1965; rpr. 1989), pp. liii–v, and in Briggs, p. 306.

61. This situation recurs in 1631 in Arthur Wilson's *The Swisser*, in which the crisis caused by the King's rape of Eugenia is resolved by the revelation that she is a woman whom he had previously courted. He is then happy to marry her, and she accepts the resolution: despite having previously rejected his advances and despite loving another man.

62. Laura Levine, 'Rape, repetition, and the politics of closure in *A Midsummer Night's Dream*' in Valerie Traub et al., eds *Feminist Readings of Early Modern Culture: Emerging Subjects* (Cambridge: Cambridge University Press, 1996), pp. 210–28 (222, n. 2).

63. Ibid., pp. 216ff.

64. This equation is made explicitly in a later play, John Ford's *The Broken Heart* (1633).

CHAPTER 5

1. See Ovid, *Metamorphoses*, vi. ll. 433–674; see also *Ovid's Metamorphoses: The Arthur Golding Translation. 1567*, ed. John Frederick Nims (NY and London: The Macmillan Co., Collier-Macmillan Ltd, 1965), vi. ll. 525–853, pp. 150–9. Patricia Klindienst Joplin reads the story thus, as a model for women's writing. 'The Voice of the Shuttle is Ours', *Stanford Literature Review* i (1984), pp. 25–53.

2. See Lamb, p. 195.

3. I have discussed this image in Chapter 3, p. 68.
4. See Golding's translation, vi. ll. 827–36, p. 158; Lamb, pp. 218–23.
5. Wendy Wall, p. 335 (n.); Aemilia Lanyer, 'To the Queen's Most Excellent Majesty', ll. 105–6 in *Salve Deus Rex Judaeorum* (1611) in *Renaissance Women: The Plays of Elizabeth Cary; The Poems of Aemilia Lanyer*, ed. Diane Purkiss (London: Pickering & Chatto Ltd, 1994), pp. 239–338 (citing by line-number). As Wall points out, such images could also be used to denigrate women's writing (p. 355).
6. Mary Wroth, *Pamphilia to Amphilanthus*, 'Come merry spring delight us' ('P.93'), l. 21 in Roberts (1983), pp. 136–7; Lamb, p. 223. Lamb also includes Wroth's other nightingale poem, from *Urania* (Roberts, 'U.34', pp. 171–2) in her analysis.
7. Lamb, p. 195.
8. See Ovid, *Metamorphoses*, vi. ll. 1–145; Golding, vi. ll. 1–184, pp. 136–41.
9. Nancy K. Miller has read Arachne's story as a 'parable of women's writing'. 'Arachnologies: The Woman, The Text, and the Critic' in (ed.) *The Poetics of Gender* (NY: Columbia University Press, 1986), pp. 270–95 (286).
10. The *OED* defines 'text' as 'lit[erally] that which is woven, web, texture' (*sb.*[1]).
11. Mary Sidney, 'Even now that Care', l. 27 in *The Triumph of Death and Other Unpublished and Uncollected Poems*, ed. Gary Waller (Salzburg: University of Salzburg Press, 1977), pp. 88–91. See Sylvia Bowerbank 'The Spider's Delight: Margaret Cavendish and the "Female Imagination"', *ELR* xiv (1984), 392–408. A.R. Jones discusses an alternative, but 'inhibiting' model of female eloquence, Ovid's Echo, in 'New Songs for the Swallow: Ovid's Philomela in Tullia d'Aragona and Gaspara Stampa' in Marilyn Migiel and Juliana Schiesari, eds *Refiguring Women: Perspectives on Gender and the Italian Renaissance* (Ithaca and London: Cornell University Press, 1991), pp. 263–77 (264).
12. For a discussion of how Elizabethan writers bring out the sexual threat in this story, see Chapter 2, p. 42, and Chapter 3, p. 62.
13. Thus it is wise not to build on Lucas's assumption that a woman writer's treatment of rape will necessarily be different from a man's (p. 56), but to approach such writing with an open mind. We have observed several 'exceptions' to the general 'rules' in male-authored rape literature.
14. Elizabeth Jocelin, *The Mothers Legacie: To her vnborne Childe* (1624), p. 39; Isabella Whitney, *The Copy of a letter, lately written in meeter, by a yonge Gentilwoman* (1567), sigs A4v, A3v.
15. Clifford Bax, trans. *The Silver Casket: Being Love-Letters and Love-Poems Attributed to Mary Stuart, Queen of Scots* (London: Home & Van Thal, Ltd, 1946), sonnet IX p. 47. The French line is 'il se fit de ce corps possesseur, / Duquel alors il n'avait pas le coeur'. 'Pour lui aussi j'ai jeté mainte larme' in *Bittersweet Within My Heart: The Collected Poems of Mary, Queen of Scots*, trans. and ed. Robin Bell (London: Pavilion Books, Ltd, 1992), p. 38. Bax discusses these issues in his Introduction, along with the controversy over attribution.

16.    *Jane Anger her Protection for Women* (1589) in *The Women's Sharp Revenge: Five Women's Pamphlets from the Renaissance*, ed. Simon Shepherd (London: Fourth Estate, 1985), pp. 29–51 (36).

17.    Elizabeth Grymeston, *Miscelanea, Meditations, Memoratives* (1604), sig. A4v.

18.    See Barbara K. Lewalski, 'Of God and Good Women: the Poems of Aemilia Lanyer' in Hannay (1985), p. 208. For a further discussion of Lanyer's celebration of female virtue see Beilin (1987), pp. 177–207.

19.    See p. 18.

20.    Rachel Speght, *A Mouzell for Melastomus* (1617) in Shepherd (1985), pp. 57–83; 'Ester Sowernam', *Ester hath hang'd Haman* (1617), ibid., pp. 83–124; 'Constantia Munda', *The Worming of a mad Dogge* (1617), ibid., pp. 125–57. The names 'Ester Sowernam' and 'Constantia Munda' are clearly pseudonymous. I therefore follow Diane Purkiss in placing them within inverted commas. See Purkiss, 'Material Girls: The Seventeenth-Century Woman Debate' in Clare Brant and Diane Purkiss, eds *Women, Texts & Histories 1575–1760* (London and NY: Routledge, 1992), pp. 69–101 (96, n. 2).

21.    Speght, 'Certain Queries to the Baiter of Women', appended to *Mouzzell*, p. 77.

22.    See Purkiss (1992) in Brant and Purkiss, p. 89.

23.    Dorothy Leigh, *The Mothers Blessing. Or The godly counsaile of a Gentlewoman not long since deceased, left behind her for her Children* (1616).

24.    At least 19 editions were published before 1640, and another four later in the century. Joan Larsen Klein points out that this is more than of nearly any other advice book for women. *Daughters, Wives, and Widows: Writings by Men about Women and Marriage in England, 1500–1640* (Urbana: Illinois University Press, 1992), p. 287.

25.    See Ann Rosalind Jones, *The Currency of Eros: Women's Love Lyric in Europe 1540–1620* (Bloomington, Ind.: Indiana State University Press, 1990), pp. 37ff; Hutson, 'Why the lady's eyes are nothing like the sun' in Brant and Purkiss (1992), pp. 13–38 (21); Purkiss (1994), p. xxxiv.

26.    Anger, p. 42.

27.    See Lamb (1990), chapter 1; Barry Waller and Margaret W. Ferguson, 'Introduction' to (eds) *Elizabeth Cary, Lady Falkland, The Tragedy of Mariam the Fair Queen of Jewry with The Lady Falkland: Her Life. By One of her Daughters* (Berkely, LA and London: University of California Press, 1994), p. 6; Josephine A. Roberts, ed., *The Poems of Lady Mary Wroth* (Baton Rouge and London, 1983), pp. 17–22; David M. Bergeron, 'Women as Patrons of English Renaissance Drama' in *Patronage in the Renaissance*, ed. Guy Fitch Lytle and Stephen Orgel (Princeton, NJ: Princeton University Press, 1981), pp. 274–90.

28.    Lamb (1991) considers them together in this context.

29.    See Alexander McLaren Witherspoon, *The Influence of Robert Garnier on Elizabethan Drama* (New Haven: Yale University Press, 1924), pp. 150ff.; Marta Straznicky and Richard Roland, 'Supplement to the Introduction' in Elizabeth Cary, *The Tragedy of Mariam*, ed. A.C. Dunstan and W.W. Greg (Oxford: Malone Society Reprints, Oxford University Press, 1914; rpr. 1992), pp. xxi–v (xxiv–v).

30. Waller and Ferguson speculate on the likelihood of Cary knowing of the existence of Lumley's play, and argue for the influence of Sidney's *Antonius* on Cary's *Mariam* (pp. 26ff.).
31. For biographical studies of Wroth and Cary, see Roberts (1983) and Waller and Ferguson, 'Introduction', respectively.
32. See Clarke, Preface.
33. There is not space here to discuss Whitney's 'Copie of a Letter' (1567), which can be related to the complaint mode: albeit as an early example preceding its strong association with sexual shame. See Jones (1990), pp. 43–8.

## CHAPTER 6

1. Tyler, 'Epistle to the Reader', in (trans.) Ortuñez de Calahorra, *Mirror of Knighthood* (1578), sig. Aiiiv.
2. Hannay (1990), p. 61.
3. Mary Ellen Lamb, 'The Countess of Pembroke and the Art of Dying' in *Women in the Middle Ages and Renaissance: Literary and Historical Perspectives*, ed. Mary Beth Rose (Syracuse: Syracuse University Press, 1986), pp. 207–26 (223).
4. See Wendy Wall, p. 337. See also Goldberg (1997), pp. 75ff.
5. See Clarke, p. 51.
6. Adaptation is, of course, as much a form of translation as literal rendition. See Rainer Schulte and John Biguenet, eds *Theories of Translation: an Anthology of Essays from Dryden to Derrida* (Chicago and London: University of Chicago Press, 1992), p. 17.
7. See David H. Greene, 'Lady Lumley and Greek Tragedy', *Classical Journal* xxxvi (1941), 537–47; Frank D. Crane, 'Euripides, Erasmus, and Lady Lumley', *Classical Journal* xxxix (1941), 223–8; Krontiris, 'Mary Herbert: Englishing a Purified Cleopatra' in *Oppositional Voices*, pp. 64–78 (68); Gary Waller, *Mary Sidney, Countess of Pembroke: a Critical Study of her Writings and Literary Milieu* (Salzburg: Salzburg University Press, 1979), pp. 105–6.
8. Lamb (1990), p. 141; see also Beilin (1987), chapter 6.
9. B.L. MS. Reg. 15. A. ix. See Harold H. Child, ed. *Iphigenia at Aulis Translated By Lady Lumley* (Oxford, 1909), pp. v–vi. Quotations from the text will be cited by line number from Child's edition. For recent accounts of Lumley's play setting it in its cultural and biographical contexts, see Lorraine Helms, pp. 48–75, and Purkiss's introduction to her edition of the text in *Three Tragedies* (1998).
10. Child, p. vii. Lord Lumley's work is MS. Reg. 17. A. xlix.
11. Ibid., p. vi.
12. Purkiss (1998), pp. 167–8.
13. See Bruce R. Smith, *Ancient Scripts and Modern Experience on the English Stage 1500–1700* (Princeton: Princeton University Press, 1988), pp. 203–5.
14. See Margaret Arnold, 'Jane Lumley's *Iphigeneia*: Self-Revelation of a Renaissance Gentlewoman to Her Audience', unpublished paper cited in Waller and Ferguson, p. 27; Helms, pp. 66–8.

15. Purkiss, on the other hand, argues that this means precisely that Lumley is *un*likely to have translated the work after 1553, given the discomfort it might have caused her father. See Purkiss (1998), p. xxv.
16. Helms, p. 49, using Lynda E. Boose, 'The Father's House and the Daughter in It' in *Daughers and Fathers*, ed. Lynda E. Boose and Betty S. Flowers (Baltimore: Johns Hopkins University Press, 1989), pp. 19–74. For a reading of Euripides' *Iphigenia* in the context of other Greek myths and the connections between violence against women and female language, see Joplin, pp. 38–43. For marriage as martyrdom, see Purkiss (1998), pp. xxviiiff.
17. See Greene, p. 540.
18. See Greene, pp. 540–1. Like Erasmus, she also gives a speech by Clytemnestra to Iphigenia. See Lumley, ll. 921–4; Arthur S. Way ed. and trans., *Euripides* (London: William Heinemann and NY: G.P. Putnam's Sons, 1920), i. ll. 1123–6; Erasmus, trans. *Hecuba, et Iphigenia in Aulide, Euripidis tragoediae* (1544), f. 66–66v. In quoting the original, I shall use Way's translation where it is sufficiently literal (citing by line number), and distinguish my own translations by putting them in italics. All translations of Erasmus are mine.
19. She follows the Greek rather than the Latin in a dialogue between Achilles and Clytemnestra, ll. 867–79. See Way, ll. 995–1000; Erasmus, f. 62v.
20. See Child, p. vii.
21. Beilin (1987), p. 314, n. 10.
22. Erasmus is not responsible for this emphasis on the mind (f. 75).
23. See Way, ll. 1510–31.
24. Erasmus too has Agamemnon refer to maidens (f. 53v).
25. The corresponding speech is Way, ll. 900–16, which Lumley has already condensed substantially. There is no precedent for her added line in Erasmus's rendition (see f. 60).
26. Here she would be simply 'κακγν' (*evil*). Way, ll. 1183–4.
27. See f. 68: 'Sed per deos caueto, neu me adegeris, / Vti talis in te fuero, qualem neutiquan / Decet esse' ('by the gods, beware, lest I become such to you, and you to me, as would never be fitting').
28. Lumley omits this from her summary (972–4).
29. Cf. Way, 'ὡσ γυναικα δει ξενην' ('*as far as an alien woman may*') (469); Erasmus too refers to 'hospitam' ('stranger' or 'foreign woman') (f. 47v).
30. Lumley, l. 559; see Way, l. 542, Erasmus f. 49v.
31. This is completely different from the original (ll. 1500–1).
32. See Erasmus f. 76v. Unfortunately, Lumley also cuts some details that would enhance this emphasis.
33. Erasmus emphasises decorum, without expanding the passage as Lumley does (f. 77).
34. Erasmus here invokes 'Fama' (gossip), but does not make Iphigenia its sole object (f. 62v).
35. For instance, a choral celebration of Eros and Aphrodite (Way, 543–88; omitted from after l. 560), and a comparison between Iphigenia and Helen (1417–19; cf. Lumley, 1226–30). While she uniformly cuts the

choral odes, the omission of non-choric material, as in the latter case, seems to serve no other purpose.

36. See Way, l. 1108, omitted from Lumley, l. 907; l. 681, omitted from l. 654; and l. 658 – 'Perish their wars, and Menelaus' wrongs!' – omitted from l. 617. She also eliminates references to Iphigenia as the destroyer of Troy rather than the saviour of Greece. See Way, ll. 1398, 1474–83, 1510 and 754–800 (omitted from after ll. 1202, 1297–305, 1319 and 708, respectively). Erasmus does not omit these references (see ff. 77, 78).

37. Erasmus reproduces the original: 'Dedo corpus hoc meu / Graeciae' (f. 75).

38. See Way, ll. 460–1, omitted from after l. 466; and Way l. 796, omitted from after l. 708. The latter is part of an omitted chorus.

39. See Way, ll. 1266, 1275, and 1381. They are reproduced by Erasmus, ff. 71 and 74.

40. Purkiss (1998), p. xxxii. Cf. Way, ll. 1510–31.

41. 'ἐγημας ακουσαν με καλαβεσ βια '.

42. 'Me non uolentem, uique raptam coniugem / Dux[is]ti' (f. 67) ('you took me unwilling, having seized me as your wife').

43. Way, ll. 1146–208.

44. The original uses the word 'ἐξαρπασας' (*snatched away*). Erasmus gives 'hic epistolam / Tuam manu uiolentus extorsit mea' (f. 43v) ('he wrenched your letter violently from my hand').

45. Erasmus uses the words 'abreptam' ('carried off') and 'abduxit' (led away') (f. 37v). Lumley also omits the emphasis on reciprocity of the original. See Lumley, ll. 94–5; Way, l. 75: 'ἐρων ἐρωσαν' (loved and was loved).

46. See p. 43.

47. Mary Sidney, *Antonius, A Tragedie written also in French by Ro. Garnier* (1592), published with *A Discourse of Life and Death; The Triumph of Death*, ed. Waller.

48. 'De vous mesme / Perdre' (531–2), 'à nous-mesmes deüe' (587) and 'mon espous est moymesme' (588) respectively. *Robert Garnier: Two Tragedies: Hippolyte and Marc Antoine*, ed. Christine M. Hill and Mary G. Morrison (London: Athlone Press, 1975).

49. The reflexive verbs are, respectively, 'de se perdre' (549) and 's'outrager' (646). The remaining phrases correspond to 'vous l'exercez sur vous' (585), 'c'est pour ne l'exercer encontre mon espous' (586), and 'inhumaine pour soy' (597).

50. Krontiris, p. 70; Lamb (1990), p. 131.

51. See Geoffrey Bullough, ed. *Narrative and Dramatic Sources of Shakespeare* (London: Routledge & Kegan Paul, 1964), v. 231; Witherspoon, p. 86.

52. Sidney has translated both 'dereiglez' (1382) (dissolute) and 'mechamment' (626) (maliciously) as 'lewd'/'lewdly'.

53. See ll. 279–82, 691–4.

54. Cf. 'd'estre nez / D'une si noble race' and 'elle a le cœur trop haut, / Magnanime et royal' (1850–1, 882–3), which neither use the term prince nor share vocabulary with each other.

55. For Elizabeth's deployment of this gender-neutral term, see Leah S. Marcus, 'Shakespeare's Comic Heroines, Elizabeth I and the Political Uses of Androgyny' in Rose (1986), pp. 135–53. Philip Sidney calls Elizabeth 'prince'. *The Miscellaneous Prose of Sir Philip Sidney*, ed. Katherine Duncan-Jones and A.J. van Dorsten (Oxford: Clarendon Press, 1973), pp. 55, 57.

56. See *Sir Fulke Greville's Life of Sir Philip Sidney*, ed. Nowell Smith (Oxford: Clarendon Press, 1907), pp. 155–7.

57. Critics have concurred with this, to varying degrees. See, for example, Janet MacArthur, 'Ventriloquizing Comfort and Despair: Mary Sidney's Female Personae in *The Triumph of Death* and *The Tragedy of Antony*', *Sidney Newsletter & Journal* xi (1990), 3–13; Krontiris, pp. 64–78.

58. Several epyllia are current by 1592, but by the time *Antonius* is republished in 1595, many more have appeared. See Chapter 3.

59. Sidney may have completed the poem in the late 1590s (see Lamb (1990), p. 138), when the complaint genre was in its heyday (see Chapter 3).

60. Clarke argues that Sidney marginalises the poet's role to give Laura greater agency (pp. 91–3).

61. Lamb (1990), p. 120; Clarke, p. 70.

62. See Daniel's *Tragedie of Cleopatra* (1594), Epistle Dedicatory, sig. A2.

63. For the political significance of these works and their participation in the Sidney project, see Clarke, pp. 99–124, 128–57.

64. For the adaptability of the complaint by other subgenres, see Schmitz.

65. Sidney's translation of Mornay's *Discourse*, paired with *Antonius* in 1592, mediates the relationship between it and the *Triumph* by foregrounding the virtue of dying well. *A Discourse of Life and Death. Written in French by Ph. Mornay* (1592). See Lamb (1990), p. 129. However, this is problematised by Mornay's condemnation of suicide; and Laura's relationship to the *Discourse* too is problematic (ibid., p. 139).

66. 'L'affanno, / Che va inanzi al morir, non doglia forte'. *Petrarca: Triumphi*, ed. Marco Ariani (Milan, 1988), ll. 46–7. Garnier's lines read 'Qu'inhumaine à soy mesme elle offense de coups' (734) and 'Plombez vostre estomach de coups multipliez' (l. 1986), respectively. Neither uses the verb *martirizzare* or *martyriser*.

67. Clarke, p. 123.

CHAPTER 7

1. Elizabeth Cary, *The Tragedy of Mariam*, ed. A.C. Dunstan and W.W. Greg (Oxford, 1914; rpr. 1992), ll. 2007–8.

2. Two versions of *Edward II* were published in 1680: the longer, folio version, *The History of the Life, Reign, and Death of Edward II* (which dates the manuscript to 1627), and the octavo, *The History of the Most Unfortunate Prince King Edward the Second*. The relationship between the two texts, and the authenticity of the latter in particular, is the subject of controversy; the folio is, however, held to be as authentic as the

possibility of intervention by its printers will allow, and it is from this
version that I work, in Purkiss's edition in *Renaissance Women* (1994),
pp. 79–237. The 1680 folio (like the octavo) publishes the work as con-
tinuous prose; Purkiss restores substantial passages to the verse which
seems to have been intended. I shall also give as verse some other
passages which seem to invite it, distinguishing my arrangement in
the text.

3.  *The Antiquities of the Iewes* and *The Lamentable And Tragicall Historie Of
    the Warres And Vtter Ruine Of The Iewes* in *The Famous and Memorable
    Workes of Josephus*, trans. Thomas Lodge (1602; rpr. 1609). For Cary's
    participation, with *Mariam*, in intellectual and possibly Catholic inter-
    est in Judaism, see Waller and Ferguson, pp. 18ff. For possible rela-
    tionships between *Mariam* and other plays on the same subject, see
    Waller and Ferguson, pp. 23–6.
4.  See Maurice Valency, *The Tragedies of Herod and Mariamne* (NY: Colum-
    bia University Press, 1940).
5.  See Michael Drayton, *Mortimeriados. The Lamentable ciuell warres of
    Edward the second and the Barons* (1596) in *Works*, i, *England's Heroicall
    Epistles* (1619); Christopher Marlowe, *Edward the Second* in *The Com-
    plete Plays*, ed. J.B. Steane (Harmondsworth: Penguin, 1969; rpr. 1988);
    Sir Francis Hubert, *The Historie of Edward the Second. Surnamed Carnar-
    van* (1629) in *The Poems of Sir Francis Hubert*, ed. Bernard Mellor (Hong
    Kong and Oxford: Hong Kong University Press and Oxford Univer-
    sity Press, 1961).
6.  Critics have read Mariam as a paragon of chastity [see Beilin (1987),
    p. 167; Nancy Cotton Pearse, 'Elizabeth Cary, Renaissance Playwright',
    *Texas Studies in Literature and Language* xviii (1976), 601–8 (604)] and
    Isabel as a victim [see Krontiris, pp. 92–5].
7.  See Dympna Callaghan, 'Re-reading Elizabeth Cary's *The Tragedie of
    Mariam, Faire Queene of Jewry*' in Margo Hendricks and Patricia Parker,
    eds *Women, 'Race,' and Writing in the Early Modern Period* (London and
    NY: Routledge, 1994), pp. 163–77 (165–9).
8.  See Waller and Ferguson, p. 43. Stephanie J. Wright argues, in the
    introduction to her modern-spelling edition of the play, for *Mariam's*
    performability. *Elizabeth Cary: The Tragedy of Mariam The Fair Queen of
    Jewry* (Keele: Keele University Press, 1996), pp. 21–3.
9.  Both works contain images of women as 'white devils', and images of
    corruption in *Edward II* recall *The Duchess of Malfi*.
10. A.C. Dunstan suggests a date of 1603–4 (pp. viii–ix). Since this makes
    Cary around eighteen, it has led at least one critic to underestimate
    the work, like Lumley's, as a 'schoolbook exercise' (Pearse, p. 604). Bei-
    lin refutes Dunstan's arguments and suggests a date range from 1606
    to 1612 in 'Elizabeth Cary and *The Tragedie of Mariam*', *PLL* xvi (1980),
    46–64 (47–8, n. 6). Unfortunately, most subsequent critics adhere to
    Dunstan's dating, with the exception of Waller and Ferguson in their
    edition (p. 54, n. 13), and Wright (p. 15).
11. See ll. 1845, 1991, 623. For Elizabeth's use of the term, see p. 147. For
    the oblique connections between Mariam and Elizabeth, Mary Tudor
    and Mary, Queen of Scots, see Ferguson, 'Running On With Almost

Public Voice: The Case of "E.C."' in *Tradition and the Talents of Women*, ed. Florence Howe (Urbana and Chicago: University of Illinois Press, 1991), pp. 37–67 (43), and 'The Spectre of Resistance: *The Tragedy of Mariam*' in *Staging the Renaissance: Interpretations of Elizabethan and Jacobean Drama*, ed. David Scott Kastan and Peter Stallybrass (NY and London: Routledge, 1991), pp. 235–50 (245). For the significance of Henry VIII's divorce as a 'social text' to *Mariam*, see Waller and Ferguson, pp. 30–5.

12.    See Catherine Belsey, *The Subject of Tragedy: Identity and difference in Renaissance drama* (London and NY: Methuen, 1985), pp. 129–48; Linda Fitz (Woodbridge), '"What Says the Married Woman?" Marriage Theory and Feminism in the English Renaissance', *Mosaic* xiii (1980), 1–22.

13.    See, for instance, *Arden of Faversham* (probably 1591) and *A Warning for Fair Women* (*c*. 1590); Edmund Tilney, *The Flower of Friendship* (1568), sig. Bvi; Robert Cleaver, *A Godlie Forme of Householde Gouernment* (1598), p. 169. See also Belsey, pp. 130–7; Fitz, p. 1.

14.    See Beilin, pp. 168–9; Ferguson, 'Running', p. 47.

15.    For Graphina as a figure of 'safe', private speech, see Ferguson 'Running', p. 47.

16.    In wishing herself a milkmaid, Mariam recalls Elizabeth I's use of this idea in her speech to Parliament in 1576, where she uses it to reject marriage. See Helen Cooper, *Pastoral: Mediæval into Renaissance* (Ipswich and Totowa, NJ: Rowman & Littlefield, 1977), p. 193.

17.    See *Antiquities*, p. 388.

18.    Clarke describes Mariam's sexual denial as a 'passive resistance' (p. 179). See also Ferguson, 'Running', p. 43.

19.    For the analogy between Mariam and Christ, see Beilin, pp. 171–6.

20.    James I said, 'I am the Husband, and all the whole Isle is my lawfull Wife'. *The Political Works of James I*, ed. Charles H. McIlwain (Cambridge, Mass.: Harvard University Press, Oxford: Oxford University Press and London: Humphrey Milford, 1918), p. 272.

21.    See William Gouge, *Of Domesticall Duties* (1622), p. 222; T. Becon, trans. Bullinger, *The golden boke of christen matrimonye* (1543), f. xx. See Constance Jordan, *Renaissance Feminism: Literary Texts and Political Models* (Ithaca and London: Cornell University Press, 1990), p. 94.

22.    William Whateley, *A Bride-Bush, or A Wedding Sermon* (1608; rpr. 1617), p. 4.

23.    Heather Dubrow argues that it thus recognises female desire. *A Happier Eden: The Politics of Marriage in the Stuart Epithalamion* (Ithaca and London: Cornell University Press, 1990), p. 25.

24.    Juan Luis Vives, *A Very Frutefvl and Pleasant boke callyd the Instruction of a Christen woman*, trans. Richard Hyrde (1529; rpr. 1541), sigs 66–66v.

25.    Cary was sympathetic to Catholicism from around 1605 and converted formally in 1626. See *The Lady Falkland: Her Life*, ed. Waller and Ferguson (1994), p. 190.

26.    See Kathleen M. Davies, 'Continuity and Change in Literary Advice on Marriage' in *Marriage and Society: Studies in the Social History of Marriage*, ed. R.B. Outhwaite (London: Europe Publications, Ltd, 1981), pp. 58–80 (78).

27. Vives (1541), ff. 91–91v. This is inconsistent with his earlier insistence that a wife cannot make a vow contrary to her husband's wishes.

28. See, for example, *The King's Book Or A Necessary Doctrine and Erudition for any Christian Man* (1543), ed. T.A. Lacey (London: Society for Promoting Christian Knowledge, 1932), pp. 111–12.

29. Vives, *The office and duetie of an husband* (1529), trans. Thomas Paynell (1555), sig. Rii–Riiv.

30. Purkiss makes this emendation, which restores the iambic pentameter lost in the original (1994, ll. 1417–18).

31. There was much contemporary anxiety concerning the power wielded by the wives of rulers over their husbands. See Jean Bodin, *Six Bookes of a Commonweale* (1606), p. 754.

32. Herod makes a similar claim for her (ll. 1757–60).

33. The context for Mariam's remark is ambiguous. She seems to refer to Doris (or a hypothetical other) as one 'who sees for truth that *Mariam* is vntrue' (1855). Dunstan's suggestion of 'says' for 'sees' (p. xi) makes this more palatable. Purkiss's punctuation links the description firmly to Doris, but does not emend the word, which retains the sense of Mariam's admission of culpability (see Purkiss, ll. 1793–4).

34. Waller and Ferguson suggest one reason for this: that both characters may be versions of Anne Boleyn (p. 33).

35. See *OED*, 'range', $v.^1$, 7 and (especially) 8: 'To change from one attachment to another; to be inconstant'.

36. Theobald cited *Mariam* in the context of the 'Indian'/'Iudean' controversy, as evidence of contemporary knowledge of the story, in his argument for the latter reading, but did not refer to the verbal similarity. See Lewis Theobald, ed. *The Works of Shakespeare* (1762), p. 339. Farmer quoted Cary's lines to support this reading. See Horace Howard Furness, ed. *Othello, A New Variorum Edition* (Philadelphia, 1886), p. 329. Waller and Ferguson note the similarity but conclude that we cannot tell which play influenced which (pp. 41–3).

37. *Othello*, ed. M.R. Ridley (London and NY: Methuen, 1958; rpr. 1987).

38. See Stephen Greenblatt, *Renaissance Self-Fashioning: From More to Shakespeare* (Chicago and London: University of Chicago Press, 1980), p. 250.

39. See Lancashire, ed. *Second Maiden's Tragedy*, pp. 215–16 (n.). See also Clarke, p. 189.

40. Cary may also have taken the 'handmaid' image from Hardyng: 'The quene was, but an handmayden in dede'. *The Chronicle of John Hardynge* (1543), clxxiiii st. 7.

41. There are 40 references to ears or tongues in *Edward*, 32 being unrelated to Isabel or to women: 14 of tongues (see, for example, pp. 86, 105), 18 of ears (for example, pp. 88, 127).

42. Spencer's 'overture [comes] to the queen's ear' (p. 165), and her tongue tries to persuade the French (p. 174). Other references relate less directly to her (pp. 177, 187–8), and after the invasion there is a reference to her and Mortimer's ears (p. 218) and an image of her 'railing' tongue (p. 202): the 'exception' which I shall discuss later.

43. Cary uses the word in this sense later (p. 196).

44. See pp. 168, 192. Nature blowing them to Orwel to avoid capture is not in the sources. *Mortimeriados* has nature working against Edward, rather than for Isabel, and its force is passive, simply resisting the author's plea to 'turne gentle wind, and force her to retyer' (l. 1307).

45. See Thomas Becon, *An humble supplicacion vnto God for the restoringe of hys holye woorde vnto the churche of Englande* (1554), sig. A7; Constance Jordan, 'Women's Rule in Sixteenth-Century British Political Thought', *Renaissance Quarterly* xl (1987), 421–51.

46. Cary's criticism of Isabel for her treatment of Spencer may derive from Hubert (st. 525). However, her praise for his patience in suffering and the 'greatness of his heart' (p. 204) is incongruous with her portrayal of his malice and may be ironic.

47. This reworks Hubert's more theoretical observation about 'Monsters' (st. 308, ll. 6–7), which lacks this gender-specificity.

48. Marlowe's attitude to her is ambivalent, while Hubert characterises her as morally aberrant, and Drayton as witch-like. Stow, Holinshed and Daniel portray her as a mediator, but criticise her after the invasion. Samuel Daniel, *A Collection of the History of England* (1618), p. 179ff.

49. See Daniel (1618), p. 183.

50. The wish not to know the details of the murder echoes Marlowe. There, however, it is duplicitous (V.ii.46).

51. The author's summary states that his 'wife and ... son ... were the greatest traitors' (p. 228).

52. The histories record that she was punished with imprisonment after Mortimer's fall.

## CHAPTER 8

1. 'The [first and] secound booke of the secound part of the Countess of Montgomerys Urania', unpublished manuscript at the Newberry Library, Chicago (Case Ms fY 1565.W 95), part i, f. 60v. I shall cite this work by part and folio number. Quotations from the published work, *The Countess of Mountgomeries Urania, written by the right honourable the lady Mary Wroath [sic]* (1621), will be cited by page number; from *Lady Mary Wroth's Love's Victory: The Penshurst Manuscript*, ed. Michael G. Brennan (London: Roxburghe Club, 1988), by act and line number.

2. See Maureen Quilligan, 'Lady Mary Wroth: Female Authority and the Family Romance' in Logan and Teskey (1989), pp. 257–80, and 'The Constant Subject: Instability and Female Authority in Wroth's *Urania* Poems' in *Soliciting Interpretation: Literary Theory and Seventeenth-Century Poetry*, ed. Elizabeth D. Harvey and Katharine Eisaman Maus (Chicago: Chicago University Press, 1990), pp. 307–35; Carolyn Ruth Swift, 'Female Identity in Lady Mary Wroth's Romance *Urania*', *ELR* xiv (1984), 328–46; and Beilin (1987), Chapter 8. The 1621 *Urania* is also available in a critical edition by Josephine Roberts, as *The First Part of The Countess of Montgomery's Urania* (Binghampton, NY: Medieval &

Renaissance Texts & Studies, 1995). Her critical introductions to this work and to Wroth's poetry (Roberts, 1983) provide invaluable information on biographical, textual and critical issues.

3. See Beilin (1987), pp. 215–16; Quilligan (1989).
4. See *Urania*, pp. 382ff. I discuss this scene below (see pp. 216–17).
5. The sea cure, pp. 192–3.
6. See Quilligan, (1989 and 1990).
7. Hackett discusses Antissia and Nereana as counter-types to Pamphilia. '"Yet tell me some such fiction": Lady Mary Wroth's *Urania* and the "Femininity" of Romance' in Brant and Purkiss (1992), pp. 39–68 (53).
8. Hackett, 'The Torture of Limena: Sex and Violence in Lady Mary Wroth's *Urania*' in Kate Chedgzoy, Melanie Hansen and Suzanne Trill, eds *Voicing Women: Gender and Sexuality in Early Modern Writing* (Keele: Keele University Press, 1996), pp. 93–110 (104, 107).
9. *The Queene of Navarres Tales* (1597) contains 16 of the stories, without the framing device. Roberts notes that the *Heptaméron* (1558) provides an analogue to the *Urania*, and that Wroth spoke French. Roberts (1995), p. xxxvi; (1983), p. 9.
10. For an analysis of Marguerite de Navarre's portrayal of rape and the impact of each narrator on the shaping of the rape/seduction narrative, see Cholakian.
11. There are eight scenes of threatened rape in the published *Urania*, featuring Antissia (p. 32), Nallinea (p. 80), Nereana (p. 165), Pamphilia (pp. 119, 429), the wife of Polydorus (p. 317), the (nameless) women encountered by the Duke of Wertenburg (p. 518) and the woman whose 'modest honor' the Duke of Savoy saves (p. 555). Rape narratives in the sequel feature Antissia (i. f. 16v), Pamphilia (i. f. 56), Sophia (i. f. 61), Melasinda (i. f. 63), the Queen of Bulgaria (ii. f. 28v), Lydia and Leatissia (ii. f. 32vff.), Cliante, whom a giant intends to force into marriage when she has grown up (i. f. 22v), and Urania and Selarina, who are saved from rape by one of Melissea's spells (i. f. 62). Further, Lupus intends to force the princess of Argos to marry him (i. f. 32v) and an unnamed maiden is in danger of rape by Philarchos (i. f. 46).
12. See Cholakian, p. 9.
13. Marguerite de Navarre, *The Heptameron*, trans. P.A. Chilton (London: Penguin, 1984), pp. 181–8. See Cholakian, pp. 117–28. This novella is included in the English translation.
14. Roberts notes that 'much of [Wroth's] mythological imagery derives from Ovid' (1983, p. 48).
15. See Ovid, trans. Golding, vi. ll. 827–36, p. 158; Lamb (1990), pp. 218–19.
16. See Ovid, *Metamorphoses*, iv. ll. 798–803.
17. Ibid., v. ll. 572–641 (638), i. ll. 553–6. For discussions of this aspect of Daphne's story, see Richlin, p. 162; Maus, pp. 202–3. Wroth's direct allusion to Daphne avoids such implications (ii. f. 48).
18. See Michael MacDonald, *Mystical Bedlam: Madness, Anxiety and Healing in Seventeenth-Century England* (Cambridge: Cambridge University Press, 1985), p. 123; Edward Jorden, *A Briefe Discourse of a Disease Called The Suffocation of the Mother* (1603), f. 13v.

19. Robert Burton, *The Anatomy of Melancholy*, ed. Thomas C. Faulkner, Nicolas K. Kiessling and Rhonda L. Blair (Oxford: Clarendon Press, 1989), i. 128.
20. Tomaso Garzoni, *The Hospital of Incurable Fooles: Erected in English* (1600), pp. 140ff.
21. See also Garzoni, p. 1. Hysteria was supposed to derive from the womb (Gk. *hyster*).
22. Katharine Hodgkin, 'Dionys Fitzherbert and the Anatomy of Madness' in Chedgzoy, pp. 69–92 (75).
23. 'M.R.', *The Mothers counsell, Or, Liue within Compasse. Being the last Will and Testament to her dearest Daughter* (1630?).
24. Phyllis Chesler, *Women and Madness* (1972; rpr. London: Allen Lane, 1974), p. 53.
25. The *OED* defines 'mad' as 'moved to uncontrollable rage; furious' (5).
26. They ensnare Amphilanthus (i. f. 48v), Leonius (i. f. 58) and Selarinus (ii. ff. 10v, 31).
27. See Michael Shapiro, 'Lady Mary Wroth Describes a "Boy Actress"' in Barroll, iv. 187–94.
28. See ii. f. 12; ii. f. 36v. Satan in Eden is commonly represented as a serpent with a maiden's face. See Beryl Rowland, *Animals with Human Faces: A Guide to Animal Symbolism* (London: Allen and Unwin, 1974), p. 144.
29. See p. 87.
30. See A.C. Hamilton, ed. *The Faerie Queene*, p. 606 (note).
31. Hackett (1992), p. 53.
32. Harvey (1992), p. 44.
33. See Swift (1984) p. 345; Roberts (1995), p. lxii. For an alternative view of Nereana as receiving poetic justice, see Hackett (1992), p. 54.
34. See Roberts (1983), p. 13; Lewalski (1993), pp. 80ff.
35. Cf. Burton, i. 302.
36. Cf. Jorden, f. 13v.
37. See Roberts (1983), p. 51; Hackett, p. 53.
38. See Juliana Schiesari, *The Gendering of Melancholia: Feminism, Psychoanalysis, and the Symbolics of Loss in Renaissance Literature* (Ithaca and London: Cornell University Press, 1992), p. 141. For an exploration of the constructed relation between women and madness today, see Shoshana Felman, 'Women and Madness: The Critical Phallacy' in *The Feminist Reader: Essays in Gender and the Politics of Literary Criticism*, ed. Catherine Belsey and Jane Moore (Basingstoke: Macmillan, 1989), pp. 133–53.
39. For an account of the two types, see Schiesari, Introduction.
40. See Burton, iii. 139ff.
41. See Roberts (1995), p. xxxiv.
42. Burton identifies 'Poeticall *Furies*' as a symptom of madness (i. 133), but gives no female examples.
43. See Maurice and Hanna Charney, 'The Language of Madwomen in Shakespeare and His Fellow Dramatists', *Signs* iii (1977), 451–60 (456) for the slippage between verse and prose associated with madwomen on stage.

44. Roberts (1983), poem N6.
45. See A.R. Jones, 'Writing the Body: Towards an Understanding of "L'Ecriture feminine"' in *The New Feminist Criticism: Essays on Women, Literature and Theory,* ed. Elaine Showalter (London: Virago, 1986), pp. 361–77 (363–5).
46. 'Sir Edward Denny to Lady Mary Wroth', 26 February 1621/2 in Roberts (1983), p. 239.
47. See Roberts (1983), pp. 31–7. She also suggests a range of dates from late 1620 to 1626 or 1629 (1995, pp. xvii–viii).
48. See Roberts (1983), pp. 32–3 (l. 1).
49. She is pictured in a 'Gowne of light Tawny or Murrey' (p. 141), embroidered with a pearl. See Frances A. Yates, *Astraea: The Imperial Theme in the Sixteenth Century* (1975; rpr. London: Pimlico, 1993), pp. 215–19. Elizabeth's assertion that she is married to her country appears in William Camden, *The Historie of the Most Renowned and Victorious Princesse Elizabeth* (1630), pp. 26–7.
50. Hackett (1995), p. 116.
51. My concern here is with the operation of these connections within the text. For the political topicality of both *Uranias*, see Roberts (1995), pp. xxxix–liv.
52. Ros Ballaster, *Seductive Forms: Women's Amatory Fiction from 1684 to 1740* (Oxford: Clarendon Press, 1992), p. 62.
53. There are rebellions in Austria (i. ff. 5, 35); Argos (i. ff. 28ff.); Hungary (the attack on Melasinda, i. f. 63); Denmark and Norway (ii. ff. 37vff.); Pamphilia (ii. f. 54v); Tartaria (ii. f. 54); and in the country of Ollo-randus's widow (ii. f. 56v). Clavorando puts down a rebellion (ii. ff. 14ff.); and the Sophie of Persia has usurped the crown (i. f. 39).
54. See Roberts (1995), pp. xlviii–ix.
55. That rape stories are potentially transformable is implicit in Donald-son's *The Rapes of Lucretia: A Myth and its Transformations* and in Kath-leen Wall's study of the Callisto rape myth. It is, of course, in the nature of 'myths' to be transformable. In this case, however, it is the narrative structure associated with rape in romance which facilitates the transformations.
56. See p. 23. For Wroth's treatment of the blason and of the 'male gaze', see Hackett (1992), pp. 56–9.
57. Cf. *Old Arcadia*, pp. 47–8.
58. Hackett (1996), pp. 104, 107.
59. Ibid., p. 99.
60. Of four examples of false rape narratives I have found, one is an illusion (*Mirror*, ii. ff. 43v, 102–102v), and in another the claim is made by a man (*Orlando Furioso*, XVIII. 34–5). In *Palmerin* an enchantress is responsible, rather than the supposed victim (i. f. 79v). Only once is the supposed victim herself the deceiver (*Orlando Furioso*, XXI. 19ff.).
61. See my discussion of Acrasia in Chapter 3, pp. 78–81.
62. This also contrasts with the scene in *Primaleon* discussed ealier in which it is suggested that the woman's resistance was not genuine. See pp. 40–1.

## CONCLUSION

1. We might compare Fenton's insistence that Julia kill herself after rape (in 1567) to Heywood's debating of the issue of suicide in *Lucrece* (1603–8), but also to the totally unquestioned and spontaneous death of Theocrine in Massinger's *Unnatural Combat* (1621–5).
2. 'Grevell''s poem in the *Arundel Harington Manuscript* is a notable exception to this rule. In the *Old Arcadia*'s rape trial, both participants in each act are on the same side.
3. Lucas, p. 56.
4. Nancy J. Vickers, 'The Mistress in the Masterpiece' in Nancy Miller, ed. (1986), pp. 19–41 (19).
5. Ibid, pp. 23–4.
6. Ibid., p. 23.
7. Benvenuto Cellini, *Trattato della scultura* in *La Vita*, cited and translated by Vickers (p. 22), modifying George Bull's translation in (trans.) *The Autobiography of Benvenuto Cellini* (Harmondsworth and NY: Penguin, 1956) (insertion mine).
8. Cellini, p. 290, cited in Vickers, p. 23.
9. This is the title of Miller's collection and of the conference in which the collection originated.
10. Edwards, p. 19.
11. See Chapter 1.
12. See pp. 125–6.
13. This requirement was abolished following a report by the Law Commission, which found that the notion of corroboration was intellectually flawed. Section 32, Criminal Justice and Public Order Act, 1994.
14. *Historia Placitorum Coronæ: The History of the Pleas of the Crown* (1678), ed. George Wilson (Dublin, 1778), p. 635. For a discussion of the implications of this contention, see F. Ferguson, p. 89.

# Index

Main references to a headword are indicated in bold.